CW00641941

KA SEFOFANE

(BY AEROPLANE)

The story of Flying Mission
By
Malcolm J. McArthur
OBE, FRCS(Eng.)

First published in 2011 by Milton Contact Ltd. A CIP Catalogue record for this book is available from the British Library.

ISBN: 978-0-9562649-6-1

Printed in the United Kingdom

Milton Contact Ltd
3 Hall End, Milton
Cambridge, CB24 6AQ
United Kingdom

www.miltoncontact.co.uk

Acknowledgements

As I look back I am constantly amazed at the many wonderful people who have filled my life with blessings and colour. Certain friends and colleagues have been included in this account and some have not. This is not because some are more favoured than others. It was simply not possible - or practical - to include everyone. Yet all have played a part.

This book would not have reached publication without direction, encouragement and assistance from The One who sent Gudrun and me to Botswana in the first place, and a multitude of people that have made up my life since before I can remember.

You have all been instrumental in some way or another, perhaps unknowingly.

Loving parents and family. School friends and teachers. Dr Alfred Merriweather for sending us the initial contact that put Botswana 'on the map'. The Revd. James Cassels, who patiently wrote answers to all our questioning letters. And a host of others, especially the Flying Mission 'family', the incredible bunch of fantastic folk from so many different countries and backgrounds, who have made up and contributed in so many ways to make Flying Mission what it became.

Special thanks, because of actual direct involvement in the book's production, go to the following. To Revd. Jason Fawcett and Rose Yates who first introduced me to computers and word processing. To Debbie Spicer who challenged me to a race - and who won by a wide margin - with her book 'K is for Keeps' about her disabled daughter, Kgakamatso (KG). To KG herself, for her question, thrown at me one morning as I was making coffee - "What are you doing? Are you capable?" - the memory of which has often returned to prod me. It was a wonderful stimulus!

To Ann Hunter for her poetry. To Stuart Mingham for his cartoons and artwork. To Revd. John and Yvonne Lubbe, who took over the Flying Mission in 2002 enabling me to have more time to write. And, more recently, to Simon and Thomasina Brown who have painstakingly checked manuscripts and done their best to teach me basic English spelling and grammar.

Two more people have made an enormous contribution to bringing this project to fruition.

Christopher Thomas, my publisher, who has advised and encouraged and provided helpful advice at many points in the process. And Narasimha Shastri, a faithful friend, who has been available at a moments notice to sort out IT problems and set me straight when my hardware, or softeware, has 'refused', usually because of my own ignorance.

One other person deserves special mention - my beloved wife, Gudrun. Without her love, dedication, constant care, and encouragement, I would never have got this far.

Thank you, one and all.

-oOo-

Erratum...
On page 174 the caption should read:
Sarah Haynes (L) and Michelle Royce (R)
took over from Gudrun as Mission
Housing Officers.

ii

1999 (Dr Alfred Merriweather) Patron
Darck, Dalene (ZM) IND STV
Edridge, Judy-Ann (NZ) AEF IND STV
Haynes, Matt & Sarah (US) Pilot
Hindley, Charles (UK) IND STV
Long, Daniel (US) IND STV
Kobedi, Onika (BW) Secretary
Mosege, Siene (BW) Estates Manager
Van Wyk, Eurika (SA) Accountant
Cutler, Dan & Judy-Anne (US) AEF Engineer
Krebs, Natalie (CH) IND STV
Lowe, Cash & Lisa (US) Care Ministries
Mannothoko, Lesego (BW) IND STV
Mpofu, Israel (BW) IND STV
Skaggs, Steve & Vonnie (US) HIV/AIDS
          Co-ordinator
2001 Boyle, Isobel (UK) IND STV
Jeary, Michael (UK) Housing Maintenance
Langford, David & Patti (US) Engineer
Lubbe, John & Yvonne (CH) Directors
Macholo, Gaone (BW) Board
Maphorisa, Joyce (BW) Board
Radowski, Jens (DE) IND STV
Scales, Julian (BW) Board
Schubert, Tim & Uli (DE) Pilot
Unrau, Julia (US) IND STV
Vos, Diane (SA) Secretary
Walters, John (UK) Board
Williamson, Andrew (UK) IND STV

2002 - Handover to John & Yvonne Lubbe 09/03/02

*   *   *

IND - Independent, STV - Short Term Volunteer
UFCofS - United Free Church of Scotland
BW - Botswana, CA - Canada, CH - Switzerland,
DE - Germany, NO - Norway, NZ - New Zealand,
P - Portugal, SA - South Africa

Flying Mission Aircraft

A2-ZGB (C185) 'The Quiet Hour', Dedicated 1978
A2-ABG (C206) 'Lephoi La Pula' (Dove of
Blessing) (Butterscotch & Toffee)
Dedicated 05/03/83
N42472 (C207) Leased from MAF, Kenya 1983
A2-FMC (C207), 'Morongwa wa Kagiso
(Messenger of Peace) Dedicated 1984
A2-FMD (C206), 'Morongwa wa Tsholofelo'
(Messenger of Hope) 1984 & Dedicated
22/11/1986
A2-AEP (C206) Morongwa wa Lorato
(Messenger of Love) Dedicated 22/11/1986
A2-AGG (C210) 'Morongwa wa Boitulmeo'
(Messenger of Joy) 1990 & Dedicated
14/04/91
A2-AIC C206 'Morongwa wa Kgomotso'
(Messenger of Comfort) 1993
A2-AHX (C206) Leased 1996
A2-AFU (C206) 'Morongwa wa Botshelo'
(Messenger of life) 1996 & Dedicated
12/07/1997
A2-AJF (C335) Leased 1997
A2-FMS (C210) 'Morongwa wa Pholoso'
(Messenger of Health) Dedicated 04/12/1999
A2-OCB (C421) 'Diphuka tsa Pgodiso' (Wings of
Healing) Dedicated 04/12/1999 in honour of
Dr A M Merriweather
A2-MJM (KINGAIR 90) 'Mercy One'
Dedicated 13/04/2007

*   *   *

Mission Organisations Flown

Africa Enterprise
Africa Evangelical Fellowship & Church
African Inter-Mennonite Ministries
Anglican Diocese of Botswana
Baptist Mission of Botswana
Botswana Adventist Medical Service
Botswana Bible Graining Institute
Botswana Christian Council
Botswana New Apostolic Church
Botswana Theological Training Programme
Brethren Mission
Catholic Mission, Maun
Christian Missions in Many Lands
Christian Women's Club of Botswana
Christoffel Blind Mission
Church of Christ in Botswana
Church World Service
Churches of Christ
Church of God in Christ
Diocese of Botswana
Dutch Reform Church & Missions Committee
Evangelical Lutheran Church in Botswana
Evangelical Lutheran Church of Southern Africa
Finnish Evangelical Lutheran Church
Interkerkelijke Coördinatie Commissie
Ontwikkelingsprojecten (ICCO)
Jesus Generation Movement
Kgologano College
Love Botswana for Christ (Campus Crusade)
Lutheran Resource Activity Centre of Botswana
Lutheran World Federation
Mennonite Central Committee
Mennonite Ministries in Botswana
Mission of Evangelical Lutheran Free Churches
Missionary Aviation Fellowship (South Africa)
Open Baptist Church
Orapa Christian Church

Pentecostal Holiness Church
Scripture Union of Botswana
Seventh Day Adventist Mission
Swedish Holiness Union Mission
Thuso Lutheran Rehabilitation Centre
United Congregational Church of Southern Africa
United Free Church of Scotland
Vereinige Evangelische Mission
Wings of Life Ministry
World Vision
Young Women's Christian Association
Youth with a Mission

Non Government Organisations Flown

German Volunteer Organisation

*   *   *

'Soli Deo Gloria'

Glossary

Aviation

AH - artificial horizon
DG - directional gyro
DME - distance measuring equipment
NBD - non-directional radio beacon
VASI - vertical approach slope indicator lights
VOR - VHF omni range radio beacon

Medical

DMO - District Medical Officer
MOH - Ministry of Health
Prostatectomy - an operation on the prostate gland

Setswana

Kgosi - Chief
Kgotla - the Chief's meeting place
Kopje - a rocky hill
Mmangaka - Mrs. Doctor
Ngaka - Doctor
Rondavel - a round, thatch roofed dwelling
Sefofane - aeroplane
Stoep - veranda

-oOo-

Thank you

Foreword

"You should write a book."

"Me? Write a book? About what?"

"About your experiences in Botswana and about Flying Mission. After all, you founded FM."

The answer to that has become well rehearsed over the years. "I didn't 'found' Flying Mission. There was a whole bunch of folk who 'founded' FM."

"Yes, but you had the idea. The vision."

"Well, I was only trying to do the job that needed to be done in the way that seemed best."

Over many years I have never been able to shift the blame to anyone else and that proposal kept being repeated. I also came to realise that many folk wanted to know not just how Flying Mission started, but also, why things were done in the way that they had been done. So, I have tried to put the story on paper. The following pages are the result.

Right at the beginning, however, a number of points must be made clear. Firstly, in telling the story of Flying Mission, I have included people and occasions to bring 'life' to the telling. What I have written, or described, is based on my memory with help from many folk whose memories - or records - are better than my own. The people were a real part of life. Where conversations, or dialogues, are included this is seldom 'word perfect' but rather it is constructed in a way that will highlight an incident, principle, policy, decision or situation... a sort of 'poetic licence'. However, every effort has been made to make the account both accurate as well as readable. Events are broadly chronological but occasionally time has been 'moulded, or merged' for the convenience of the telling and to keep from extending into many volumes.

I have not consciously intended to 'do anyone down', or cause hurt or offence. If this happens I beg for forgiveness in advance. If the record is too technical in places then please feel free to skip the page! My purpose has been to record what happened in a way that will inform, encourage, stimulate and challenge the reader and help him, or her, to understand how exciting life can be. For this reason several accounts have been included that are not perhaps part of the   actual 'Flying Mission' story.

Flying Mission has not been exclusively an aviation ministry. It has always been intended that it should be a 'servant' organisation and as such it has sought to meet the needs of those being served. Yes, aviation has been a large part. However, with the arrival of the HIV/AIDS virus the care of orphans and other vulnerable people quickly added new dimensions to the Flying Mission activities. At one point motor cars seems to need constant attention and, for a time, there was a 'care ministry for vehicles' that also had a training element for local young men and was enormously appreciated by those who used the service.

Questions may be raised as to whether some of the 'stories' should have been included. However, they have been inserted in order to give the reader a little background to our life and work in Botswana. Hopefully they will either provoke thought, or produce a little light relief and perhaps a smile, as well as providing insight into a beautiful country with its wonderful people. A country that, after living in it for more than 40 years as we have, has become home.

-oOo-

Contents

-oOo-

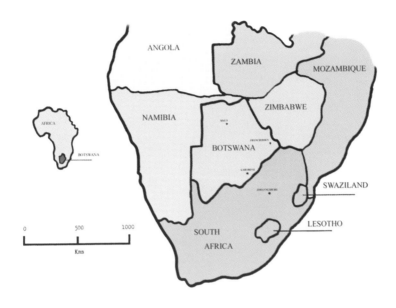

Botswana and its neighbours in southern Africa

Botswana became a British Protectorate under Queen Victoria. In 1966 it gained 'independence' and subsequently became one of the group of Southern African Development Countries (SADC)

*   *   *

A Kalahari highway

Provision

Though the way may seem uncertain
Though you doubt you've heard My call
Take each step I lay before you
    I'll provide.

Though you fear that you will fail me
Though you know your emptiness
Take each morsel that I hand you
    I'll provide.

Though you know you're weak and powerless
Though you tremble at your lack
Take My Word and My empowering
    I'll provide.

Ann Hunter

Ann Hunter first came to Botswana in 1980 with her husband,
who worked in the Police Radio Unit. Ann was appointed to
the position of Flying Mission Office Supervisor in June 1998,
and became the Mission's Prayer Co-ordinator in 2003, a
position that she continues to hold at the time of writing this
book.

*   *   *

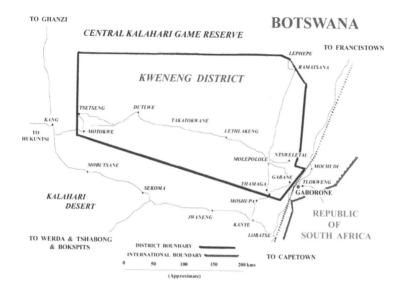

The Kweneng District of Botswana is the district in which Molepolole is situated.

Molepolole is the largest village in the region and it was the responsibility of the Scottish Livngstone Hospital to look after the medical needs of the entire area. Medical and mission visits were made regularly to all the remote settlements in the district.

Lephepe was famous for its wells and it was the last watering place for Dr David Livingstone's oxen on his travels to the north.

※　　　※　　　※

CHAPTER 1
BACKGROUND

-Δ-

For a full understand of why Flying Mission (FM) was begun I shall have to 'back up' a little to give you the complete picture.

In August, 1968, my wife - Gudrun - and I were seeking a position in a mission hospital. We were young, energetic Christians with a keen desire to serve our Master, and after an interview with the Overseas Committee of the United Free Church of Scotland (UFCofS), we were accepted for the positions of mission doctor and midwife at the Scottish Livingstone Hospital (SLH) in Molepolole, Botswana, in southern Africa. (Botswana is the country. The people are the Batswana, one of whom is a Motswana. The language is Setswana.).

*   *   *

From the first day, we loved it. The medical work was challenging. The Mission Team was made up of wonderful people. We soon fell in love with the Batswana and their country. Yes, there were frustrations and difficulties. Yes, there were times when we felt like throwing a tantrum and walking out, never to return. Looking back I am amazed at the patience of the senior missionaries who were responsible for orientating us and instructing us in the ways of Africa and the Batswana.

1

*An old man selling wooden spoons in
Molepolole*

The Planning

On September 30th 1966 the Bechuanaland Protectorate, located in the centre of Southern Africa, acquired independence and Seretse Khama was elected the first President of the fledgling state of Botswana. Until then, the British Protectorate Administration had had its headquarters in Mafeking, in what is now the Republic of South Africa.

On our arrival in August 1968, Botswana was an underdeveloped country. For the most part flat, and some 1000 x 1200 km in area, with a population of around 1.2 million. Little had been done to discover and make use of the vast resources that are available today. The majority of Batswana were subsistence farmers devoted to their cattle. Some drifted to South Africa to work in the gold mines. Deep in the Kalahari were the Makgalagadi tribe of people and the Bushmen - 'hunter gatherers' - later known as the Basarwa, or Rural Area Dwellers. Gaborone boasted about a kilometre of tarred road. The highest building was the two-storied British High Commission. The Capitol Cinema had recently been opened. There was one bank - Barclays - a Post Office, a few small shops and the Station Hotel. The 'station' building was a corrugated iron shack a few yards from the railway tracks with - at night - a paraffin 'hurricane' lamp hung on a pole. A train arrived once or twice a week, usually at around one o'clock in the morning, from Capetown, or Bulawayo.

Gaborone International Airport was a dirt strip located between the new 'town' and what had come to be known as Gaborone Village - an area where the Protectorate Administration had built a small number of rambling colonial homes for the few officers who had to live in the territory - the District Commissioner, the Commissioner of Police, the Medical Officer and a handful of other folk. In those early days, when walking from Gaborone Village to the station - about 45 minutes walk - it was advisable to carry a rifle to protect oneself from prowling lion.

In 1968 the main method of travel was the railway, operated by the Rhodesian Railways between Mafeking and Gaborone, in the south, and Francistown and Bulawayo in the north. The railway ran along the Eastern border of the country and along this railway line lived most of the million or so of the Batswana population. A gravel road that ran beside the railway line also linked the Botswana centres of Gaborone and Francistown. Other villages like Molepolole, Kanye, Serowe and Maun, all located farther West, were reached by gravel roads, or dirt, or sand tracks that became progressively worse the further West one travelled.

At Independence in 1966 it was predicted that Gaborone was unlikely ever to have a population larger than 30,000 and, at Independence, the British Government had built a small hospital with some 250 beds and named it 'The Princess Marina Hospital' after Princess Marina who had been the Official British Representative at the Independence celebrations.

Upon our arrival we had been quickly introduced to the bitterly cold August winds and the bone shaking 'corrugations' and penetrating red dust of the rough gravel 'road' out to Molepolole.

Expecting to live in a 'mud hut' we were greatly surprise by the clean, well-built hospital and staff houses of the first Scottish Livingstone Hospital (SLH). Dr Shepherd began the medical work in 1931. Dr Alfred Merriweather had taken it over, in 1944, and developed the original two clinic buildings into a busy 180-bed hospital with a maternity unit, medical and surgical and children's wards and an operating theatre suite. There was also a small chapel. Later, male and female TB wards and a new outpatients department were added and, by 1975, the Scottish Livingstone Hospital (SLH) accommodated 280 beds and was regarded by many Batswana as being the finest hospital in the country. Some of our patients travelled from far in the north, by-passing Government hospitals on their way, to attend the SLH.

Part of our duties at the hospital were outstation visits - on a weekly basis - to the network of Mission Clinics set up by Dr Alfred Merriweather around the Kweneng District. The more distant villages and settlements scattered to the West of Molepolole, in the Kalahari Desert, were visited on a monthly or three monthly basis.

4

Loading the 7-ton Bedford truck for a Desert trip

These expeditions - and that is really what they were - lasted anything up to ten days depending on the stamina of the Team (including the vehicle that was either the 5 or 7 ton Bedford truck), the rate at which the medicine chests emptied, or the finding of a critically ill patient who required urgent admission to hospital. Such trips were an exciting change from the usual hospital routine.

Flying Mission was begun as a direct consequence of these excursions to take medical care and the Christian Gospel to the people living in the remote regions of the Kalahari.

*   *   *

First Gear

The 7-ton Bedford truck ground slowly along the deep ruts in the scorching red sand.

Gudrun was enthroned in the cab beside the hot steel covering the roaring motor. I had opted for a spell on the back, away from the fuming engine, and Temalo, our cook, was wedged between my knee and a sack of mealie meal with a towel over her face. Another sack of grain applied itself to the curve of my spine and functioned as an excellent shock absorber when the truck wheels bounced over a rock... of which there were many. Two patients were likewise wedged between a door - that was protecting them from a large roll of barbed wire - and a roll of bedding. The door was destined for a Small General Dealer in some distant Desert village. Mmanti, one of the two nurses on this trip, was invisible except for the top of her head. Moruti, the Evangelist, likewise, was buried in comfort beneath layers of towels, suitcases, sacks of corn, 'pockets' of oranges and a couple of chickens awaiting execution.

The truck's gears shifted occasionally out of first gear and into second gear before a labouring engine forced Milton, the driver, to change reluctantly back down into first. The consumption of diesel was terrific. Forward movement was 'peanuts'. The 7-tonner had required 'digging out' on several occasions during the afternoon.

Everyone longed for Dutlwe to emerge from the shimmering, heat haze somewhere out front even though we all knew we would have to set up clinic, hold a short service and hand out medicines and pills, as well as administer 'the needle' to anything up to 50 patients, before we could relax around a wood fire to indulge in some of Temalo's culinary creations before finally crawling into our sleeping bags.

High above us in the azure sky were three black specks slowly rotating in the cloudless heavens. Three vultures. Wings spread effortlessly to ride the warm updraft of an invisible thermal. What a simple, silent and magnificent way to travel... compared to our noisy, inefficient, smelly struggle across the burning hot Kalahari sands.

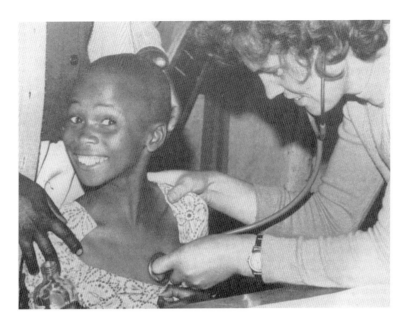

Gudrun examines a young patient at a Desert clinic.

Oaee! An old lady thinks.

A halt to replace a broken fan belt

Seeing patients in Motokwe

Later, as Gudrun and I talked of the day's events a thought presented itself.

"You know, Honey, these salt pans... The one at Takatokwane, and now here at Dutlwe... they're all quite large enough and flat enough to land a small 'plane on."

"Well. Why not suggest it to Alfred?"

"We should. We must."

*   *   *

Back in Molepolole I wasted no time in putting the idea to Dr Merriweather, sitting in his office. Dr Shepherd, the hospital's founder, gazed down on us from a faded, framed photograph hanging on the wall.

"Alfred, that Desert trip was fantastic. Gudrun and I loved every minute." I chose words with care. "But it was tiring and the travelling was so time consuming! I was not trained in digging trucks out of sand. Have you considered using a light aircraft for these visits?"

"But Malcolm, there are no airstrips in the Desert." Dr Alfred Merriweather had travelled the Desert tracks and knew the people of the Desert, and almost all of the remote Kalahari settlements well, after doing a medical survey for the Bechuanaland Administration many years before. "And would there be any advantage?"

"Well, it would be cheaper and a great time saver."

"Cheaper? Than a Bedford truck?" A triumphant smile suggested that he considered the argument won.

"Certainly. For one thing an aircraft flies in a straight line and for another thing it would not suffer the same wear and tear that a truck does on those atrocious tracks in the Kalahari." I was not to be deterred. "The capital outlay would be higher initially but in its lifetime an aircraft will fly much farther than any vehicle on the ground. How many miles do you get out of a truck on those Desert tracks before it falls apart You would need at least 20 vehicles to match the distance an aircraft would fly."

"Mmm. That makes the cost look a bit different. The passengers would be more comfortable too. We'll have to think about it."

9

As I left the office I had the strong impression that Dr Shepherd, in that faded photograph, winked.

*   *   *

Alfred did think about it, and, at the end of our first year in Molepolole, when Gudrun and I returned to the UK for further specialist studies, he promised two things...

"Well... Malcolm. We'll see what we can do to find money for an aircraft for you. Bread for the World might be interested. And for you, Gudrun, I'll make sure that, when you two get back, there will be a new, and more comfortable, bed."

By the end of our first fifteen months in Molepolole, Botswana had become home. Gudrun and I both believed we had found our life's work but we had also become acutely aware that further training would be beneficial. We therefore returned to the UK, for Gudrun to train as a Midwifery Tutor and me to complete my surgical training for the Fellowship of the Royal College of Surgeons in London.

It was 1974 before we got back to Molepolole and there had been changes. The new bed was there but sadly, no aircraft. A new outpatients block had been built and the Scottish Livingstone Hospital had become a shining example of what a mission hospital should be. However, the United Free Church of Scotland was now struggling to make ends meet. The Ministry of Health was already covering the costs of drugs and salaries for the Batswana nursing staff. 'Localisation' was a word in frequent use and it was felt by those in authority in Scotland that the time had come to hand over the Scottish Livingstone Hospital into local hands and, in 1975, this was accomplished.

*   *   *

"That one Ngaka"

Handover left the Mission personnel with two options, either to return home, or, to enter Botswana Government service. Doctor Merriweather and I opted to become Government Officers and to continue under the new administration. Isobel Johnston, the Matron, and Marion Peter, the Sister Tutor of the Scottish Livingstone Hospital School of Nursing, departed back to Scotland, and Ngaire Reid, a nurse from New Zealand who had been a part of the team for over a year, decided to take a posting with the District Council.

Ngaire had come to Botswana under the Africa Evangelical Fellowship (AEF) with the idea that God wanted her to work amongst the Bushman of the Kalahari, and, after a period of orientation in the village clinic in Mmankgodi (previously one of the Scottish Livingstone Hospital's outstations and now a Clinic run by the Kweneng District Council) Ngaire was posted to the village of Kang to set up and run a new District Council clinic. Kang is situated some 400 km West of Molepolole, deep in the Kalahari.

Dr Merriweather and I continued working at the Scottish Livingstone Hospital. However, it was not long before a brown envelope bearing the words 'ON BOTSWANA GOVERNMENT SERVICE' across it arrived in my hands. It contained a request that I transfer my services to the Princess Marina Hospital in Gaborone. The Princess Marina Hospital (PMH) had become the main Referral Hospital for the country and the expatriate Government Surgeon who had been serving there had departed.

This was to be a major change. Gudrun and I had believed that Molepolole would be our life's work. It had become home. We had adopted a family of Batswana children. We were happy in Molepolole. But, as Alfred pointed out, we really had no option but to comply with the wishes of our new 'Employer'.

Reluctantly, very reluctantly, Gudrun and I packed our belongings onto our Chevrolet truck and moved to the 'big city'.

However, this move was part of a plan Masterminded by a much Higher Authority than even the President himself.

Years later the first Molepolole hospital was replaced by a new, larger, modern Government hospital that, however, still proudly bears the name 'Scottish Livingstone Hospital' in big brass letters at its entrance.

When I settled into the work at the Princess Marina Hospital I found myself to be the fourth Government Medical Officer on the staff. In those days the team consisted of a Physician, an Anaesthetist, a Gynaecologist and a Surgeon. My surgical duties required me not only to attend to surgical patients at the PMH, but also to visit the hospitals in the surrounding towns and villages of Mochudi, Molepolole, Lobatse and Kanye, and, later, to hospitals and health centres all over Botswana.

Gudrun occupied herself doing voluntary work in the Deborah Retief Mission Hospital in Mochudi, some 40 km north of Gaborone. On our weekends off, and during holidays, we would make it a point to try and visit Ngaire, who by then was setting up the clinic in Kang. Such visits were made possible because of our one-and-a-half ton Chevrolet truck, and, even with that mighty vehicle, reaching Kang would take some 12 hours because of the deep Kalahari sand and the poor 'roads'.

Little did we appreciate that the stage was now set. The Divine Hand had been at work moving people into position for something we had never imagined...

*   *   *

Sethunya

After rain the Kalahari Desert can burst into a profusion of blooms. The normally dry, brown veldt can change to lush green grass, and small Devil Plants can carpet the ground with golden blossoms. Sethunya is the Setswana word for flower.

She was a little Desert flower. I cannot remember her name, but I remember her as Sethunya. She was a small girl. She was one of the 'little people', known as Basarwa, or Kalahari Bushmen. And she played an important part in the beginning of the Flying Mission.

*   *   *

"Malcolm, I hate to interrupt the paving project but I've got a patient for you to see." Ngaire had in her hand one of the standard pink, outpatient cards used by all the Government health facilities. "She's a Bushman girl and I think she's broken her arm."

Gudrun and I were visiting Kang for a few days and had driven out to the Desert in our white, one ton, C30 Chevrolet truck, taking stores to Ngaire who had set up, and was now running, the new clinic in this remote Kalahari village. The nurse's house was a 'prefab' built on a cement foundation set in the deep sand and we were laying a small area of paving outside the front door on which to sit in the evenings.

"Surely. I'll come. Honey, don't you go lifting those paving stones by yourself. I'll be right back."

"Don't worry. I won't." Gudrun tapped one of the flat, twelve-inch by twelve-inch cement paving slabs that we had brought with us from Gaborone, into position. "I'll take a break and make some coffee."

Ngaire led the way to the clinic situated about fifty yards from the nurse's home. It was a long building and, like the nurse's house, it was a 'prefab'. A wide, covered 'stoep', or verandah, ran the length of the front, and a small group of folk was sitting clustered about the door that led into the consulting room. They were chattering in the strange, clicking

14

language of the Desert peoples but fell into an expectant silence as we approached.

"You go in." Ngaire handed me the card. "I'll go and find Janet to interpret for us. I think she's sweeping out the Maternity Ward. Hey, the sand here in Kang gets in everywhere here. One of us seems to be sweeping much of the day!"

Moments later, Janet, a local Kang lass who was the clinic's General Duty Assistant, came in leading a young girl by the hand.

"Ngaka, (Doctor) it seems that she had a fall and has hurt her arm."

The girl looked at me with large, brown eyes. She solemnly parted the grey blanket that was draped about her shoulders and held out her bare arm. I held her delicate hand and ran my fingers gently over the smooth, pale, brown skin. There was a classical 'dinner fork' deformity at the distal end of her forearm and she winced ever so slightly as my fingers passed over the damaged bone.

"Well, she's got a fractured radius." I looked up. The clear, brown eyes looked at me steadily. "The deformity is quite marked and it really needs reduction. She'll need an anaesthetic. We'll have to take her back to Molepolole with us when we go. But that won't be for a couple of days and it'll be a long, painful trip."

"And goodness knows how, or when, we'll be able to get her back to Kang."

"All right. Janet, if you can explain to her relatives just what the matter is and then, I think, admit her with her mother and we'll make a plan." Ngaire's mind was already 'in gear'. "We'll make sure she has a good night's sleep and get her well doped up before the journey and she shouldn't be too uncomfortable."

On my way back to the nurse's home, trudging over the hot sand, I wondered what it would be like to be taken away from one's home by strange people who did not speak one's language, and with a broken arm. Every jolt would stab excruciating pain into that already throbbing bone.

*　　*　　*

15

A Bushman girl with her horse

Later that afternoon we sat on the newly laid paving in front of Ngaire's house sipping tea...

"Gudrun." Ngaire had a remonstrative tone to her voice. "You've been working much too hard. You're supposed to come here for a quiet weekend and you kill yourself laying paving stones."

"Well, while you were seeing to that little girl I thought I'd just finish off the project, and it really was not very hard." Gudrun's eyes twinkled. "There were only three paving stones left and it was easy levelling the sand."

"Ah... You see, my wife is a German Officer." I slurped my tea. "And a German Officer can do anything!"

"Well, I think you're very naughty doing all that hard work." Ngaire was adamant but, at that moment, our attention was taken up by a buzzing sound that grew steadily louder.

"That sounds like Heine Strumpher." Ngaire put down her mug. "He's the Afrikaans trader who owns the Kang trading store. He's a farmer too. Anyway," she got up, "I must get back to the clinic and see the last few patients." With that she departed,

We learned later that Heine had a big cattle farm up near Ghanzi, as well as another farm down in South Africa, near Stella. He also owned his own Cessna aircraft.

Ngaire returned a couple of hours later as Gudrun was finishing the preparations for supper.

"Wow, Gudrun, that supper you are cooking smells delicious!"

"It's all ready. Come and sit down. You must be exhausted."

"Not really. There were no big problems after that little girl with the broken arm. And Janet's a good helper. But let's say grace and then I'll tell you some news."

We thanked The Lord for His abundant provision, and, while Gudrun dished up, Ngaire began in her soft New Zealand twang...

"After finishing the clinic Janet and I were clearing up when who should walk in the door? Heine Strumpher!"

"And then?"

"Well you won't believe this, but tomorrow he's flying into Gaborone for some meeting that he has to attend. He wants to leave early and get back the same day. I asked him if he could take our little patient and drop her at Molepolole. He said 'no problem', and, if you wanted to go along, Malcolm, you could even set that fracture and he would collect you on his way back. You could all be home in time for supper."

"Now that's an example of Divine planning and co-ordination."

"Yes, but the next bit you won't like." Ngaire's eyes sparkled teasingly.

"Go on. But, Honey, let me have a bit more of that lovely stew first, please."

Gudrun ladled out some tasty bits of beef as Ngaire continued.

"Well, I know you were planning a lie in and a leisurely start tomorrow."

"Yes."

"Heine wants you and the patient down at the landing strip behind the store at five thirty sharp. He wants to be off at the crack of dawn." She laughed. "So... it's your turn to make the morning tea tomorrow!"

"All right..." I feigned acute misery and defeat. "I'll make the tea tomorrow."

*　　　*　　　*

The alarm clock shrilled in the darkness and the cold morning air demanded a rapid throwing on of warm clothes.

I found that Ngaire was already up with our little patient, and after a mug of hot coffee and a slice of toast it was only a short walk over the crunching sand in the grey dawn to the airstrip behind the store.

"Good morning Heine." Ngaire made the introductions.

"Good morning Ngaire. Good morning Doc. It's great that you can come along."

"Heine, this really is most kind of you."

"Not at all. I have to go anyway and there's plenty of room."

Heine threw a bucket of water over the windshield of the Cessna 210.

18

...the grey light gave way to a sparkling Desert morning

Sethunya, with a blanket wrapped tightly around her, and I in my anorak, stood shivering while he finished the pre-flight inspection as the grey light gave way to a sparkling Desert morning.

"Right Doc. Let's go. We'll put your little patient in one of the middle seats. You can be in the front right seat. That way you can point out the hospital when we get to Molepolole."

Ngaire made sure that Sethunya was settled comfortably and then stood back. The doors were closed and Ngaire waved. The propeller began to turn and the engine coughed and fired up. Moments later we were airborne and, as Heine banked the little aircraft, we had a fine view of the round, thatched huts dotted about beneath us, and the enormous, glistening, white Kang salt pan away to the southwest.

"It's worth making an early start." Heine adjusted the throttle setting and tail trim. "By nine o'clock the thermals get going and things can get bumpy, even in winter. I'll take her up to around seven thousand feet. That's usually comfortable and it makes it easier to see where we are."

As we climbed higher into the blue, cloudless sky I gazed out of the window. The Kalahari seemed to shrink and change character and turn into a vast, tawny hide with the occasional white hole in it where a salt pan had formed.

Once the initial excitement of flying had worn off, the drone of the engine became hypnotic and Sethunya was soon nodding off. Ngaire had given her some pain killing medication that made her a bit dozy too.

"There's Tswaane Pan. And that'll be Dutlwe up front." Heine looked at his watch. "We should make Molepolole by about eight o'clock."

"That's great. It should be easy to attract attention if you fly over the hospital a couple of times. I'm sure they'll send a driver down to the airfield. The Matron will see to that."

The minutes ticked by. Takatokwane Pan and Village passed under the port wing. Then, a few minutes later the few huts of Maboane slid past to our right.

"Doc... I shall probably be through with all I have to do by about two o'clock. How will that suit?"

"Oh Heine that would be wonderful." I did some mental gymnastics. "If there's no other emergency blocking the operating theatre we should be able to get that bone straight and have the arm in plaster before lunch. But, if you don't mind, we'll wait for you to buzz the hospital again before we come down to the strip."

"No problem Doc. Once you've shown me where the hospital is, I'll have no trouble finding it the second time round."

In what seemed no time at all the corrugated iron roofs of the Scottish Livingstone Hospital were gliding below us and Sethunya was wide-awake, peering out of the window. Heine circled twice and I could see Station, one of the drivers, climbing into the small Land Rover. The touchdown was bumpy, but the airstrip was little used and most bush strips seem bumpy after a smooth flight. As we climbed out, Station pulled up beside the wing.

"All right Doc." Heine helped Sethunya out of her seat. "I'll aim to be back around two. I hope the 'op' goes well."

"Thank you Heine. That's been a big help. We'll do our best to be ready."

The roofs of the Scottish Livingstone Hospital

We watched as the propeller began to turn and then, suddenly, the engine sprang to life and a cloud of red dust began blowing out behind the tail fin.

There was a gentle breeze and, after a short roll, the little Cessna took eagerly to the sky and shrank rapidly in size as it made a beeline for Gaborone.

"Ehe Ngaka... That is a wonderful nonyane (little bird)!" Station looked thoughtful. "How was Gaborone this morning?"

"Ho, Station. We did not come from Gaborone this morning. We have come from Kang."

"From Kang? No! That's in Kgalagadi?"

"Ee Rra (Yes Sir). Kang. We were in Kang with Sister Ngaire at the new clinic and this little girl came yesterday with her broken arm. Mr. Strumpher offered to bring us to Molepolole so that we can reduce the fracture. He says he will come to collect us again at about two o'clock... So we have to be quick."

"You say that you came from Kang? This morning? And it is only a quarter past eight now." Station's jaw had dropped in amazement. "Does that flying machine also travel in the night?"

"Ee Rra... It can travel at night but we came from Kang. This morning."

"But Kang is 400 kilometers away. It takes at least twelve hours to get there even when the road is good." His amazement continued and I could see that he had doubts.

"Nyaa Rra (No Sir). We left at six thirty this morning. That aeroplane is fast and it also flies straight. It does not have to follow a winding, bumpy road."

"Aoaee Ngaka! One hour and forty-five minutes? From Kang to here?"

"Ee Rra... But come, we must be going." I could see this story would be all over the hospital by the time we had Sethunya's bone straight and her arm in plaster.

"One hour and forty-five minutes..." As the Landrover ground its way back to the hospital, Station was still awed at this new technology.

After an X-ray and a smooth anaesthetic the reduction of the deformed arm went perfectly. By lunchtime a second X-ray had confirmed a satisfactory position of the bone and the new white POP (Plaster of Paris) was dry and already becoming a marvel in the eyes of its young owner.

Lunch over, at around three o'clock, the buzz of a single engine aircraft had us scurrying to the Landrover with Sethunya wrapped in her grey blanket and clutching a rather ragged doll that had been given her by Sister Kgosientsho, the Sister in charge of the Children's Ward. Station whisked us back to the airfield.

"Doc, I'm sorry I'm a bit late..." Heine Strumpher was standing beside the open door of the aircraft. "These meetings! Folk are never on time. But we've still got plenty of daylight. And anyway, tonight it's almost full moon. I often fly at night when there's a good moon. It's great fun!"

I could see Station's jaw dropping again and visualise the afternoon's gossip round the hospital staff...

*   *   *

Aerial view of Kang and the airstrip behind the store

Patients waiting outside Kang clinic

23

Sethunya was a model patient. She came to Ngaire for regular check-ups, walking by herself the several kilometers in to the clinic from her parents' grass hut in the bush on the outskirts of Kang.

I'm sure she had her family enthralled with her stories of 'the bird', and Molepolole, and how she had been 'killed' and brought back to life again and I suspect her POP was the envy of her siblings.

Ngaire reported to us on a later visit back to Kang, that the arm had healed beautifully.

"That POP of course rapidly took on the colour of the Desert dust and sand, and when she finally came to have it removed it was very ragged. And... guess what?" Ngaire's eyes glinted naughtily as she held us in suspense.

"I've no idea. Tell us."

She brought a number of her special friends with her." Ngaire could hardly contain her laughter.

"Go on... Tell us about it!"

"Well, your little Sethunya told us that the plaster had been very useful." The story was spun out for our benefit. "She learned early on that it was a great tool for clouting her brothers. But then, when she came to have it removed, she did have one complaint. She said that it itched terribly, and you'll never guess what I found."

"Well?" I had a sudden horrific vision that I had inadvertently left some bit of surgical equipment in the plaster as I had applied it. A surgical swab, or some instrument, left in the wrong place has brought a red face to many a surgeon over the years. Until then I had (and thankfully also since then I have) escaped such embarrassment. But such a mistake is an easy thing for the unwary to make in situations where staff are not highly trained, or supplies are limited and one often has to improvise during a difficult surgical procedure.

"I see what you're thinking." Ngaire became serious. "No. It was nothing that serious. When I cut the plaster off I found seven 'little friends' - bugs of some sort - crawling about underneath it. I killed them all very quickly!

*   *   *

24

Mother & child at Motokwe

That was really the first of the medical flights that I was involved in. But it brought home to all of us just what a wonderful, and useful, tool aviation could be in the Kalahari Desert.

Flying Mission was not to 'take off' for a few years after that incident, but, before Gudrun and I took our next home leave back in Europe, further developments were beginning to take place. The Divine hand was preparing for many more exciting things to happen.

-oOo-

The Divine hand was preparing for many more exciting things to happen

CHAPTER 2
PREPARATIONS FOR
FLIGHT

-Δ-

The beginning and later development of Flying Mission can be likened to the flight of an aircraft... From the untying of the tie-downs, through pre-flight preparations, start up, taxiing out to a holding point, right through the different phases of take-off, climb out and cruise.

In Botswana, before any flight leaves the ground, the pilot must open, or 'file', a Flight Plan setting out the planned route, the aircraft type and details such as the fuel endurance, the proposed altitude of flight, the number of passengers being carried and a host of other information. This immediately becomes of great importance should the aircraft have to make an emergency landing in some remote spot and a search and rescue operation be initiated.

Filing a 'flight plan' requires careful preparation - including an evaluation of current weather reports - before its submission to the Control Centre.

Looking back, it seems to me that a 'flight plan' for Flying Mission had been in the preparation for a long time. Furthermore, it was being put together by a Divine Hand for the take-off of the Mission and for its flight into a future of service in many, widely different areas.

Let me take you on this 'flight' of the Flying Mission and try to explain some of the details, difficulties and excitements that have been encountered.

27

The Flight Plan

After sighting those wheeling vultures, from the back of the 7-ton truck while crawling across the Kalahari sands, it took several more years of 'preparation' before all was in place and Flying Mission became a reality. In fact work had been in progress on 'the project' for much longer than I had ever realised.

My first contact with aeroplanes had been watching in amazement, in 1945, as wave after wave of silver DC3's had roared over the Kuching Japanese internment camp in which my father and mother and I had been held for three years. The Dakota aircraft had flown low and slow dropping leaflets and supplies of food by billowing, white parachutes. That wonderful, deep throbbing sound reverberated off the wooden huts and embedded itself firmly in my memory.

Some weeks after our release, my parents and their now 3-year-old son were airlifted by DC3 to the island of Labuan, off the coast of North Borneo, for rehabilitation before being repatriated to the United Kingdom. Before the flight I had been stuffed with chocolate by well meaning Australian soldiers who had also given my Dad a smart, white, silk shirt to wear. White silk, chocolate and flying in a DC3 do not mix well. My first flight ended about an hour after my Dad's newly acquired - and only - shirt had been covered down the front with several layers of the best, half digested, Cadbury's production. In later life it was an incident I was not allowed to forget!

Was this the start of a promising flying career? Or, was it begun on stepping out of that DC3 and seeing row upon row of sleek De Havilland Mosquito fighter/bombers drawn up in business like lines on the warm tarmac in the bright tropical sunshine?

Whatever... There is no doubt that all I ever wanted to be was either a doctor, or a pilot, and, when failed A level examinations forced a more successful re-take 6 months later then, the subsequent delay, before being able to start medical school, was a perfect opportunity to beg my Dad to put up two hundred pounds to enable me to procure a Private Pilot Licence (PPL).

Again, looking back, it is obvious why I did the training in a three seat, fabric covered Auster which was a 'tail dragger', and not in one of the more expensive and much more 'docile', and easier to fly, Cessna 150's that sported a nose wheel and required much less skill to wrestle back to earth in an elegant, smooth and safe manner. What was apparently built-in, hereditary Scottish prudence undoubtedly had a place in the Divine planning.

"Now, remember..." instructor 'Wilbur' Wright would intone... "Keep your toes on the pedals and your heels up and off the brakes. Keep the nose straight..." The ground loop was a thing often talked of with animation but it was not one of my achievements. Neither did I ever forget Wilbur's injunction when approaching over the pine trees... "Keep the speed up and the engine running or you'll be caught in the downdraft and stall into the cricket pitch." Nor his wise murmuring in relation to keeping a sharp look out for other traffic... "Remember... it's the one that you don't see that will spoil your day."

Wilbur told me more often than anything else... "Stay below the TMA!" (Terminal Movement Area of London's Heathrow Airport.) How I managed to get round a solo, cross country flight from Denham to Portsmouth and Shoreham, and back to the grass, 'pocket handkerchief' size field at Denham, without a radio, without touching the mixture control (which I knew nothing about) and without clipping some large passenger aircraft, or having red flares fired at me for breaking some rule of the air somewhere along the route, remains a mystery. The skies over the lush, green English countryside were, of course, much less crowded in 1960, and, keeping well below the London TMA - and other air corridors - at all times, probably helped to keep me out of trouble.

At five pounds an hour to hire an aeroplane, plus the mandatory flying club membership subscription, as well as the costs of travel to get to an airport, the Private Pilot's Licence was not of much use to a medical student on a meagre grant who was soon to be married. Flight training was followed by severe lessons in economics, as well as the expected lectures in anatomy and physiology. Somehow I managed to notch up the required 5 hours flying per annum to keep the licence current for a couple of years before being forced to acknowledge that there were other priorities.

However, the weeks of flight training were to bear fruit. God's economy is never wasteful.

*   *   *

Once Gudrun and I had transferred from Molepolole to Gaborone in 1976, and after the first flight with Heine and 'Sethunya', the possibility of re-instating the Private Pilot's Licence presented itself and it seemed that it might be useful. Accordingly, I took some brush up lessons at the Kalahari Flying Club, was introduced to a Cessna 150 and learned how to use a radio to report to, and take instruction from, the control tower. An introduction to a Cessna 172 followed and we began making periodic weekend visits to Kang, 450 Kilometres west in the Kalahari, by air. The arrangement worked well until one day, in 1977, when I went to book the aeroplane for the weekend, I was informed, "I'm sorry, the Club is being sold and the aircraft are no longer for hire."

Somewhat sadly, I made my way back to the Princess Marina Hospital and sat down in my office to open the mail. Then occurred one of those most perfect of Divine timings.

Within minutes there was a knock on the door. A gentleman entered who introduced himself as Mervyn Mason. He said he would like to talk about flying. I offered him a chair and a most amazing thing happened. Mervyn explained that he was the Seventh Day Adventist Mission Hospital Business Manager and that he had recently had to pay an insurance bill for an aircraft, 'The Quiet Hour', a Cessna 185 that belonged to the Mission.

Mervyn told me that the aircraft was named after the American singing group that had originally raised the funding to purchase it. He had had to pay a large bill for the insurance and felt it would be better to try and recoup a little of the expense rather than leaving the aircraft standing idle. The Seventh Day Adventist Mission Hospital had no pilot at the time. He proposed that we use the aeroplane and pay the

Seventh Day Adventist Mission whatever we felt was a reasonable figure for the use of it.

What an offer!

A short while later we were seated in the office of Mr. Bob Hampshire, the Safety Officer for the Botswana Government's Department of Civil Aviation, who informed us that "Yes, that's a great idea, but the aircraft has been standing for almost a year and it will need an airworthiness inspection first." Bob had leaned back in his chair and stroked his handlebar moustache. "The snag is that the only engineer who can do that inspection is based in Francistown. But, wait a minute. He's coming down from Francistown this weekend! I'll telephone him and we'll fix it for you."

On the following Saturday morning, during the short flight from Gaborone to Kanye in a Cessna 172, Bob Hampshire had thrust into my hands the Owner's Operating Manuel of a Cessna 185 saying, "You'd better take this. It'll be useful."

We had found The Seventh Day Adventist Mission's Cessna 185 standing silent, forlorn and tucked away in a small hangar at one end of the Kanye airfield. The name 'The Quiet Hour' was stuck onto the side of the engine cowling in neat, italic lettering.

My first impression of the 185 was that it was enormous. G-AGVJ - the fabric covered Auster that I trained on had only three seats. This machine, A2-ZGB, had six. The Auster had no electric starter. To coax it to life required the concerted effort of a pilot manipulating the magneto switches at the orders of a 'prop swinger' out front, who seemed to be courting a quick death. The 185 roared to life at the twist of a small key.

After cleaning off a few bird droppings and checking the wing tanks for water in the fuel, the Aviation Engineer who was with us had done a slow and careful inspection. The engine was started and, after warming up, it was run to maximum RPM a couple of times.

Cessna 185, A2-ZGB at Kanye

Ailerons and flaps were checked and seemed to be in good order. The aircraft was pronounced airworthy for a flight back to Gaborone. Further detailed checks would have to be performed there before Bob could officially stamp a new Certificate of Airworthiness.

As we stood before this monstrous aircraft, admiring its dark green paint scheme and graceful, curving lines, Bob Hampshire turned and handed me the keys with a curt "All right... I suggest you taxi the beast up and down the field a few times to get the feel of it before you take off. Once we see you're safely airborne, we'll take off and follow you back to Gaborone."

Oh my! It had never occurred to me that Bob Hampshire would not fly this machine back to Gaborone himself. Of course, by the time the 185 was gathering speed for the actual take off there were a few more hours in my flying log book than when that Auster and I had puttered over the large, silver gasometer that was the main landmark at Rickmansworth, and the green fields of England that had surrounded Denham airfield.

The name 'The Quiet Hour' was stuck onto the side of the engine cowling

The step up to flying a Cessna 185 was a quantum leap. And, thankfully, the Divine Controller had organised a perfect day with hardly any wind. Even so, the landing back at Gaborone was a tense moment. A 185 is renowned for its ability to 'dance' at any altitude below 10 feet above ground level and my training in a 'tail dragger' proved to have been a most worthwhile investment.

'The Quiet Hour' was certainly far from quiet but it was fast (we - the aircraft and I - were able to fly rings around Bob Hampshire and the Aviation Engineer in their Cessna 172!) and the aeroplane was extremely sensitive to the controls. On that 20-minute flight back from Kanye to Gaborone a love affair was begun.

*   *   *

The Cessna 185 proved the perfect 'bush' aeroplane. With a high wing configuration, power in abundance in the 6 cylinder Continental engine, excellent performance and load

33

carrying capacity, long range fuel tanks and 'balloon' tyres mounted on fixed landing gear, it was ideal for the long flight distances and the short, rough Desert landing strips of the Kalahari. It was the perfect machine for Flying Mission's first aircraft.

Flying Mission, or 'FM', as it soon became known, was about to get airborne.

Doctors Winters, Rempel and McArthur, all of us pilots and working for the Botswana Government, and based at the Princess Marina Hospital, were delighted with the aircraft. So also was Jay Aeschliman, the first full time Flying Mission pilot/mechanic, when he arrived later in 1981, seconded to Flying Mission by Mennonite Ministries.

*   *   *

Pre-Flight

Before any flight, it is worth spending time on a careful pre-flight inspection of the aircraft, to check that the airframe and power plant are in good order. Mental preparation is necessary to prepare the needed maps, airfield approach plates and, for night flying, a torch, as well as a check on the weather. A good pilot will systematically walk around the aeroplane and look for signs of damage - nicks in the propeller, dents in the fuselage, or perhaps a flat tyre - and remove covers that have been placed over air intakes and pitot tubes, and undo the tie downs. This pre-flight preparation and inspection should be unhurried and thorough if a flight is to be completed safely.

*   *   *

Frank Winters was a highly specialised ophthalmic surgeon from California. John Rempel was a general surgeon from Canada. We often indulged in a coffee break between surgical operations. In Sister Dikeledi's office, where we collected for such periods of refreshment, the table was frequently littered with patient's notes, mugs, a pot of sugar, a jar of Nescafe, an assortment of teaspoons and a bottle of milk.

"John, what've you done with the kettle?"

"Frederick the porter took it to make his tea." John got up and leant out of the glass door. "Hey, Frederick! Where's our kettle got to?"

Moments later an apologetic Frederick appeared. "I am sorry Ngaka. When the nurses in the autoclave room saw it they also wanted to use it." Frederick handed over the missing equipment, smiling happily. "I've filled it for you, and I've sent Gabriel for your next patient from the female ward." He departed in response to a call from Dr Bate, our Polish Anaesthetist, who was checking the Boyles anaesthetic machine in one of the operating theatres. Frank placed the somewhat battered electric kettle on the table and gingerly pushed the plug into a socket in the wall beside the desk. "We should get a new cable for this. Just look at all this insulation tape!"

"You know, we've been talking about a Flying Doctor Service." John spooned out Nescafe into three mugs. "I was talking with Bill Wood in the Ministry of Health the other day."

"Bill Wood? Who's he?"

"Well, you know that the Ministry of Health has set up a department to liase with all the mission hospitals and clinics. The idea is that this department can oversee grants that are given to the missions. Take your own hospital at Molepolole. By the time it was handed over to the Government it had been receiving Government funding for several years for such things as drugs and even the salaries of some of the Batswana nursing staff."

"Yes."

"Right. Well, Bill Wood is now running the office that's helping to set up what is being called the AMMB - the Association of Medical Missions of Botswana. All Government dealings with missions will, in future, be channelled through this new department. That way every mission will be treated the same and the Deborah Retief Memorial Hospital in Mochudi, say, won't get more funding than the Bamalethe Lutheran Hospital in Ramotswa."

"Mmm... Sounds a good idea."

After wheezing asthmatically for a while the aged kettle began, at last, to burp and spurt steam.

"Yes. You know that Primary Health Care is all the rage these days." John carefully poured boiling water into the waiting mugs. "Who's for sugar?"

"Please."

"Bill's keen that, rather than starting a Flying Doctor Service, it should be a Flying Health Service."

"There you go." Frank's eyes lit up.

"Well now, last time we were in Kang visiting Ngaire we got to hear about her new District Medical Officer (DMO). He's Norwegian and has been working in Zambia for the Flying Doctor Service up there. He's fed up with spending so much of his time here on bumpy roads and he'd really love to fly round his district. Perhaps one day we could be flying the DMO's round their districts. Maybe a Flying Health Service is not such a bad idea."

"Sounds great. And we'd really be able to build up our flying hours!"

"Doctor Winters." Doctor Bate's head appeared round the doorpost. "Bernadette has your patient with the cataracts asleep and waiting for you."

"OK. I'm coming." Frank drained his mug and got up. "The problem is that we're all medics and we're employed to be surgeons, not taxi drivers."

"He's right Malcolm."

"Yes, and another thing. I think we should keep the flying separate from Government." John and I had both worked with missions. John had been with the Africa Evangelical Fellowship (AEF) in Zululand and Gudrun and I had been with the United Free Church of Scotland at Molepolole. "Missions think, and do, things very differently from Government."

"That's true. And, on reflection, all the clinics in the Kalahari District are District Council Clinics but they're actually all staffed, at the moment, by mission nurses. That last mercy flight I did to Hukuntsi, the two Sisters there are from some German mission in Wuppertal, and Ngaire is AEF of course."

36

"Shouldn't we have a talk with Roy Davidson - he's a Southern Baptist missionary and also interested in flying? And some of the other mission folk should be included."

"Let's do that. Ah, there's Gabriel with my lady for removal of a breast lump. What have you got now?"

"I'm through for today. That last little guy was a tendon release for his clubfoot. It straightened up nicely. I'll go and check patients on the ward."

"Do me a favour and cast an eye on my man with the bladder irrigation and give the tube a squeeze. He's not bled much after his prostatectomy but I don't want him getting any blockages."

"Will do."

* * *

Start Up

After a couple of weeks things began to come together and, as usual, over steaming mugs of coffee, plans were nurtured in Matron Dikeledi's office between operations.

"Hey you guys. I have something to tell you."

Frank and John looked expectant.

"You know how hard it has been for us trying to get the Government Accounts Department to cough up travelling expenses when we use an aircraft to travel. Well I think we may get a break."

"Oh. Why?"

"Well, I was called in to see the Big Man yesterday."

"Oho!" Doctor Grazyna Bate, who came from Poland, put down her mug and leaned forward with mounting excitement. "You been swinging on that chandelier in the State House again?"

"Yep. I had to check the Presidential blood pressure."

"I cannot think why they choose a surgeon to check a blood pressure!" Dr Bate laughed. "And Lady K probably gave you tea in her special best china tea cups. Tell us all about it."

37

"Now Grazyna. Don't get jealous. You know perfectly well that they only call me in because Dr Merriweather is away on leave and they know me from Molepolole, and, yes, in fact Lady Khama was there and I did get tea."

"Well go on. Don't keep us in this terrible suspense."

"We got talking, and Seretse was asking about our work here at the Princess Marina Hospital. He likes to keep up to date with everything so that he can keep the Cabinet on their toes. And, somehow, Lady Khama got to asking me about how we travel round the District Hospitals and the subject of flying came up. Lady K was all for it. Seretse too, and, when I mentioned that we were having a problem getting approval from the Finance people for flights for our work Seretse's comment was that 'Yes, there are some people there in Finance who think that flying is just a rich man's hobby'. Lady K got quite worked up and I think our beloved President might well do something to loosen the string around the moneybags. I have a feeling that there may be a change of attitude in the pipeline. He certainly appreciates what we are doing."

"Wow Malcolm. That's great!" Frank was delighted. "I always thought The Lord had a special reason for getting you into visiting State House. I can see that things are beginning to move..."

"You see, Dr Bate," John pushed the plate of fat cakes toward Grazyna, "I keep reminding you that 'The Lord moves in mysterious ways'."

"Yes certainly I can see that." Grazyna laughed. "I just hope that, if our President ever needs an operation, you won't be told to do the anaesthetic and me the surgery!"

"Don't worry. Dominus providebit!"

"Yes. God certainly does provide. But John, we've been thinking of talking to various folk about a Flying Medical Service." Frank was looking thoughtful again. "Could we manage to fix a meeting sometime fairly soon? I think there are a number of mission folk who'll be interested."

John Rempel looked up from writing up his operation notes. "Sure. What about tomorrow evening if we can get word around to everyone? It'd have to be at our place. I don't think we can fix a baby-sitter that quickly."

"No problem. I saw Ngaire at the AEF headquarters and she told me that Marlis and Inge from Hukuntsi, and Marianne from Bokspits, are all in town at the moment."

"I don't think we've got anything on tomorrow evening." Frank looked thoughtful again. "Joy may have something but I can certainly manage it. What time?"

"Let's say seven thirty? Is that all right with you, Malcolm?"

"Sure. I'll give Don Genheimer a call. He'll want to come and he'll have some useful ideas."

*   *   *

Taxiing Out

"Well folks." Frank called the meeting to order. "Now that you've all had time to grab some tea, or coffee, and some of Lorna's excellent cookies, we want to run an idea passed you and get some feed back."

There was a general stir as people wriggled to get comfortable, or sipped their beverages, and Frank continued.

"First of all, thank you for coming. I know that many of you find it hard to make time in the evenings. Secondly... Thank you, Lorna and John, for allowing us all to take over your sitting room." He smiled round benignly and went on. "I think you are all aware that John and Malcolm and I fly aeroplanes and some of you also know that we've recently been offered the use of the Seventh Day Adventist Mission Cessna 185. The SDAs have made us a most generous offer. Their aircraft was originally donated to them to use for making mission and medical trips into the Kalahari. They had a Doctor Wical who was a pilot and who flew this airplane. But Doctor Wical returned to the USA a while ago and the SDA Mission now has no pilot. Their 'plane has been standing idle for almost a year. They have noted that we have been flying out to the Desert and they have suggested that we could use their aircraft if we pay for the costs of the flights. The suggestion has also been made that we set up some kind of Flying Medical

Service and, because John and Malcolm and I are all Christians, we thought we should put the idea to as many mission people as we could and see what people felt about the idea and, if it is right, to see how to go forward with this thing. We of course are Government Officers. We do fly in the course of our work but we'd all like to see this aircraft used to extend God's Kingdom as well as for medical purposes. So, that is why you have all been invited here tonight. Now, Don, you have been with the Africa Evangelical Fellowship for many years and I believe the AEF also use aircraft in their work. Would you like to make any comments to get the ball rolling?"

"Thanks Frank. Yes..." Don Genheimer gave us a bit of his own background and outlined something of the AEF flying programmes. From time to time others chipped in with comments and ideas and experiences.

"I sink zis is a great idea." Marianne Dumjahn had been Matron of the Bamalethe Lutheran Hospital in Ramotswa and had recently taken a posting to run the clinic at Bokspits in the far southwest corner of Botswana. "You know it vill take me two days to get back to ze clinic in Bokspits. If zer vos such a service it would take me back in just a few hours."

"Yes, and for us also." Marlis Schwarzwaelder, also from Germany, was always full of stories of Desert road travel and the long hours of driving. "Often we have to drive at night, too, to get an emergency patient to Lobatse Hospital. A airplane would be so much better."

"Mission Aviation Fellowship (MAF) did come to Botswana some years ago and they did a survey to see if it would be worthwhile for them to work in Botswana but they thought there would not be enough flying for it to be worth it."

"Mmm, and I have also seen a proposal put to Government by AMREF, the African Medical Research Foundation in Nairobi. Doctor Michael Wood was asked to come and assess the possibilities of setting up a Flying Doctor Service. It was a detailed proposal but nothing came of it."

"What we have in mind is not just a medical service but something that would also be of benefit to churches and missions here in Botswana. A Christian ministry with the primary aim of extending Christ's Kingdom."

Refuelling A2-ZGB at the old Gaborone airport

Dr Merriweather helping to unload a patient

The discussion was lively and, gradually, a plan came into focus.

"Ladies and gentlemen I propose that we ask Don Genheimer to look into procedures and to report back at a meeting to be planned once the initial investigations and preparations have been made." Frank brought the evening to a close. "But first of all I think we should ask The Lord for His direction and blessing on this whole project. It could become something big."

A time of prayer followed. A proposal was put to a vote and a decision made to move forward with the setting up of "a Flying Mission". The meeting was then adjourned.

Don subsequently did his homework and, a short while later, a further meeting of interested parties resulted in the recording of "Members present" and the formation of an Executive Committee to administer and run the new venture.

The propeller had begun to spin. Forward movement was beginning... Slow at first, but it quickly picked up speed.

*   *   *

Taking Off

To sit at the end of a runway with an idling engine does not result in flight. It requires further effort to push the throttle forward... and faith that the machinery will not only lift off and climb enough to clear the fence at the end of that runway... but also take one on to the intended destination.

*   *   *

Gudrun was recovering from major abdominal surgery. I was sitting at her bedside trying to collect my thoughts and watching her dozing under the effects of the post-op medications, when there was a gentle knock and Mervyn Mason poked his head around the door.

"Oh Malcolm. What happened?" His eyes widened.

Over the next few minutes I filled him in with the details of Gudrun's surgery.

"Wow! That's too bad. I'd come back later but I really need to talk with you about 'The Quiet Hour'."

At the sound of our voices Gudrun stirred and opened her eyes, saw Mervyn and smiled weakly.

"Honey, Mervyn's looked in because he wants to talk about 'The Quiet Hour'."

"Hello Mervyn. I'm sorry to be like this. But you two talk and I'll just listen."

"Well, I'd be grateful. You see I have to take an answer back to our Mission Board this afternoon."

"Sure, Mervyn. Pull up that chair and tell us what the problem is. Are we not paying enough rental for the aircraft?"

"Oh, no! Nothing like that." Mervyn settled himself in the chair and leaned forward. "Actually the arrangement we have with you to use our Cessna 185 is working nicely and everyone is delighted. But are you sure it's all right for me to stay for a while?"

"Mervyn, go ahead. I'm fine. Really." Gudrun was wide-awake and keen to hear what the Business Manager from the Seventh Day Adventist (SDA) Mission Hospital in Kanye, had to say.

"Right. I'll be brief. In a nutshell, our Board has decided that we are unlikely to be able to get another pilot in the foreseeable future."

"And?"

"Doctors Mueller and Wical, who used to fly the aeroplane out into the Kalahari to do clinic trips, left us some time ago to return home. We had hoped to find a replacement pilot but, after a year of trying, we've not found anyone." He paused. "The fact is that some of the Board members are pushing to sell the aircraft. Now, you are using the 'plane for what it was donated to us for - medical trips into the Kalahari. So, I at least want to give you the first option to buy the aircraft."

There was a stunned silence. The IV fluid dripping into Gudrun's arm continued to drip steadily and silently. The familiar clatter of the hospital seemed to become quiet.

"Well, Mervyn." I was at a loss for words. Yes, 'The Quiet Hour' was a wonderful aeroplane. Also it was now being used for flights out into the Kalahari for visits to the new clinics at Kang and Hukuntsi. The rugged build of the Cessna 185 model was exceptionally suited to the rough, bush airstrips of the Desert. The high wing configuration allowed a good clearance of any bushes that might be growing close to the landing area and the other bonus was that the pilot, and passengers, had some shade from the hot sun. Being a tail wheeled aircraft, the single propeller was high off the ground during taxiing and that saved it from damage from flying stones and gravel. The long-range fuel tanks and the big 'balloon' tyres were enormous assets for long distances and for landing in deep sand. It was a most suitable aeroplane for what we were doing, but there was one major problem.

"Mervyn. We do have one big difficulty." I was going to give it to him 'straight'. "We do believe that this 'plane is ideal and fits perfectly with what we believe God wants us to be doing. But..." I paused for a moment, "what sort of figure have you got in mind if we were to buy this aircraft?"

"I was hoping you'd come to that." Mervyn's eyes twinkled and a smile spread across his face. "I am a Business Manager after all! We think the aircraft is worth about twenty-nine, or thirty thousand rand."

"Mmm. At this point we don't have a bean, let alone thirty thousand rand. Honey, what do you think?"

"Malcolm, I can't help feeling it's right." Gudrun's voice was clear and steady from across the white sheets. "I think we need to pray about it."

"I think that would be the way to go forward." Mervyn's smile widened.

In the unlikely situation of that hospital room, we bowed our heads and asked God to make clear to us what He wanted us to do and, after we had each sent up our requests, we sat for a while in silence.

"Mervyn, Gudrun and I have been thinking of this kind of mission service for some time. It was absolutely miraculous timing the way you appeared when you came that first time to offer us the use of 'The Quiet Hour'. I believe The Lord wants us to go forward with this. I don't know how it can be paid off, but, if you allow us to continue to use the aircraft as we have been, paying you the rental, as we have to date, then, as money comes in, we will pay it off. However, I think it may take up to six months. Would your Board be happy if we pay it off over six Months?"

"I'll put it to them." Mervyn was serious now. "We'll see what they say."

"Yes. And, in the meantime, let's all continue to pray much about it." Gudrun was becoming quite excited. "If it's what God wants then it will happen somehow."

Mervyn departed. Gudrun went back to sleep. I pondered.

*   *   *

The Seventh Day Adventist Mission Board did approve.

Gudrun recovered well and was soon out of hospital and back to her usual, lively self.

We wrote a newsletter to our friends, telling of Gudrun's surgery and mentioning that we had been offered an aircraft for mission and medical work and requesting prayer for the 'project'.

Life went on much as before. But not for long...

"Honey... The post today has an interesting letter in it."

"Oh. From whom?"

"It's from the Springfield Mennonite Church in Pennsylvania."

"Well... What do they want?"

"They've sent us a cheque for one hundred American dollars... 'to put toward an aeroplane'!"

"How did they know we were buying an aeroplane?"

"I've no idea!"

We never did find out. And, over the next six months there was seldom a day that went past that we did not receive a letter from somewhere in the world containing a cheque, or a money order, or a promise of some kind of support for what was later to become known as the Flying Mission. Often we knew the givers, but, just as often, we had never heard of them before.

Of course The Lord provided a lot more than just the finance. It was amazing how just the right person would walk into our lives at exactly the right moment.

"Malcolm, you need to open a bank account..." John Freeman of the Africa Evangelical Fellowship had mission administration experience that was invaluable in setting up account books.

"To open a mission bank account you need a constitution." The Bank Manager was wonderfully helpful. "Richard Lyons, can fix that for you. He's a lawyer."

"You'll have to get registered with the Registrar of Societies. The mission should be set up as a charitable organisation." Donald Genheimer, also from the Africa Evangelical Fellowship, had years of experience in mission service in Africa.

It was not long before Flying Mission had a legal Executive Committee, a few Members and its first three volunteer pilots - John Rempel, my surgical colleague at the Princess Marina Hospital, Frank Winters, the eye surgeon, and myself and over the following months Frank, John and I used 'The Quiet Hour' for our visits to the more distant hospitals and clinics.

Periodically, requests came for one of us to do a 'mercy flight' to a Desert clinic to bring in a patient with some kind of medical, surgical, or obstetrical emergency. Soon requests came from the District Medical Officers for us to make specialist expertise available to patients in the more remote areas of the country. On such visits to the rural areas, it became apparent that flying would be an enormous help to the District Medical Officers themselves, saving them much time and energy as their own duties normally took many days of tiring travel by road.

*   *   *

Frank Winters & his Nurse arrive at KANG

"Mervyn. I have another cheque for you..." became an often repeated phrase.

Gifts came from many people and organisations. We were amazed and humbled. And, two weeks before the six months deadline for payment was reached, that aeroplane was paid off in full.

"Dominus providebit."

Thank You Lord!

-oOo-

!Xabaile

CHAPTER 3
AIRBORNE

-Δ-

To sit at the holding point of the runway awaiting take-off clearance is the culmination of hours, days, and sometimes weeks of preparation. Have all the checks been made? Is the aircraft airworthy? Is there enough fuel in the tanks? Does the pilot have the correct maps for the route to be flown and instrument approach plates for the destination airport and an alternate landing point should it not be possible to reach the planned destination? Has the load been positioned and fixed to keep the aircraft centre of gravity within safe margins?

Then, as the pilot eases the throttle forward and the motor roars the aircraft begins to move. Acceleration increases and at that moment when the lifting force generated by airflow over the wings exceeds the weight and drag, flight begins. Vibrations from the wheels running over the tarmac, or sand and gravel, is replaced by smooth flight.

Once airborne doubts may still arise. Can that fence at the end of the runway really be cleared? Or those treetops a little farther away? Faith can expect to be tested.

*   *   *

*The dedication service in Kang for 'The Quiet Hour'.
This was led by Moruti (Pastor) Africa Katai from the Kang
church, and Pastor Roy Davidson who founded the Gaborone
Open Baptist Church*

In some ways, looking back now, the start up of Flying Mission and its subsequent 'take off' were haphazard from a human point of view. Certainly the way the Mission has grown and developed is far beyond anything that was envisaged in the early days and yet there seems to have been a purposeful oversight and progression to the point where it is today.

Yes there were times of doubt and questioning but the obstacles were overcome. Altitude was enough to 'clear the fence'... and the treetops too. Many exciting and wonderful experiences were in store.

*   *   *

Weights

It was one of those days. A jangling operating theatre telephone in the background added to the tension.

"There, Bright. Slip your finger into that plane of cleavage. Work your finger round right and left till you have the whole tumour isolated and loose on the urethral 'stalk'. Then cut it flush with scissors."

"Ho! It comes easily!" Bright's smile showed his white teeth to perfection.

"Ngaka, Dr. Merriweather is on the 'phone." Sister Dikeledi, the Operating Theatre Superintendent had sidled up behind me. "There has been a police radio message to collect a woman with an obstructed labour from Hukuntsi. Can you fly out and collect her?"

"Yes I think so. Bright, can you finish off here? Just remember – use the largest De Pezzer catheter you can get and keep the irrigation going well till it clears of blood. And don't warm the irrigation fluid... it will only make bleeding worse."

"Sure, I'll manage." Bright Bagwasi was always keen to try any surgical procedure. He was quick to learn and, a few years later, he would earn a Fellowship of the Edinburgh College of Surgeons. At this point he was proving himself a capable assistant and could easily finish what was left of the operating list for that day. There was nothing major now that we had done the prostatectomy.

As I drove out of the hospital gates, a weight seemed to lift. It had been a hard morning. The thought of a flight out to the Desert promised some time to think. The route was familiar. The weather was perfect. Daylight was sufficient if I got away smartly and all went without a hitch. However, I was still tense and 'keyed up' from the surgery.

When I parked my vehicle at the airport and walked out onto the tarmac the Cessna 185 somehow looked expectant. I put my briefcase with maps, plotter and a torch onto the co-pilot's seat. Pre-flight walk around was uneventful, if a bit skimpy. But I had a lot on my mind and wanted to get away quickly. The 'plane was already fuelled. Start-up was normal.

"Gaborone Tower, Alpha Two Zulu Golf Bravo request taxi clearance for Hukuntsi please."

"Alpha Two Zulu Golf Bravo cleared to the holding point zero eight..." There followed the usual figures and the instruction to "Call ready for take-off."

"Zulu Golf Bravo, Roger." The throttle was half open and the engine roaring. I checked the RPM expecting the normal enthusiastic lurch forward... But nothing happened.

A bit more throttle. A lot more noise. And vibration. And then, at last, a sluggish movement.

"That's funny." I thought. "Am I dreaming? Why doesn't this 'plane move? Brakes are off ... Oh well, we seem to be going now."

But it took forever to get to the turn at the end of the taxiway. The little 'plane that was usually so eager to fly, was somehow really sluggish today.

How dumb can one get?

"Tail trim neutral. Throttle friction nut tight. Mixture rich, and fuel on and sufficient." I intoned my way meticulously through the pre-takeoff checklist.

"Gaborone Tower, Alpha Two Zulu Golf Bravo is ready for take-off."

As I finished speaking into the microphone and released the transmit button it suddenly dawned on me what the problem was. That skimpy pre-flight examination. With too much on my mind, and wanting to hurry, I had not untied the tail weight - a 50 litre oil can that I had scrounged from Noel Fitzgerald in the Kalahari Air Services and Charter (KASAC) hangar and had filled with concrete with a big iron hoop set carefully into the top of the heavy mixture.

"Zulu Golf Bravo is cleared for takeoff zero eight. Wind..."

The rest of the take-off clearance was lost on me as I embarked on my next stupid exercise of the day, throttling back to idling, setting the parking brake and hopping out onto the tarmac.

It was the work of only a few seconds to untie that weight and roll it into the grass beside the taxiway for later retrieval. But, when I turned around, I found that the now unrestricted aircraft was inching forward and beginning a turn to the left.

Of course, I managed to jump in and regain control... I think even before the controller realised what had happened, because he repeated his instructions and by that time I was 'back in business' and able to hastily acknowledge the takeoff clearance.

"Zulu Golf Bravo, roger, and we are rolling for takeoff on zero eight. Left turn out."

The throttle advanced smoothly. The engine roared - again. But, this time, there was a most satisfying surge forward and, moments later, the tail lifted. We were on our way.

After those two mistakes, and a little time to think things through, the day got rapidly better. The flight was uneventful. The patient was duly collected and brought back to Gaborone - where she later was delivered safely of a lively infant.

Once I had shut down the Cessna 185 in the usual parking spot, I walked out to the run-up area, retrieved the tail weight out of the grass and rolled it back to its place on the apron. Then, after fixing the rope from the weight to the tail tie-down ring on the under surface of the fuselage, I walked round the aircraft fixing tie-downs on the wings too and, after making sure all was secure, I headed for home thinking about weights - and my stupidity at forgetting to untie that one on the tail.

Tie down weights have their uses. When the aircraft is parked, those weights tied onto the tail and the wings have saved our Cessna 185 on several occasions when other light aircraft on the airfield have been blown about and suffered some severe damage. A high wind, or the passage of a 'dust devil', can easily flip a light aircraft over onto its back.

I learned some lessons. The experience was a vivid reminder of the effects of sin and that, as Christians, we 'should throw off those sins which so easily beset us... and run with patience the race which is set before us'. That 50 litre oil can filled up with concrete and tied onto the tail was a wonderful example of how sin is an impediment in life. And the weight slows one down horribly.

A couple more bits of advice from the 'textbook of life' came to mind as well... The first... "He that believeth shall not make haste." And, the second... "Let all things be done decently and in order."

*   *   *

A Curled Prop

The Cessna 185 is an aeroplane of character. Parked on the ground, the nose is held high and the propeller has a much better clearance than the average nose wheel aircraft. This is one of the features that makes it an ideal 'bush' aeroplane. The 'prop' is less liable to sustain damage from gravel sucked off the surface of a rough airstrip. But there are occasions...

"John, Malcolm." Frank Winters had popped his head round the door of Sister Dikeledi's office. "Are either of you planning anything with the 185 this afternoon?"

"Not me Frank." I had a stack of paperwork to get caught up with.

"Nor me," echoed John Rempel. "I've got a patient with a fractured forearm that needs plating and I've still got a prostatectomy to do."

"OK then, I'd like to go and get some practice with 'roll on' landings. There's a nice steady crosswind breeze coming from the north west."

"Ho... Brave man!" John leant back in his chair. "Rather you than me. That 'plane has a will of its own on a calm day, let alone in a crosswind."

"Ah, it's not that difficult. First get her descending nicely under power. Then keep your upwind wing down a little and keep her straight with the opposite rudder. When you touch down, push the nose down to keep her on the deck and watch for the tendency to swing into the wind. That large tail surface acts like a weather vane if you're not careful."

"Yeah, and the other trick that's useful is to land as diagonally across the runway as you can - into the wind."

"Thanks you guys. I guess it's like doing a corneal graft. Once one gets the hang of it it's easy really..." Frank departed for the airport.

John went off to scrub for the prostatectomy and I headed for the pile of paper in my own office... Reports... Letters... The weekend duty roster...

*   *   *

Some two hours later, having cleared my desk, I was about to head home when the telephone jangled.

"Hey Malcolm." It was Frank. "Can you come over to the airport? I need to show you something." He sounded serious.

"Sure. I'll be there in about five minutes." I hung up wondering what Frank had found. The C185 was an old aeroplane. When we first began using it we found that the fuel bladder in the left wing had a small leak and it eventually required the installation of a new bladder. There always seemed to be something that needed attention.

A short while later I was on the tarmac and enjoying the cool breeze. There - parked at the fuel pumps was 'The 'Quiet Hour' looking splendid. Nose jauntily high. Dark green paintwork gleaming in the late afternoon sunshine. Frank was leaning against a wing strut.

"Thanks for coming Malcolm." Frank looked sombre.

"No problem, Frank. It's always nice to get out of the hospital and walk in fresh air. How did your crosswind landings go? Have you perfected the art of a smooth, roll on landing?"

"You know Malcolm, I thought I had done just fine." Frank brightened a little. "Like you guys suggested, I set up a nice long final approach. And that trick of holding the wing down and slipping in... It's great. My trouble is getting that nose forward the moment she touches down. Push forward a moment too late and wow... You can bounce! And once that starts it seems to go on."

"That's right. One almost has to fly it on. In fact, to really get the hang of it, it's worth finding a long, wide runway where there is minimal traffic. Then just fly along the runway simply bouncing gently. That way one can get a really good 'feel' for a precise roll on landing."

"Yeah. Well I thought I was doing quite well, but I must have had a really hard landing." Frank mopped his forehead. "When I got here to the pumps to refuel the BP fuel attendant asked me what had happened to the prop!"

"And...?"

"Well come and look."

Leaving the shade of the wing we strolled forward to the nose of the aircraft.

"Look at that." Frank pointed to the tips of the two propeller blades. "I have no idea when that happened. I heard nothing unusual. And it was only when our friend here pointed it out that I saw these two curled over tips."

"Wow, Frank!" I gazed in amazement at the gracefully curved propeller tips. "That's about the end four inches... bent backward... pretty well ninety degrees..."

"That's right. And I am so sorry Malcolm." Frank was the picture of abject misery. "I honestly have no idea when it happened. Yes, I suppose I did do some pretty bouncy landings, but I didn't think they were that bad, and, as I say, I never heard a thing that would have suggested all that damage."

"Don't be upset Frank. At least you didn't get hurt. Let's go and find Noel, over at Kalahari Air Services and see what he says about it."

*   *   *

"Yes, Doctor Mac." Noel Fitzgerald looked grave. "Do you want the good news, or the bad news first?"

"Let us have both Noel... Please."

"Well, the good news is that I can get a new prop for you from Jo'burg fairly quickly." He paused.

"And the bad news?"

"The bad news is that, when Bob Hampshire from the Department of Civil Aviation came to inspect the prop, he wanted to know exactly how it had happened and I told him what Doctor Winters had told me. "

"And? "

Some airstrips were a little rough (Cartoon: S Mingham)

"Bob immediately said that, because the damage had been done with the engine running at more than idling speed, he had no option but to order the engine be stripped to inspect the crankshaft and cylinders for damage. He also wanted me to do a thorough check on the landing gear."

"Oops! That sounds bad." I had a sudden vision of a large bill coming our way.

"Yes, I'm afraid 'Oops' is about right. "Noel ran his fingers through his wavy hair and grimaced. "I've already done the landing gear. No problems there. Hey, that undercarriage must have really splayed out for the prop to hit the tarmac like that. But the engine... We'll have to send it to Jo'burg, and that's going to take time... And money."

*   *   *

In the Bible, in the book of Romans, the apostle Paul reminds us that '...in all things God works for good with those who love Him.'

The 'apparent' disaster of having to have that engine stripped was indeed a costly exercise. However, once the engineers in Jo'burg had the machine disassembled and in bits they found that a number of the parts were not the standard, high quality Continental Engine parts but, instead, some badly worn, replacement bits and pieces of dubious origin that had been put in by some 'bush mechanic' during an earlier engine overhaul. The verdict was that, if the engine had continued to run, it would not have been long before it would most probably have given trouble and, perhaps even, have seized up... Not an ideal thing to happen when flying over a remote area of the Kalahari Desert!

Yes... The apostle Paul was right... 'in all things... God works for good with those who love Him.'

"Thank you Lord."

*   *   *

P & G Factors

The 'P factor' needs explaining for anyone who does not have aviation training. If the following information if hard to understand I apologise, and there is no penalty for skipping on to the next paragraph.

'P factor' is the term applied to the effect of the slipstream from the propeller as it flows back in a corkscrew fashion over the tail plane meeting the vertical fin at an angle of attack. This generates a sideways aerodynamic force, which tends to yaw the nose of the aeroplane. The pilot can balance this yaw effect with opposite rudder pressure. The slipstream effect is most pronounced under conditions of high power and low airspeed (e.g. during take off and climb) when the 'corkscrew' is tighter and its 'angle of attack' at the fin is greater. The direction of the yaw resulting from the slipstream effect depends on the direction of propeller rotation. If the propeller rotates clockwise when viewed from the cockpit, the slipstream from the downward moving propeller blade passes underneath the fuselage and strikes the fin on the left hand side causing a tendency for the nose to yaw to the left. Counter-clockwise, rotation has the opposite effect.

Having got the technicalities out of the way let me get on with the story!

*   *   *

We were standing on the tarmac beside 'The Quiet Hour' sharing thoughts and ideas and enjoying the warm afternoon sunshine.

"Malcolm, that singing group in the USA that originally collected the funds needed to buy this aircraft for the Seventh Day Adventist Mission."

"Yes, John?"

"Well, 'The Quiet Hour' was a great name for them, but hardly for this aircraft." John Rempel had run his fingers along the propeller's leading edge seeking nicks. "It's certainly not what folk must think of this 'plane. When we take off in this the whole of Gaborone knows about it. This thing roars!"

"I guess that's typical of a Cessna 185. It's just a noisy bird."

"That's true, but, on the other hand, that's because there's plenty power in the engine." Frank Winters ran his hand lovingly over the dark green paintwork. "She climbs like a homesick angel, and that's a big blessing when we have to get out of some of the strips we have to land on. Although, on the ground... she does behave a bit like a wild horse!"

"Well it's a tail-dragger. It's different from an aircraft with a nose wheel." My own training on a tail wheel Auster had prepared me for flying the Cessna 185. "You have to keep on your toes all the time. Let it get out of hand - even for a moment - and you can be in big trouble fast."

"Sure... And don't forget the 'P Factor'." Frank had many hours flying under his belt and had owned his own aircraft back in the USA. "Bill Scott in the Department of Civil Aviation reminded me of that the other day. Remember... When you open the throttle for take-off, as you build up speed, she'll try and swing her nose to the left... and, if you let her start that, you'll have a real job to bring her back in line."

"Thanks Frank. I'll try and remember."

'... the dark green paintwork.'

"And hey... bringing the tail up adds another problem to do with a gyro effect if I remember rightly."

"That's correct. With the prop spinning, when you raise the tail you're actually trying to turn the 'prop disk', which results in a tendency to swing the prop disk sideways at ninety degrees to the vertical tail movement."

"Yep... And that's on top of the P Factor. I'd forgotten that." Frank laughed. "This aircraft's got real temperament. Wow... ground loops... you guys ever done one of those? That's a landing problem of course because of the long fuselage. One of the Kalahari Air Service pilots told me that when he had to fly a 185 up from Cape Town, by the time he landed at Gaborone, he'd managed to do three ground loops, one at each of his refuelling stops! What fun. They say that the ground loop sorts pilots into two categories - those who have... And those who will!"

"At least the prop has a good clearance. We would have a lot more problems like this if the prop was nearer the ground." John had found a small nick in one blade. "I'll ask

Noel to file this out. Is it OK by you two if I fly to Ghanzi in this machine tomorrow?"

"Sure. Enjoy the trip."

"OK, with that encouragement I'll go and do a couple of circuits and get the 'old lady' refuelled and tied down for the night." John climbed in and Frank and I retreated to a safe distance.

"Yeah... We could stand here all day and talk, about airplanes. It's such a lovely afternoon. Not too hot." Frank ran his fingers through his hair. "But I need to get home. Joy will be wondering where I am and little Sam will no doubt be up to some mischief."

He sauntered off and I watched, as John taxied to the holding point of runway zero eight. The windsock hung limply. 'The Quiet Hour' lifted her voice and began her take off roll. The tail came up and, seconds later, she leapt into the cloudless, blue sky.

*   *   *

"It's for you Ngaka." Sister Dikeledi handed me the telephone. "It's the switchboard. They have Doctor Rempel on the radio from Ghanzi."

The patient's condition, the surgery we had just finished and the operation notes I was in the middle of writing, were pushed to the back of my mind as I took the receiver.

"Eee Ngaka, we have Doctor Rempel patched through from the police radio. Can you speak with him please?"

"Malcolm. Is that you? Over." It was John's voice. The crackling atmospherics made it hard to hear him.

"Yes John. Go ahead. What's the problem? Over."

"I made it to Ghanzi just fine and I finished seeing all their patients in good time. But I've had some... " His voice faded behind a burst of severe crackling.

"Sorry John. I lost you. Please repeat. Over."

"I was saying that I had trouble on take off. Over."

"Ehe. What sort of trouble? Over."

A further burst of unintelligible noise blocked him out.

"Say again please. Over."

61

Ditonkie (Donkeys) qualify as obstacles.
(Photo: J Calhoon)

Gradually, over the switchboard's connection to the police radio network, I got the story. The combinations of a brisk cross wind, some goats where they should not have been, and that P Factor had ended in a swerve off the gravel runway. After a valiant attempt to bring the aircraft under control, and realising that he had lost the battle, John had managed to stop the engine before the C185 had ploughed into a fence post. It seemed that he had got away with only one bent propeller blade. It could have been much worse. Thankfully, no one was hurt.

* * *

Noel Fitzgerald, when I 'phoned him, was full of sympathy. "No problem Doc. I'll fly up to Ghanzi in the morning. We've got a spare prop in the KASAC hangar. I'll take that along and, so long as there's no more damage, we'll be back by lunchtime. It's a good thing he shut down the engine before the prop strike, otherwise it would have meant stripping the engine again. But I'm sure it'll be OK."

And it was. The prop change went without a hitch. There was no other damage and the engine ran as smoothly as ever. The goats had long disappeared. The fence post survived to continue service as a fence post. And John - he had added 5 hours Pilot in Command time to his log book as well as chalking up first hand experience handling a C185. He had also been orientated to the 'G Factor'... Goats running out onto the runway!

*   *   *

'The Angel' always remained homesick, noisy in the air, and like a wild horse - hard to control - whenever she flew near the ground. But we loved her.

The moral of the story? Well... a little sin - if it is not dealt with quickly - can lead to disaster. It's much better to keep on one's toes and correct a problem with one's direction of travel before it gets out of hand and runs away with one. And, of course, make sure there are no goats (or donkeys) in your vicinity, check the wind and correct for drift, and aim to keep exactly to the runway centre line. That way one can be sure of God's protection and one has the best possibility of reaching one's destination safely.

*   *   *

In the Wet or A2 - WHO

Whisky Hotel Oscar was a Rheims 'Rocket'... A 'souped up' Cessna 172 with an adjustable pitch prop. The aircraft was well equipped for 'instrument flying' in bad weather. But those were the days before I had my Instrument Rating.

The registration letters reflecting the World Health Organisation, for whom the owner of the aircraft worked, were painted in bold white on the blue fuselage. It was a trim and energetic little machine and it was available for rental to us through the new Kalahari Flying Club in Gaborone.

*　　*　　*

The rains had come. The Batswana rejoiced and began scattering to their 'lands' as was usual in the weeks before Christmas. There would be much activity ploughing, now that the soil was moist and crops could germinate.

Gudrun and I had planned a weekend trip to Kang. Ngaire was away on leave and Joy, a nurse from South Africa connected with Ngaire's Mission - the Africa Evangelical Fellowship - had stepped in to help out. We had promised the Mission Director that we would 'keep an eye on her' and be supportive.

The flight out was uneventful. Whisky Hotel Oscar behaved perfectly. The weather was clear. The weekend went well. Joy was managing the clinic nicely. We planned to get back to Gaborone early the next day.

"Malcolm, I wonder if I could come back to Gabs. with you?" Joy looked at us hopefully over supper. "It would mean that the clinic driver wouldn't need to drive me out and I would be very happy to have the extra day for shopping."

"Sure... No problem."

"And would there perhaps also be enough room for Tshimologo... He's our Tuberculosis (TB) Assistant. He also needs to get to Gabs."

"That's fine... so long as the two of you don't have too much luggage. Tshimologo won't want to bring a goat or something?"

A rain lily

"Oh no... at least I don't think so. But I'll check."

"That would be a good idea. The last lad I gave a lift to was Keoagile. I was going to fly from Molepolole to Gaborone and he asked if he could come. He said he wanted to visit his mother. I thought he just wanted a flight and didn't bother to ask about luggage. He turned up with a large cardboard box and said he would be really grateful if he could take it with him as the kombi drivers were refusing because it took up too much space. I had no other passengers so there was plenty of room. But I discovered later the real reason why the kombi drivers were refusing to take that box."

"Well... Why?" I knew Joy would be inquisitive.

"By the time we landed the 'plane was full of a most horrible stench... And there was a big, dark red stain coming through the cardboard of the box."

"Oh yuck...no!"

"Yes you've perhaps guessed. When Keoagile took the box out of the 'plane he placed it carefully on the tarmac and lifted a flap to show me. It contained a whole cow's head. He was so grateful. He said his mother would be absolutely delighted and it would make a fine feast!"

"Well... you know I said I'm sure Tshimologo won't want to bring any animals." Joy put on an appealing look. "I was going to ask if it would be all right if I take my cat along."

"Joy I'll be happy for you to take your cat if you sedate it somehow and keep it in a box or basket. One of our pilots once had a cat jumping all round the cabin."

"What happened?"

"Well, the cat became more and more agitated and active and in desperation someone opened a window and the thing was out in a flash..."

"Oh no!"

"Yes. And I don't want to have to cope with that sort of situation."

As it happened, the flight next morning had plenty excitement of another sort...

*   *   *

66

Keith & Jo Irvine's little dogs were always exemplary passengers

Monday dawned clear. A beautiful, sparkling Kalahari morning.

By eight o'clock we were packed into Whisky Hotel Oscar. As usual, we bowed our heads in prayer to ask The Lord for protection and safety for this flight and, a short while later, we were airborne and banking gently over the glistening whiteness of Kang pan and onto our heading of 112 degrees for Gaborone.

"That salt pan is big ... And the cattle down there look soooo small!" Tshimologo took in every detail.

"Yes, and look... There is the road to Phuduhudu." Joy tapped the Perspex of the window. "It looks so straight from up here. I'm glad we're flying and not bumping down there on that road. Just think, we would only get to Gaborone sometime late this evening... If we had no punctures or other problems."

"How's the cat?"

"Fine." Joy peeped into the wicker basket in which the pet had been imprisoned and seemed satisfied.

"Well we should make it by about nine thirty." I settled to my time and distance calculations in preparation for a call to the Johannesburg Control Centre. "I'm climbing up to nine thousand feet where it should be nice and smooth."

My passengers settled down. Gudrun dozed. Joy cradled her imprisoned cat. Tshimologo kept craning to look out of his side window.

Twenty minutes out from Kang I made contact with Jo'burg on the short wave HF radio and gave them my route details and our estimated time of arrival in Gaborone. They did not report anything of note. However, I could see the beginning of some grey cloud ahead.

By the time we were overhead Dutlwe that cloud was looking distinctly solid and by Takatokwane I began descending to keep within sight of the ground. A short while later Jo'burg informed me that Gaborone was reporting rain, but by that time we were well passed our 'point of no return' as far as fuel. Anyway, it would not be the first time I had had to land in rain and Molepolole was a good alternative airfield if need be.

As the cloud base lowered so did we. By Lethlakeng - some fifty miles from Molepolole, and about ninety-five from Gaborone - we were well below five hundred feet and rain was beginning to streak the windshield. The sun had long departed and we were sandwiched between a grey-green world above us, and a brown, soggy mass of bush passing below. However, the sand track stood out clearly and I knew from many road trips that there were no major hills or obstructions between Molepolole and us.

"My Darling." Gudrun was awake and peering ahead. "Do you think we'll make it to Gaborone?"

"We shall see my Sweetie." I pointed forward. "That's Molepolole ahead. We'll have a look at the airfield before we go on."

"The rain is getting heavier."

"Mmm. We'll be fine." The altimeter was wagging an accusing finger at me. We had descended lower... much lower. I estimated the tops of the telephone poles passing beneath us to be about fifty feet away. Every now and then visibility dropped to zero in every direction except down.

"...get your head down ... and pray!"

"There's the hospital to the right and if we turn a little left... there... there's the airfield."

The rain increased as the completely waterlogged strip of Molepolole passed below us and I made the decision to press on.

Because we were flying so low I had not managed to make contact with the Gaborone Control Tower. However, Whisky Hotel Oscar's VHF radio came to life abruptly.

"Whisky Hotel Oscar, Gaborone Control."

"Gaborone, Whisky Hotel Oscar. Go ahead."

"Whisky Hotel Oscar, be advised that Gaborone is now closed. We have a cloud base of two hundred feet and periodic heavy rain. If you are near Molepolole you should land there."

"Gaborone, Whisky Hotel Oscar is overhead Molepolole at this moment and it looks a little too wet to land here. I can see it is clearer toward Gaborone and I'll come on in if I may."

"Whisky Hotel Oscar. I repeat. Gaborone is closed." The controller was adamant.

Rain lashed the windshield in front of us reducing visibility drastically although the side windows were nice and clear.

"Malcolm you told him Molepolole was just a little bit wet but the whole airstrip is under water!" Gudrun was horrified.

"Whisky Hotel Oscar. I repeat. Gaborone is closed. You must land at Molepolole."

"Gaborone, Whisky Hotel Oscar. Roger."

"There Honey... You see that gap in the cloud. It's lighter on the other side... And once we are over these low hills on the Gabs. side of Moleps. we'll be home and dry."

"But..."

"You get your head down... and pray!"

Ten degrees of flap, and bringing the throttle back a little, slowed us nicely. We were over a tarred road now and I knew that it had some straight bits that would make a good place to land... if we really had to.

As the wet, thorn bush covered hills rose toward us, the cloud ahead lifted a little and the rain eased slightly.

"There... We may not be 'home and dry' but we are almost home!"

My passengers sat mute. The Kopje (a rocky hill) just West of Gaborone was now easily visible... And the Gaborone dam behind it. And, there to the left, was the town and the airport. A welcome sight!

"Gaborone Tower Whisky Hotel Oscar is left base."

"Whisky Hotel Oscar." There was a pause. "Whisky Hotel Oscar is cleared to land."

"Thank you. Whisky Hotel Oscar."

Moments later we were parked in the usual spot.

"Whisky Hotel Oscar is closing down. Thank you very much."

"Whisky Hotel Oscar, please report to the tower." The order was curt.

I pulled out the mixture control and the engine died. Silence descended... but only for a moment. Suddenly everyone was talking at once...

"Ooops! My Darling. He doesn't sound too happy with you!"

"Oh Malcolm... I've never been so frightened in all my life..."

"Oaee Ngaka. That was wonderful! We flew just like the birds. It was fantastic!"

"Well... let's thank The Lord for answered prayers"

"Yes... Thank You Lord."

*   *   *

"Now Doctor. Explain yourself." The Controller was not amused. He went into a long and detailed accusation and listed all the terrible things that would happen to me. "This airport is closed on account of the weather. Anything could have happened..."

"Well, it really was wet at Molepolole. I thought we'd very probably nose over in the mud if we tried to land there. And by that time I could see that Gaborone was clearing enough to get to easily."

"But I told you Gaborone was closed and that you must land at Molepolole!"

"Yes. But you weren't flying the 'plane!"

"I'm very upset with you. You really had me over a barrel!"

"Well... I am sorry. I really am."

I was sorry too... but just occasionally - very occasionally - it may be better to choose to ask for forgiveness rather than for permission.

While Gudrun's prayers are almost always answered this was a flight to remember. And it was one that helped me decide that to get Instrument training and an Instrument Rating would be an excellent idea.

"Yes... Thank You Lord."

-oOo-

71

'The desert shall blossom...' (Isaiah 35:1)
Flowers at the edge of the Kang salt pan

CHAPTER 4
CLIMB OUT

-Δ-

Flying, like anaesthesia, is often described as 'periods of 90% boredom separated by periods of frantic activity, with occasional laughs'.

The 'climb out' phase of a flight is busy. From the point of aircraft lift off to the settling down at altitude to cruise there is always plenty to keep the pilot occupied.

Rate of climb, instructions from the control tower, heading changes, engine oil pressure and temperature, and a host of other details need to be monitored closely, as well as any traffic that may be in the surrounding air space.

The moment one is established on track, at correct altitude and speed, and with the cowl flaps closed and trims adjusted, flight takes on a different quality.

Flying Mission had its moments on 'climb out'... and we all had much to learn.

The following accounts include descriptions of some of the highlights, excitements and hilarities of mission and medical flying, as well as the satisfaction after a job well done is completed.

The adage that 'any pilot who walks away from the aircraft after any landing has done well' holds true. However, there is a greater and added sense of fulfilment after a successful mission or medical flight has been accomplished with the knowledge that pain has been relieved, or a patient

73

has at least been brought to a place where it can be relieved and, hopefully, health can be restored.

To be in 'the service of The Master' is a wonderful privilege.

*   *   *

Communication

Being able to communicate can be a big help and, when Ngaire was posted to Kang to start, and run, the new clinic, her Mission Board was anxious that she should be able to communicate with the Mission Office, in Pietermaritzburg, in case she had a problem and needed assistance.

Kang is situated 400 km west of Molepolole and, apart from a trader who visited his store only periodically, Ngaire - from New Zealand - was on her own and unable to speak any of the local Kgalagadi languages. A few folk spoke English but the majority did not. Her medical work relied heavily on the clinic staff for translation.

John Freeman was sent to see what the Mission - the Africa Evangelical Fellowship - could do to make Ngaire's situation a little easier.

"Ngaire, tell me, when you have a weekend off, how would you get to Gaborone?"

"I'd have to get a lift to Lobatse and then either get another lift or take the train. Or I have to take my 'week end' when we have a serious patient that we have to take to Lobatse or Gaborone!"

"Can't you get a bus from Kang?"

"A bus? From here in Kang?" Ngaire laughed. "You must be joking! There are no buses that come to Kang. The only vehicles that come to Kang are the cattle trucks taking the Ghanzi farmer's cattle to the slaughterhouse in Lobatse. Occasionally we get a Government vehicle coming through. The Central Medical Stores truck comes from Gaborone once a month to bring us medicines and drugs and stuff and Heine, the trader, sends his big truck to Lobatse for stores about every two weeks."

The local trading store sold only basic foods and, in addition, what the local cattle farmers and hunters needed... a few tools, some cooking utensils, some cheap clothing, saddles and a variety of ammunition.

"I see... And if you have a real emergency what do you do?"

"If it were a real emergency then I'd have to send our clinic driver with the ambulance. But that means we'd be without any transport here for a couple of days."

The Desert clinics were equipped with an ambulance - usually a Toyota Landcruiser, or a Ford F250 one and a half ton truck. The roads were terrible and even these sturdy vehicles often did not survive for long.

"So if you needed to get a message to us in Pietermaritzburg, what would you do?"

"Well, I'd write a note and send one of the clinic staff to the store with it." Ngaire smiled. "Most vehicles stop at the store and the folk there would hand the letter to a driver to post in Lobatse."

"I see... So communication with the outside world can be a bit difficult."

"Well, it's better than in Livingstone's time when a letter to Cape Town could take up to 6 months, by ox wagon."

Later, back in Gaborone, John was anxious to make a plan.

"Malcolm, how can we best help?" John's Aussie accent was marked. "I mean, we've got this girl way out on a limb out there. Anything could happen to her. Yes, I know she's a committed Christian and, as Christians, we believe God is keeping His eye on us. But at the Mission Headquarters we feel we need to be as responsible as we can be to ensure Ngaire's well-being and safety. You know the Kalahari. You've had some experience of working here in Botswana. What would you suggest?"

"Well, Gudrun and I do try and get out about once a month and we take out what we think would be of help, but, apart from basic foodstuffs, it's sometimes hard to know what she needs."

"Mmm. I think we need to start raising funds for a personal vehicle that she can use when the clinic ambulance is away."

"It'll have to be a 4-wheel drive."

I'll check that out." He scribbled a note in his diary. "You know I used to be interested in 'ham radios'. What about if we could fix up some kind of radio link?"

"That might work. When I was at school we had a 'ham' radio shack on the roof and one guy was really into it. But I think you need to take an exam in Morse code. I was never able to manage Morse at the speed needed to pass the exam."

"Yeah, but that was for a 'ham' licence. A lot has changed. I think we could arrange something. I was looking at an HF SSB (High Frequency Single Side Band) radio that Motorola were offering and that was for communicating between rural communities and police stations. If we got something like that for Ngaire, would you and Gudrun be prepared to operate a set from here, in Gaborone, and be our link?"

"Sure..."

The link was soon established and the idea of such communication was very quickly taken up by Ngaire's District Medical Officer, Dr Tachezy, for his other Desert clinics. That Africa Evangelical Fellowship radio link was the beginning of the development of a radio network for all the Government clinics, a system that rapidly became known as the 'Roger, roger' and proved an enormous asset for both medical and nursing personnel, and their patients, all over Botswana.

Also, it was not long before a green, three quarter ton 4 wheel drive Chevrolet truck for Ngaire's personal use was standing outside her little house in Kang.

*　　*　　*

76

*John Freeman balancing precariously to set up the antenna
at Kang clinic*

District Medical Officer Flights

A fly wandered erratically around the rim of one of the empty coffee mugs on the table. In the distance a donkey brayed.

"I really think it's time." Doctor Pavel Tachezy, the District Medical Officer for the Kgalagadi District, ran a hand over his neat beard. "I mean I'm spending more of my days being bounced on these terrible roads than I spend seeing patients."

"What are you suggesting Doctor?" Ngaire voiced the question that was in the minds of each one of us.

The fly continued its painstaking exploration. The thermometer on the wall registered 35 degrees Centigrade. The donkey had quietened down. Two o'clock in the afternoon in a Kalahari village in the heat of summer is definitely a time to 'siesta', but the District Medical Officer (DMO) was on one of his rare visits and it was worth taking the time to talk.

"Well, Malcolm, you and Gudrun have come out from Gaborone for the weekend." Pavel paused, took off his spectacles and stroked his forehead. "You left Gaborone at seven this morning and got here by eight forty-five. You've seen as many patients as I have and you've also done some minor operations."

"So?"

"So? It took me two days to get here from Tshabong. Yes, I passed through Hukuntsi on the way, and saw the patients that Inge and Marlis had there for me to see. But it has been mostly time spent cooped up in my Landcruiser being slowly hypnotised by watching the thorn bushes passing the window."

"Mmm... I hope you're not suggesting that your visit has been a waste of your time."

"No no! Far from it. I'm saying that there must be a better way of doing this." The Norwegian doctor leant forward. "Malcolm, you and Gudrun have come out here for your weekend off."

"Yes. That's true. But we have been good friends with Ngaire ever since our time in Molepolole." Gudrun waved the fly off the mug rim. "We enjoy working together."

"Yes, I can see that. And I'm not suggesting you shouldn't come!" The fly had returned and Pavel took a swipe at it. "But listen. In Zambia I was working with the Zambian Flying Doctor Service. We were based in Lusaka and our team would be flown to the outlying clinics every week. They used Britain Norman Islanders... twins... slow and noisy but with good performance on short, rough airstrips. . We would have myself as the doctor, a nurse and often, a specialist in surgery or ophthalmology. We would be back in Lusaka by the end of the day, and be able to take seriously ill patients back with us to the hospital."

"You mean you could be based in Gaborone rather than in Tshabong and work from there?"

"No. But I'm thinking that it might be something to consider, flying a specialist out to Tshabong and then doing a two or three day trip round Werda, Bokspits, Middlepits, Hukuntsi and here to Kang."

"Yes, I see."

"At the moment I come to Hukuntsi and Kang twice a month. It takes me a minimum of four days each visit, most of that time driving. When I do the Bokspits side it's the same. And that's so long as we don't have a puncture or a breakdown. If that happens we can be stuck for days."

"Yes it sounds a good idea. I'm sure Frank Winters and John Rempel would be happy to visit the Kgalagadi clinics. But how would such a trip be funded? It has been quite a battle with the Ministry of Health (MOH) and the Accounts Department to get our own specialist flights to Maun and Ghanzi paid for."

"Ah. But you see I work for the District Council and they don't come under your MOH."

"Ehe..."

"Ehee! I don't think funding would be a problem. The Norwegian Development Agency, NORAD, pays my salary, and don't forget that NORAD is heavily into Primary Health Care in Botswana. It was NORAD that funded the building of this clinic and most of the ones in Kgalagadi. The Bokspits clinic was put up by Bread for the World, but that was when the Bamalete Lutheran Hospital in Ramotswa was providing health care to the Southern Region."

"Ngai... I think we need some more coffee..."

"That sounds a splendid idea." Pavel stretched himself. "And, while the kettle is boiling, let me tell some other news. After seeing the short wave radio that Ngaire's mission has installed for her here, I've been looking into the possibilities of getting such radios installed in all the Desert clinics. It would make my job easier to keep in touch with the clinic Sisters, and, if we can install one at the Princess Marina Hospital too, then we could have specialist help available for consultations on difficult cases. It could be very useful."

"Ehee... This discussion is beginning to go somewhere!"

* * *

And go somewhere it did. Back at the Princess Marina Hospital the following week, I put the idea to John and Frank who were both enthusiastic and it was not long before Dr Tachezy persuaded us to arrange a trip round his Kgalagadi District. It was the beginning of a service that was to grow rapidly and, when Dr Tachezy submitted his report later in the year at the annual District Medical Officer's conference, the DMOs of the other regions of Botswana quickly saw the benefits that a flight service would bring in terms of savings in time, energy, and vehicle wear and tear not to mention the added bonus of specialist support, and they also began clamouring to be able to use a flying service. The idea of radio networks linking peripheral clinics to their District Medical Officers and the referral hospital was also accepted with alacrity and was soon being implemented all over the country.

Later on, in addition to the flights for the District Medical Officers, the eye teams of the Christoffel Blind Mission took advantage of the availability of a flying service to reach the rural areas. Flights for surveys and for the treatment of patients with eye disease became frequent. Personnel of the German Volunteer Service also became 'frequent flyers' in order to visit their personnel and projects in a number of remote locations.

However, we three 'pilots' realised very quickly that the time had come to pray for a full time pilot/mechanic for the Flying Mission. The situation was becoming urgent, but a Divine Planner already had the solution in hand...

One day Gudrun and I stopped by two friends for tea. Ed and Irene Weaver were working in Botswana with the African Inter-Mennonite Ministries and, during the course of our visit, the need for a full time pilot became a topic of discussion.

"Oh that shouldn't be a big problem." Ed was immediately interested. "I'll contact our 'home office' and see what they can do. I'm sure they will help find a suitable person."

"That'd be wonderful. But it will have to be soon. Frank, John and I just cannot do our jobs properly if we are going to be called out on mercy flights and, if these District Medical Officer flights take off - and it looks as if they will - we'll not be able to cope at all. What about support for such a person? We don't have money to pay a salary."

"Well such a person coming out under Mennonite Ministries (MM) would either find their own support, or be given their support by MM. MM would then second that person to serve with Flying Mission."

"Ed that sounds a wonderful idea.'

"Let me work on it. I'll have to talk it over with Larry Fisher the MM Director. But I'm sure we can work something for you."

*   *   *

Medical Districts (shaded areas) and routes of the DMO flights in 1985. The Central District was added later

A welcome committee

Nurse Shana examines a patient

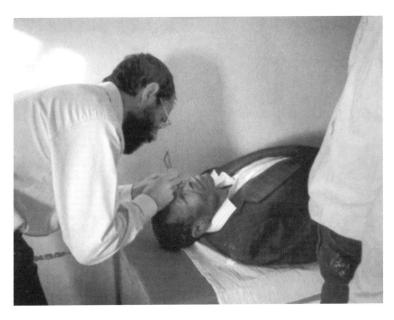

Dr Brian Savage at work in a rural clinic (Photo: F Schmidt)

Steve Mayer checks a patient's vision
(Photo: G Vermeer)

"Modimo O Thusitse"

Sunday the 8th of February. 7.50 am. Time for my daily radio 'scheds'. Rain is tapping at the window. An unusual start for a day in Botswana where the sunrise is normally brilliant and clear. I sit at my desk, twirl the knob on the Marconi radio and take mental note of the cloud cover... solid and low, low enough to close the airport. This sort of morning we get only once or twice a year. Seconds later I am talking to Sister Ngaire in Kang and then to Staff Nurse Miriam in Hukuntsi. These two clinics are situated 400 and 500 km respectively to the west of Gaborone, deep in the Kalahari Desert. No problems today. Both are reporting continuous cloud cover, but the clouds are high and they have had no rain. I call the hospitals in Maun and Ghanzi. No answer. This means a quiet Sunday.

My hand almost reaches the on/off switch when I hear the voice of the Staff Nurse in Tshabong. Her tone, even when mixed with static, tells me that she has trouble and I have a momentary vision of her worried face before the microphone. Her problem is a woman who has been in labour for 48 hours with no progress. The Staff Nurse has been trying to get a message to us over the Police radio network since last night. Yes, the baby seems all right so far.

The situation is clear. The patient will probably need surgery. The doctor who runs the Tshabong Health Centre is away on an out-station trip and is not expected back for two days. The only ray of sunshine in the bleak picture is that Tshabong, 550 km to the southwest, has cloudless, blue sky. If the Gaborone Control Tower will permit me to fly out of Gaborone then I can take operating instruments with me to Tshabong and, if necessary, operate there.

It is not long before the Controller is aware of the situation. He agrees that Gaborone is officially closed. However, because it is an emergency, and because I have detailed knowledge of the country, he will let me go... but definitely no passengers!

Minutes later I am at the controls of the Flying Mission Cessna 185 droning westward over the Molepolole road. Behind me the seats are piled with packs of surgical instruments from the Princess Marina Hospital. The road is sliding backward fifty feet below me. Rain is lashing the windscreen. I pass the Scottish Livingstone Hospital but am barely able to make out the corrugated iron roofs as rain sheets down. I console myself that the road is wide and straight, that I can land on it if necessary, and that there are no high masts or hills in the Kalahari.

After 45 minutes flying the cloud base lifts and the rain stops. I glimpse the Jwaneng diamond mine passing under the port wingtip.

From now on there are no radio beacons to help with navigation. There is no longer the comforting voice of the Gaborone Controller to talk to. The only sound is that of the steady beat of the six cylinders in front of me. Visibility is improving... but reveals only an expanse of sand with a sparse covering of grasses and the occasional thorn tree and game trail. I am conscious of being in the hands of my Creator.

A view of the Jwaneng diamond mine on a clear day

Suddenly I see a small patch of blue sky. Soon I am climbing to a safer altitude and can breathe more easily. I remember the many times that I bumped along the Desert tracks in the Scottish Livingstone Hospital truck on the monthly trips to Motokwe... becoming intimately acquainted with the Kalahari... and I thank God for His training programme which prepared me for this flight so many years ago.

We (an aeroplane has its own personality after being one's companion on a difficult flight) touch lightly down at Tshabong at 11 am and are greeted by the relieved Staff Nurse. I am whisked to the Health Centre by ambulance and as I gently feel the distended abdomen and watch the tired face of our patient it is obvious that surgery is needed without delay. After a prayer we arrange our 'operating theatre' in the small maternity ward. The patient's bed is the operating table. The Staff Nurse and her assistants are delegated duties. An intravenous infusion is set up. The baby's heart is checked... still beating, but irregularly and much more rapidly than normal. The patient is weak from her unrewarded efforts.

Time is running out and we have only moments to act if disaster is to be averted. It is a tense moment. Tshabong Health Centre is not geared for major surgery, but, with Gaborone airport closed, there is no alternative.

The powerful drugs are injected slowly. Our patient closes her eyes and grunts. The nurse holding the torch moves closer, The knife slices into the smooth, brown skin and, 36 seconds later, a wriggling infant is dangling in the air by his heels and beginning to take stock of his new surroundings! Speed is essential. We have no blood transfusion service and every drop of the spurting fluid is precious. Leviticus Chapter 17 and verse 11 springs to mine! "The life of the flesh is in the blood." The wound is closed rapidly and 40 minutes after she shut her eyes on the world our little mother is stirring and wondering what has happened. The miracle of Caesarean section is over. The slow process of healing is commencing. The new life is gasping its way into reality.

7.50 am, ten days later. I am sitting at my desk. The sun is shining. The sky is blue. The radio crackles... the voice of our Staff Nurse is happily reporting that mother and baby are well... and, that the grandmother has named the baby...

"Modimo O Thusitse". "God has helped". My mind goes back to that wet morning. I think of the difficult flight. I remember the anxious moment when the mother's blood gushed from her open womb. The happy faces after surgery was over. The sight, when I eventually flew home, of the Thamaga River in full flood.

Yes, God had helped... and it was wonderful to know that everyone who had enacted that small drama had been aware of His help. Our first major operation in Tshabong. Modimo O Thusitse!

*　　　*　　　*

An old apple box made a wonderful incubator for a premaure baby at the Hukuntsi clinic

A Cap & a Mag

It was a blue cap. Like the one in the picture opposite. The latest in nurse's uniforms. And Marlis wore it with aplomb.

We had landed in Kang for the weekend, on one of our monthly flying visits, when I had a weekend off.

As I tied down the Cessna 185, a white Toyota Landcruiser, with the letters KANG CLINIC painted on the door, pulled up in a cloud of dust and Ngaire climbed out.

"Welcome, Ngaka." Ngaire was always happy to see us. "And Gudrun... I am glad that you could make it this weekend! I hope you managed to get that curtain material I asked you about over the radio. I'm desperate for curtains. Oh, and I have Marlis with me."

"Ehe... Dumela Marlis. What are you doing here?"

Marlis and Inge were two German mission nurses who were posted in the next village, Hukuntsi, some 90 km to the west of Kang.

"Vell I am on my vay back from Lobatse." Marlis' German accent was readily distinguishable. "I had to take down a patient to ze psychiatric hospital and I don't like to drive in ze dark in ze Desert so I also am staying with Sister Ngaire for tonight."

As we unloaded our weekend bags and the pile of shopping that Ngaire had asked us to bring - as well as the bag full of curtains - we exchanged the latest news from the big city of Gaborone and in no time we were piled into the vehicle and bumping away from the airstrip leaving the green and white aircraft in solitude.

"Marlis... That's a posh new hat you're wearing."

"She got it in Lobatse." Ngaire swerved to avoid a pothole. "It's part of the new uniform for District Nurses. We're all getting them but mine hasn't arrived yet."

"Yes. It's actually ver nice." Marlis chortled on about her visit to Lobatse and shortly we pulled up before the clinic nurse's house.

"As always, welcome to my humble home." Ngaire led the way inside and directed us where to put what. "Now... first of all some tea and then we can make decisions."

Over mugs of the steaming brown fluid we discussed plans for the weekend. As I expected there would be a collection of patients that had been saved for the benefit of a surgical eye to be run over them. But then came an unexpected invitation.

"Marlis has to get back to Hukuntsi tomorrow and she has suggested that we might all go over for a visit." Ngaire's New Zealand lilt grew stronger as she outlined her idea to us. "I thought that it would be great to visit Hukuntsi and spend some time with Marlis and Inge. But it would take too long to go by road. So... I was wondering - Malcolm - if we could all fly across. How long would it take do you think? Would it be a possibility?"

"To fly from Kang to Hukuntsi? That takes about 30 minutes. Yes we can do that easily. We have plenty fuel on board."

"Well that's settled then. We can leave after an early lunch."

"Fine. But just remember that we have to be back by sunset. That's six thirty." I did a quick think. "Actually we can make it easily by then. Six thirty is Gaborone sunset time and we're four hundred kilometres west of Gabs. And there's a good 15 minutes useful daylight after the sun sets."

"Yes, and Inge will be so ver happy." Marlis' eyes sparkled. "We might even persuade Inge to play her trumpet for us."

"Inge... plays the trumpet? I didn't know that."

"Oh yes. Inge plays ze trumpet ver well. And it is most useful. When we go on ze outstation trips to places like Tshutswa ven we get zere Inge always stands in ze shade under ze tree and she plays her trumpet and ze whole settlement knows zat we haff come." Marlis laughed. "Ze system works ver well."

The plan was all worked out. It would be a fun time... Little did we know what excitements were in store for us.

*   *   *

90

The next day presented a cloudless, blue sky but with little wind. Perfect.

"Honey, if you sit up front right we'll put Ngai and Marlis in the two middle seats."

There was a climbing, wriggling session, as everyone got comfortable.

"Marlis... Have you got your seat belt fixed? Ngai can you check please."

"Yes I am ver fine." Marlis was excited at the prospect of a flight. "But vait a moment. You are ze Pilot. You should be vearing ze hat!"

The posh, new, blue, nurse's hat was placed firmly on my head and we all laughed.

"Right... let's go."

Pre-take off checks were uneventful. Engine run-up was smooth. Magnetos were functioning normally. Control movements were full and free. There were no donkeys, or goats, on the airstrip. As the throttle was opened there was a surge of power. The aircraft was eager to be airborne.

Speed built up rapidly. Rotation and take-off were uneventful. Almost immediately I adjusted for cruise settings, retracted the wing flaps and closed the engine cowl flaps.

"There... Hukuntsi... Here we come."

We were far from anywhere and the radios had been quiet. We had the sky to ourselves. Because it was only a short hop I had levelled the 'plane off at an altitude of 5000 feet. Why waste fuel and time climbing higher and only have to come down again. Anyway... we might see some game.

There was some turbulence. After all it was mid-day. But it didn't seem much.

We were fifteen minutes out of Kang. Gudrun was dozing as she usually did. The two middle seat passengers were quiet... Probably enjoying the view as I was...

A bit more 'chop'. Nothing too bad. The Cessna 185 was always a bit lively. Anyway it felt a bit like being in a sailing boat... A rather nice rolling sensation...

"There's Lotlhake Pan passing on our right." I dipped the right wing gently to edge closer hoping there might be some game. "No... no animals today."

"Malcolm... " I felt a tap on my shoulder and turned to see a very green Marlis and, at that instant, her cheeks filled. As Ngaire scrabbled in a seat pocket for a sick sack poor Marlis was desperate. She seized the first available solution to her immediate predicament... The posh, new, blue hat was snatched from my head and, in an instant, was promoted to an infinitely more useful role.

Even with all the aircraft vents wide open it quite impossible to cleanse the atmosphere and we sat in silent sympathy.

No matter... Hukuntsi was in sight. In minutes we would be on the ground.

I busied myself with the let down, trying my best to keep it as smooth and short as I could... But hey... What's this? The EGT (Exhaust Gas Temperature) gauge was 'going bananas'. Fuel flow... was as expected. RPM... seemed steady. Manifold pressure... no problem there... Oh well... We were within reach of the field anyway.

The landing was normal. Hukuntsi was a bumpy airstrip... A lot of hard calcrete lumps in the otherwise soft sand... "Marlis... I am sorry about that. It was a little turbulent."

"There..." I swung the nose round into the parking area and before I shut down the engine I did the usual magneto check. And then the problem was identified, for the engine spluttered and almost quit when the left magneto was turned off. We were not going to be going anywhere fast for a while in this 'plane!

Inge was waiting for us beside the airfield gate.

"Welcome to Hukuntsi. You are in good time."

"Thank you."

"Did you bring the Bibles we wanted?"

"Yes of course. But I've also got a patient for you. Marlis is suffering from the flight."

"No problem. I'll look after her. Let's get unloaded and I'll organise some tea."

It was not long before we had our 'patient' safely back home where recovery was rapid and, once Marlis was herself again, we recounted to Inge four different versions of the story of the hat with increasing colour and laughter at each telling.

Bibles for Hukuntsi clinic. Handle with care!

It was then that I broke the news of the magneto failure.

"Ladies... I have an announcement."

"Yes... What's the trouble?"

"Trouble? Who said anything about trouble?"

With all eyes turned expectantly to me there was a hush.

"It's just that we're going to have to go home by road. I'm sorry to have to tell you that we won't be flying back to Kang today. As we were coming in to land..." I explained the nature of the problem and tried to answer the resulting questions as best as I could.

"Well, it's good that you tell us now." Inge did not seem at all phased by the new situation. "And I think The Lord has an answer to the problem. The trader at the store told me this morning that he is going out to Lobatse in his truck later today. I don't think he has left yet."

"Now that would be a real provision."

"Yes, I think so. Let's pop down and see if he is still here."

A short trip along the sand track and the new plan was agreed. The truck had not yet departed and it could take Ngaire, Gudrun and myself back to Kang, and then I could continue with it to Lobatse where I would have no difficulty in finding transport back to Gaborone.

"Of course it vill be dark soon. But zat does not matter. It is a big truck." Marlis had recovered her usual sparkle.

The afternoon slipped by all too fast and it was with reluctance that we said our 'good byes' with promises of a repeat visit.

*   *   *

Of course the posh, new hat was not ruined. Neither was the technical problem with the aircraft any real disaster. The return trip just took longer than expected.

If I remember rightly, we got back to Kang on the five ton truck of the trader who ran the Hukuntsi store. Gudrun and Ngaire stayed in Kang and I continued on with the truck heading for Lobatse.

The trip was reasonably uneventful. However, somewhere between Phuduhudu and Morwamosu we hit a large, unexpected pothole. Painful noises then came from 'up front' and, after investigation, the cause was found to be a broken engine mount. No real problem. We agreed that I would be transferred to the next passing vehicle and take with me details of the necessary spare part to, somehow, get back out to the broken down truck. The driver and his other passengers would camp beside the truck.

My next lift arrived some hours later and it got me a further 200 km, to Kanye, where Liesel - the wife of a volunteer engineer whom we knew from Molepolole days - took pity on me and drove me back to Gaborone.

It took me two days to organise a pilot / mechanic, along with a new magneto for the aircraft and a replacement engine mount for the truck. After locating the stranded vehicle and dropping the engine mount to the driver, we flew on to Hukuntsi, replaced the faulty magneto, held an impromptu Sunday School for the crowd of admiring kids that came to watch, and flew back to Gaborone collecting Gudrun in Kang on the way.

I learnt another lesson that day. We worked hard to replace that faulty magneto, and, although the sky was completely overcast - all day - I got severely sunburned. From then on a good hat became a permanent part of my equipment.

*   *   *

Banana

The Desert night was clear as crystal and cold as polar ice.

The little family was huddled round the flickering flames of a small fire made from pieces of wood collected from the veldt that afternoon before sunset. Tales had been told. The children had drifted off to sleep, lying close to the fire and snuggled against each other for warmth under a thin blanket. The two adults murmured of the day's happenings.

High overhead, a satellite passed silently between the Pleiades and Orion the hunter. In the distance, a jackal's cackling laughter spilled into the still night air, prompting startled cries from a small collection of crowned plovers standing somewhere on the white, crusted surface of the Kang salt pan. A gentle wind rustled nearby thorn bushes. The fire crackled and hissed gently at intervals.

After a while, the two adults added another piece of wood to the embers, and they also lay down and slept.

Silence descended, that absolute silence only to be found in remote parts of the earth where modern civilization has not yet managed to take root and the land is waterless, and even the plants and animals struggle to extract a meagre living.

*   *   *

Several hours before dawn, the small boy had stirred. The story was unclear. His mother had been woken by his moans and had found him unconscious and lying across the glowing embers of the fire.

"So she brought him straight to the clinic." Janet, the General Duty Assistant had found the mother and the moaning child patiently waiting on the clinic stoep when she had come on duty and she had immediately called Sister Ngaire. "The burns are deep."

"Let's have a look." Sister Ngaire gently lifted the ragged, whitish, cotton cloth to reveal an extensive burn on the little boy's hand and forearm. "I see. What a mess! All right. Let's get a dressing on and we'll get the Doctor to have a look when he next comes and then we can decide what will be best. And let's give him something for the pain."

A short while later, the damage was described over the radio for my opinion.

"The burn is extensive. It's covering most of the outer surface of the little boy's forearm and hand and it's deep in places." Ngaire's voice came through clearly. "I suspect it'll probably need a skin graft at some stage."

"OK. For the moment I suggest you do daily wet dressings with EUSOL (Edinburgh University Solution) until the dead tissue has come away. Once there are some signs that healing is beginning, we can think further. In any case, Gudrun and I are planning a trip out to you one weekend soon. I'll see him then and we can make a plan."

"Super. Oh, and if you are coming out soon I'm running low on some stuff. I'll give Gudrun a shopping list on the 'sched' tomorrow morning if that's all right."

"Sure. Is that all?"

"For now, yes."

"Alright. We'll be over and out."

* * *

The following morning, after noting down the shopping list, we discussed the situation. The dressings were going as planned and the little patient had had a comfortable night.

"What he really needs is admission to a 'burns unit' and some specialist nursing care." Ngaire had experience of such things back home in New Zealand.

"Yes Ngai. But you are in a remote village in the Kalahari and the nearest place with a unit like that would be Johannesburg."

"I know. But nursing burns really is a specialist job and needs almost 24 hour attention if it is to be done properly."

"I'm sure you and Janet and Edna are doing your best and he's probably getting more attention than he'd have here at the PMH (Princess Marina Hospital). He'd likely be stuck in a corner here and get one dressing a week, and none too gentle at that. And I wouldn't try and graft him for a while, not until all the sloughs are off and he's developed some good clean granulations."

"Well, we'll just have to do what we can with what we've got."

The decision was made to keep Banana - that was his name - in the clinic and Ngaire and her 'team' would look after him.

*   *   *

Later that day a cattle truck from Ghanzi rolled into Kang village and stopped in a cloud of dust outside the one shop. The driver and his passenger climbed out of the cab.

Passengers, or hitch hikers, are usual as the big trucks taking beef cattle to the abattoir in Lobatse are often the only transport to pass that way for days on end, and such lift opportunities are seldom left unused.

After a short while, the two emerged from the shop. The driver had pointed the way across the sand track toward the clinic before climbing back into his cab to continue on his journey to Lobatse.

The young woman, who had light brown hair and a fair complexion, walked the short distance to the clinic, made her way through the collection of waiting patients and knocked on the door.

*   *   *

97

The next morning, I switched on the radio wondering what the latest report about Banana would be like.

"Kang, do you copy Gaborone Village?"

"Yes Gaborone Village, we copy you loud and clear." Ngaire's voice jumped the 400 Km that separated us with ease.

"Ehee. Good morning to you."

"Eee Rra. And you won't believe this." Ngaire's voice sounded excited. "There's been a real miracle."

"Tell me about it. Did Banana's arm heal up overnight?"

"No. But we now have a 'burns unit' here in Kang!"

"Oh. What's happened?"

"Yesterday we had a visitor. She came through from Ghanzi on a cattle truck and when she heard that there was a clinic here in Kang she came to have a look and see if she could be of help. Her name is Heidi Kerhahn and she's travelling round Africa on holiday. She's from Canada and she works as a nurse in a special burns unit in Vancouver. When she saw Banana she just stepped in and took over. She's a real provision and she's agreed to stay until he's better and show us how to nurse him!"

"Aoaee! That was Divine timing."

She says to ask you to please bring some vitamin E capsules when you come. Banana is to have Vitamin E applied to the burn. She says it will speed his recovery."

Over the following days, Heidi worked wonders and Ngaire was full of her praise. Janet and Edna had an excellent teacher and Banana's wounds cleaned quickly under the expert care. After only a few days, Ngaire reported that he was ready for a skin graft.

*   *   *

"Honey, do you think that we should go out to Kang this weekend? They're saying that Banana is ready for grafting. Would we have room to bring him back with us to Gaborone?"

"You mean the boy with the burned arm and hand?" Gudrun sipped her mug of coffee. "We'd have enough room I think. Would the mother come too?"

"It would be better, although I don't know what would happen to her other kids. I guess the father would have to look after them."

"We've a lot of stuff to take out to Ngaire. You said we might also be able to take back Wagamang. That little girl who was sent to the Red Cross Hospital in Capetown and has come back fitted with a pace-maker. But coming back we should have space."

"You know Honey, I'm thinking that if we go out to Kang next weekend I could perhaps persuade Sister Dikeledi to let me take a skin grafting pack."

"You mean you could do a skin graft in Kang?"

"Sure. Why not? It sounds as if he's all ready, and if this nurse Heidi is there, she will be happy to assist and look after the post-op dressings."

"Won't he need an anaesthetic?"

"Yes, but I can take some Ketamine. We could manage it. I think."

"Well, it would save him a long journey. And his Mum."

"It would be wonderful. And Wagamang's family will be delighted to have her back again too."

*　　*　　*

And that's what happened. Sister Dikeledi - the Operating Theatre Superintendent at the Princess Marina Hospital was happy to provide the packs.

"Now Ngaka, don't lose anything! Make sure all these instruments come back and make sure the nurse out there cleans everything properly when you've finished."

Doctor Bate - the Anaesthetist - happily handed over some ampoules of Ketamine. "Be careful! It's strong stuff," she had laughed cheekily. "But I suppose you know what you are doing."

Ngaire and Heidi turned the labour room in the small clinic maternity block into an operating theatre. Janet and Edna, joined by Ivy, came to watch. The Ketamine worked beautifully and we took a lovely graft from Banana's thigh.

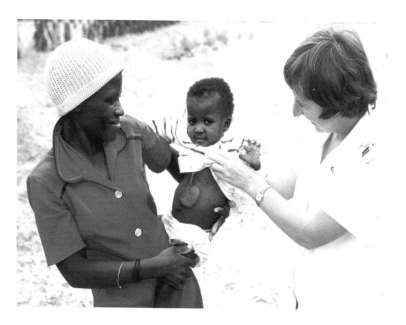

Wagamang - gping home with her pacemaker

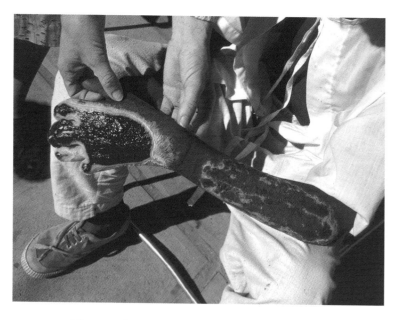

The graft to Banana's forearm took well

It all went like clockwork and Heidi kept saying, "I can't believe that this all happening and that I'm in Darkest Africa!" The graft to Banana's forearm took well. His hand was done later. Heidi's expert nursing care and her vitamin E dressings were superb, and eventually Banana's hand (and thigh) healed beautifully.

*   *   *

Of Sheeps and Ribs

"Larry, I wonder if you can help?" Larry was my last hope.

A call for help had come from the nurse at Bokspits... a small settlement right at the farthest southwest corner of Botswana, where the borders of South Africa, Botswana and Namibia (formerly South West Africa) now meet. A desolate place perched on the bank of the Nossop 'river', a dry riverbed that was flushed by a flash flood perhaps once every ten years.

The clinic at Bokspits was run by Schwester Marianne, a wiry, energetic, German nurse who, after serving for several years as the Matron of the Hermansburg Mission Hospital at Ramotswa, when her position had been localised, had opted for further service as nurse at Bokspits.

Schwester Marianne was not daunted by the remoteness of Bokspits. In fact she loved it. Bokspits was located in the area that fell to the Ramotswa Hospital where she had served as Matron and, in the same way that the Scottish Livingstone Hospital, at Molepolole, had run its 6 monthly trips into the remote Kweneng and Kgalagadi districts, the Hermansburg Mission had run similar visits further south to the string of tiny villages of Werda, Tshabong, Middlepits and Kuis, most of them along the Nossop river bed. Bokspits was the farthest settlement they visited.

Schwester Marianne had looked forward to her posting there as many of the people in the area spoke only Afrikaans and Schwester Marianne's German heritage made communication easy. She thrived in the remote Desert life and had become fluent in the local mixed speech of Setswana, Sekgalagadi, English and Afrikaans.

"Bokspits? That's the back of beyond!"

"I know. But our 185 is down for maintenance and you are our last resort." I knew that Larry was a keen pilot and that he also had access to a C210 that had been given to the Department of Wildlife by a German donor organisation.

"What's the problem?"

"The nurse there wants a young boy picked up. It was hard to understand her. The radio was full of atmospherics. I think he's got a broken arm."

"Well it's a sandy strip and the 210 only has small wheels. We may get stuck. All right. We better get going. Bokspits will be about three hours flying time. I'll meet you at the airport in about fifteen minutes. I'll have to find my maps. If you file the flight plan I'll get the 'plane refuelled."

"Great. See you there."

*   *   *

The flight had been smooth. The retractable undercarriage of the Cessna 210 gave it extra speed and the absence of a wing strut gave one an unobstructed view. The villages of Kanye and Tshabong slid below us on time and from there the dry Kalahari Desert changed in nature and became a rolling sea of reddish sand dunes dotted here and there with a flotsam of stubborn thorn trees and sparse clumps of brown, straggling grass.

"There's the Nossop." Larry pointed ahead and to port to what looked like a winding groove in the parched landscape. "It's about the only recognisable landmark around here."

"Yes I can see that." I unfolded the map on my knees. "But it's hard to miss. One is going to hit it sooner or later flying in this direction."

"That's true." Larry made a slight change in our heading and reset the directional gyro. "I'm sure this compass is out of adjustment. Every time I fly this 'plane it seems worse. I know the magnetic variation in southwest Botswana is large, around 17 degrees, due to large iron deposits but, even taking that into consideration, I seem to end up way off course at times. Anyway, once we get to the river we'll turn right and I think we won't be too far out."

A short while later we banked toward the west as the village of Middlepits passed below us.

"If ever you land on that strip" Larry jerked his finger toward the Middlepits airstrip, "just make sure you don't come in too low over the river bed. The downdrafts can be surprisingly strong."

That information got filed in my brain for future use. The well marked out airfield below did indeed end at the edge of a cliff that looked steep and jagged.

"We've made good time."

"Yes. We picked up a bit of a tailwind after leaving Werda. And there... you can just begin to see Bokspits."

Sure enough, a small flash in the distance could shortly be identified as a corrugated iron roof. Soon the clinic building, the small 'General Dealer' store and the few small huts that made up the metropolis of Bokspits emerged from the shimmering haze.

"I'll buzz the strip to check for sheep and donkeys."

Larry brought the throttle back and we began to descend gently. "Goats are the intelligent ones. They get well clear of the runway as soon as they hear a 'plane coming. Sheep are stupid. They just run about in circles. And donkeys... at Hukuntsi once there was a donkey on the strip. I buzzed him once and he stayed right where he was... right in the middle of the strip. Then I came down really low. I almost clipped his ears and then he got the message and took himself off. But, would you believe it... by the time I got round to my final approach he was right back where he had been! Eventually some of the locals saw what was going on and came and chased him off for me. That one was stubborn." He eased the aircraft onto short finals and we did a low inspection run.

"Looks nice and clear today." The engine roared and, as we climbed back up to circuit height, we swung round over the clinic buildings. The Toyota Land Cruiser ambulance was backing out of the gate as we were levelling off downwind.

'That one was stubborn.'
(Cartoon: S Mingham)

"Gear down..." Larry began chanting his pre-landing checks and flipped the undercarriage lever. There was a gentle thudding as the wheels extended. "And locked... and we have three green lights."

Wing flaps and propeller pitch were adjusted expertly to steepen the glide and, moments later, after a small burst of power to soften the touchdown we arrived back on planet earth.

Larry opened the windows for a breath of air and taxied to the end of the sandy runway where the aircraft was turned ready for our departure and the motor shut down. The propeller hesitated and shuddered to a standstill.

"Ah gut. You haf made it." Schwester Marianne was the picture of efficiency in her dark blue uniform. The wind was playing with her silvering hair. "I have ze tea ready for you and also some fruit cake."

We were shepherded into the Landcruiser and whisked to the clinic by the no-nonsense ex-matron. However, over steaming mugs of tea she relaxed a little and we were given a full account of the local news as well as of how the clinic came into being.

"Zere... now more tea?"

"Thank you Sister but we have a long flight ahead. The 'plane has no toilet and we can't stop on the way."

"Ah yes. Let me tell you about my little patient." She presented the case history and outlined what had been done. It was a detailed case history - delivered with Germanic precision. "So... I haf put ze plaster of Paris on him but zere was a big wound and I am sure ze bones are not in ze good position."

"It sounds as if you've done an excellent job." I was always amazed at what mission nurses in out of the way places could do for their patients. "We'll get him X-rayed and if necessary we'll have another bash at a reduction. I'm sure he'll do well."

"Vell I hope so... But let me tell you something. And see if you know ze answer. Ze sheep farmers here they have a problem."

"Oh. What's that?" Larry was a vet and his interest was roused.

"Yes vell, you see the farmers here they raise ze Karakul sheeps."

"Yes I know that."

"But do you know that zese sheeps are mostly ze black sheeps but there are also some white sheeps?"

"Yes I know that too!"

"Yes well, ze farmers here in Bokspits zey tell me zat zey haf studied zese sheeps. Of course zey are interested to breed ze best sheeps." Her eyes had a naughty twinkle. "Zey tell me zat zey haf found that ze black sheeps zey eat much more zan ze white sheeps."

"Go on." Larry's interest was really roused and he forgot his tea as he leant forward to hear about this new discovery.

"Yes, vell, I sought that you, being a vet, would know about zeze sings and be able to tell us why ze black sheeps in Bokspits eat more zan ze white sheeps."

"I'd have to do some research into that. It's fascinating." I could see Larry was hooked and he was having thoughts about writing a scientific paper that might have great implications in animal husbandry. "Can you give me any details? Some exact figures perhaps?"

The truth of the situation dawned as I watched Schwester Marianne's face. She was obviously delighted at the way she had been able to lead Larry right up the garden path and mirth was spilling from her blue eyes.

"Er... Larry! I think I see the problem."

"What problem? Oh..." A smile spread over Larry's face and then he burst out laughing.

"Ah you haf it!" Marianne was delighted. "Yes, of course it is simple. But you know... Everyone I tell zis to has a good laugh when zey realise zat it is just because there are more of ze black sheeps in Bokspits so of course ze black sheeps eat more zan ze white sheeps. Now... I vould happily show you around ze clinic. It is a fine building built wis a donation from Brot Fuer die Weld (Bread for the World) - but I sink you don't haf ze time."

"Yes... thank you Sister. We would love to see round but we cannot stop the sun from going down!" Larry was still smiling at his own obtuseness, but was also anxious to get moving.

"Ah yes. Right. I shall call ze driver."

And so it was that we were again packed into the Landcruiser and whisked back to the airstrip where our patient was made comfortable in the middle seats of the 210 and well padded with blankets. After saying our thanks for the tea, Larry and I climbed aboard and got started up with a minimum of fuss.

"Ready for take off?"

My thumb came up to indicate I was ready.

"Right... Brakes off... And let's go."

The engine roared. Dust swirled. The little 'plane seemed to twitch and buck in a frenzy of excitement. But, even under full power, we remained stationary and after some 30 seconds of struggle Larry brought the throttle back and the engine quietened.

"Well, I guess we're bogged down. Like I said, the 210 wheels are meant for tarmac not sand. You'll have to dig us out."

"OK." I eased myself out of the door. "But you should think about getting balloon tyres like we have on the 185."

"It wouldn't work. Tyres like yours wouldn't fit into the wheel wells when the undercarriage retracts. And anyway, I hardly ever land this machine in the Desert. We use it mostly for game counts."

A little clearing of the loose sand from around the wheels and we'd have no problems... I thought. Some investigation revealed that the nose wheel had been blown clear by the slipstream from the prop. But the two main wheels - that were of standard size but much smaller than the main wheels on our 185 - were well dug in with a big ridge of red sand piled high in front of them. It did not take too long to clear the sand ridge but each wheel had also worked itself into quite deep hole.

"OK Larry. Try again... And take her forward to that part of the strip where they've put the calcrete down. You can stop there and you won't get bogged down."

Larry did his best, but to no avail. Almost within seconds of applying power the slipstream piled a high ridge of loose sand right up in front of the two main wheels and, with the added problem of the depressions that had been formed by the rocking wheels, the aircraft would not budge. After two or three tries at full power Larry stopped the engine and climbed out.

"We'll just have to push her out. The problem is there's not much to push on except the wheel struts. If this were a 206 with big wing struts it'd be easy. Anyway, let's give it a try."

By this time a small knot of onlookers had collected and it was not hard to recruit volunteers. I positioned them carefully, one with me, and two on the other side of the 'plane.

Larry climbed back in and fired up the engine again. The four of us pushers bent to the wheel struts and applied all the push that we could. Larry applied full power. The roar increased to a crescendo. The blowing sand stung our hands. The aircraft strained... And suddenly, like a cork coming out of a champagne bottle, the Cessna 210 fought free of the sand. My stalwart pushers and I stood up and cheered as the 'plane surged forward.

Looking down on the 'road' to Bokspits and the sand dunes

BAM... Something like a charging rhino hit me in the back and knocked me forward.

After putting our weight behind the undercarriage, the four of us, as we stood erect, had been neatly mown down by the tail plane and we were all left sprawling on the soft sand.

Looking back it could have been much worse. We might have had four broken necks or severe head injuries. But after getting up and dusting ourselves off no one seemed the worse for wear and we saw that Larry had brought the freed 'plane to a halt on some firmer ground about fifteen yards further on and he was climbing out.

We thanked everyone profusely and returned to our seats. In no time at all we were again nosing upward into the blue heavens and heading for home over the red sand dunes. However, I could not get comfortable and felt a little like a wriggling tadpole stranded on a log, with an ache in my back where the 'charging rhino' had hit me.

The return flight was uneventful. The young boy was handed over to a nurse with the ambulance who took him away to the Princess Marina Hospital, and Larry went home happy to have added over 5 hours to his flight log.

The next day - after a hot bath and a good night's sleep - my back seemed improved. The job at the Princess Marina Hospital was as busy as ever and it was only when there was a lull and a peaceful moment that I was bothered by an aching reminder of the trip to Bokspits. Life went on as usual. However, after almost two weeks of reminders - at times quite sharp reminders - it seemed right to investigate the situation and, feeling rather foolish, I placed myself in the capable hands of Mrs. Bareki, the senior radiographer, and submitted to a chest X-ray.

"Tjo tjo tjo tjo Doctor..." Mrs. Bareki emerged from her darkroom as I was struggling to put my shirt back on. She stuck the freshly processed films up on her viewing box. "I think you have a reason for your aches and pains."

"Oh... What's the problem then?"

"Look here..." She pointed to ribs 2 and 3 on the right side at the back. "You've got two fractured ribs. Thankfully there is no pneumothorax. But you should be on sick leave!"

Ouch! To think... I could have been swinging in my hammock with Gudrun fussing over me... For a whole two weeks. Perhaps even longer...

*   *   *

Trims

Once airborne, the trimming of the aircraft controls can make a big difference to the amount of effort that a pilot has to exert to keep the aeroplane in a balanced state. The small trim tabs on the wings and tail plane need careful adjustment to maintain a steady state of flight both directionally and vertically and to maximise the speed and efficiency of the aircraft. The trim surfaces are small but their effect is enormous.

*   *   *

The 'flight' of Flying Mission has required constant 'trimming' over the years to ensure that what is being done is what needs to be done... and to make sure that the Mission is performing efficiently.

We have always regarded the Mission as a 'servant' to missions, churches and the Ministry of Health and a servant seeks to serve effectively and meet the needs of those served.

By June 1980 Flying Mission was registered with the Botswana Government's Registrar of Societies as a Charitable Organisation. The Mission's elected Executive Committee was meeting regularly. The Bank Account had been established and was 'in the black'. However, there were occasions when 'The Quiet Hour' was down for maintenance and a flight was urgently needed. It was usually possible to find someone willing to do the flight, or, loan an aircraft for the purpose, but it was not long before the question of acquiring a second aircraft for the Mission was raised.

*   *   *

Butterscotch & Toffee - Part 1

"They say it's due to be ferried over from the States in about three weeks." I looked at the letter. "It's got long range fuel tanks and balloon tyres for work in sandy conditions. It's got an HF Radio and the usual avionics. But what an awful colour scheme - 'butterscotch & toffee'!" I looked up at the Committee. "I really feel that if we are going to spend a hundred thousand Rand on an aircraft then we should be able to choose a colour scheme that looks nice... Light blue or something."

We had finished the business and the Flying Mission Executive Committee was about ready for tea. The details of the Cessna 206 aircraft that I had just read out to them had been sent to me by Comair, the Cessna Dealership in Jo'burg. In every respect it was an ideal 'plane except for those two details, the colour scheme, and the asking price, of a hundred and ten thousand Rand.

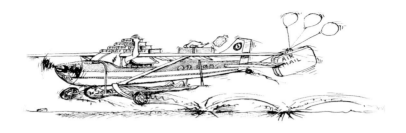

... an ideal 'plane...
(Cartoon: S Mingham)

"I still think we should keep looking for a 206" Roger Schultz drawled. "It really would be a good 'plane for the Mission." A great guy, he had vision.

"You know a 206 has large double cargo doors and it would make loading - especially of stretchers - a real breeze. The 185 really is a problem if you have a large patient."

"Well... Let's put the details to one side and wait until some helpful donor asks what we need!" Ngaire Reid usually had good ideas.

"Yes... And we need to be praying about it." Don Genheimer, the Director of the Africa Evangelical Fellowship was closing his briefcase. "That's the most important thing we can do at this stage. And as Hudson Taylor said - 'God's work done in God's way will not lack God's supply'".

Prayer is not a 'penny in the slot' affair... but sometimes it works in strange ways. And this time I was to learn that God has a great sense of humour.

*   *   *

Some months later I was working in my afternoon surgical out-patient clinic.

"Ao, Ngaka... it's so hot this afternoon. The amply proportioned Motswana nurse who was assisting me wiped her forehead as she summoned the next patient. "We've been working so hard and there are still so many to see!" She surveyed the patiently waiting line of sweaty bodies with a degree of despair.

"Never mind Mama. I'll try and be quick."

The telephone on the desk shrilled into life and the nurse picked up the receiver.

"Who?" And, covering the mouthpiece she eyed me uncertainly. "He says he's Mr. Hampshire or something."

"Yes. I'll speak with him." My heart sank. Bob Hampshire was the Safety Officer in the Government Department of Civil Aviation. We got on well but he was an absolutely stickler if anything was wrong. I had visions of having committed some unforgivable sin when last flying the Cessna 185.

"Malcolm... yes, it's Bob here." He sounded friendly enough. "I just wanted to say that I've heard that Flying Mission is looking for a second aircraft. I think I have just the one for you. It's a Cessna 180, owned and run by one of the safari companies up in Maun. A good little 'plane. No damage history. It would suit you nicely."

"Bob... That's very kind of you." I was relieved. "But we decided some time ago that we wanted to find a 206. But thank you anyway."

"Oh... well... in that case you should go down to the airfield now. Sladden the builder is selling his 206. Wants to trade up for a twin. That's a good little 'plane too. Just a year old... so it's had all the bugs worked out of it. Go and have a look."

"All right. Thank you Bob." I placed the receiver back on its cradle and tried to refocus my mind on the deformed foot of the baby held on his mother's knee. He was just under 10 months old and beginning to stand.

"Yes Mma. This foot is badly deformed but I think we can help." I wrote the details on the blue out patient card. "Can you come into hospital later this week?"

Oaee Ngaka. I am from Dutlwe. It's far!" The mother looked helpless. "Can I not just stay in hospital today?"

"Ehe... Go siame. Yes... all right." I handed the papers to my nurse. Somehow we would find a space. "Mama, send them to the children's ward and I'll work him in on Friday's list." Operations for 'club foot' were becoming one of my specialities... "Mma, I think we can make him walk well. But you will have to help us and you must begin now by bending that foot gently toward its right shape... All the time." Mother and baby were in for a six-week stay in hospital for the surgery and then for careful follow up with repeated changes of plaster splints. But we had been having good results and I felt sure the outcome for this little boy would be satisfactory.

Mother and baby departed for the ward and, gradually, the nurse and I worked through the line of remaining patients. By about five o'clock we were through.

"Ngaka... That was a long clinic." She hunched her shoulders and arched her back. "It seems that even when we try and book patients they still come without appointments!"

"Eee... Mma. Thank you. You've worked hard. It's time to sleep!"

Thankfully, I headed for the airport. It was good to be in the fresh air and warm sunshine.

Parking the car I made my way out to the tarmac enjoying the sense of space after spending the afternoon in the cramped and occasionally odorous clinic.

Yes...there was the line of aircraft drawn up along the security fence. There was the green and white Cessna 172 that used to belong to the Kalahari Flying Club. The one that I had used to get my flying licence reinstated a while ago now and the one that we had used for several months to fly to Kang. It was a two and a half hour flight in a 172 and that meant that the moment we landed the bushes beside the landing strip were definitely appreciated by the passengers!

And yes... there was a Cessna 206. In fact it was the only one in the line.

It seemed in first class condition. I could see the balloon tyres we needed and, squinting through the windows at the panel, I saw that it was well equipped with radios and all the equipment needed for flying in instrument weather conditions. It also had a 'short wave' HF radio...necessary for Desert flying to remote areas. Walking round the machine, admiring the neat lines and clean, smart paintwork I could not help feeling that this aircraft seemed familiar. It was as though I had seen it somewhere before.

113

"Hmm. It looks in good nick Lord." I conversed with God. As I looked at the distorted view of my face in the curving, shiny, chromed propeller boss, the smile looking back at me was extra wide.

"Is this the one for us Lord?"

Then... the penny dropped.

"No... I cannot believe... It can't be!"

You will have guessed... That smart, beautiful colour scheme was 'butterscotch and toffee'. It really did look super. And it was an absolutely wonderful colour scheme for an aircraft that was to be flying in the Kalahari Desert. It could not have been more perfect.

*   *   *

Butterscotch & Toffee - Part 2

Bob Hampshire was not surprised that I got straight back to him.

"I think it would be a good aeroplane for you." He said. "You need to contact Johann Langenneger. He's the one organising the up-grade deal. He's in Jo'burg. Here's his number. I'd 'phone him as soon as you can. That aircraft won't sit about for long."

A few days later Roger and I met Johann at the airport. It was a crystal clear morning with heavy dew on the long grass and a cloudless Botswana sky.

Johann walked us round the 'plane doing a pre-flight inspection.

"Doc..." Johann was draining a fuel line to check for water, "have you flown a 206 before?"

"Yes, a couple of times." I had used the bright yellow 206 that had belonged to the Flying Club on a couple of occasions. It had been much more sedate than the 185.

"Well then, I think you should fly the first couple of circuits and let Roger sit in the back. That way he can get the feel of being a passenger and you can see what a lovely 'plane this is to fly."

Moments later, Roger and I were settling ourselves into our seats and buckling up. Johann talked us through the start up procedures and the engine came to life.

"Ooo! That's quiet. The 185 would be much noisier!"

"You'll find this machine is much more sophisticated in every way." Johann prattled on as a good salesman should. "Doc... I like that. You actually looked to see if the flaps came down. You'd be surprised how many folks just test the lever and don't check the actual flaps!"

Radios clicked to life. The 'da da dit, dit da dit' of the Gaborone radio beacon came reassuringly over the loud speakers in the ceiling. Johann adjusted the squelch on the VHF radios. The VHF omni-directional navigational aid (VOR) needle swung slowly to right of centre. The brakes came off and we rolled forward.

"Gaborone Control, Alpha Two Alpha Bravo Golf would like clearance for circuits please."

"Bravo Golf is cleared to the holding point zero eight for circuits. QNH (the aeronautical term for the atmospheric pressure) is 1018. Wind zero niner zero at 5 knots. Report ready for take off."

"Alpha Bravo Golf."

The nose dipped as I gently checked the brakes while taxiing. Controls were full and free in their movement. The engine hummed contentedly. Our Cessna 185 had been described by Frank Winters - the eye surgeon - as 'a wild horse on the ground... and a homesick angel in the air' and when one took off in that 'plane the whole of Gaborone knew it. This aircraft was different. A real 'lady'.

Run up over I was cleared for take off. The nose came into line with runway 08. The throttle moved easily forward in my hand. There was a surge of power. The hum increased to a gentle roar. Moments later, the tarmac sank away and we were climbing steadily into the, as yet, still morning air. In another hour turbulence would begin and reach maximum around two to three o'clock in the afternoon, making for an uncomfortable ride for any passengers.

That circuit was beautiful. No rattles. A smooth, clean response to all the controls. There was an abundance of power. Everything worked exactly as it should.

115

" I can't get over how quiet it is!"

"Yes... the sound-proofing on these newer models is pretty good."

"Bravo Golf is right hand down wind. Request touch and go."

"Bravo Golf call finals."

The starboard wing dipped. Gaborone dam moved slowly round to the window on my side. Kgale Hill came to just right of ahead. The throttle came back. The engine purred quietly. One notch of flap... Two notches...

"Bravo Golf is turning finals zero eight."

"Bravo Golf cleared touch and go."

"Bravo Golf."

A third notch of flap. Speed coming back... eighty knots... seventy knots... sixty knots. A scream from the stall-warning indicator. A gentle kiss from Mother Earth, the throttle went forward smoothly to be followed by that wonderful surge of power and we were again floating skyward.

On the down wind leg, I glanced back to see Roger relaxed, comfortable, gazing toward the ceiling with his eyes shut and a smile hovering on his face.

*   *   *

'Lephoi La Pula'

"Johann... do you take milk and sugar?" Gudrun placed a tray, laden with mugs, on the coffee table and looked up.

"Yes please... both. And those things on that plate look delicious."

"Have some. They're flapjacks. I made them this morning while you were flying." Gudrun handed him the plate. "And I'm dying to hear how it all went."

"Honey... it's a beautiful little 'plane."

"I'll back that." Roger's face was a picture of enthusiasm through the steam coming off his coffee. "And

116

another thing. Your husband flies beautifully. I almost went to sleep!"

"The problem is that we need to know the answer to a crucial question." My Scottish nature was surfacing. "Johann, tell us what the deal is."

"Well now..." Johann settled back into the armchair and slurped his coffee. "Mr. Sladden wants to up-grade to a twin. We have the twin he wants and he's asked us to sell his 206 for him. What do you think it's worth?"

"About ten thousand Rand." Roger was quick off the mark and his eye held a twinkle as he popped another piece of flapjack into his mouth "Of course you will say that it has good avionics and it's in excellent condition. But remember... Flying Mission is a charitable organisation and we don't have enormous amounts of money. Why don't you come clean and just tell us what you feel its worth?"

"All right." Johann placed his mug on the coffee table. "Seeing that you've been straight with me, I'll be straight with you. We're looking at sixty-five thousand Rand. That's a good price and it's fair. We might even knock a bit off for you folks. But that's not my decision."

"That's better than what Comair were asking for their 'plane." I looked at Roger.

"I would like to get a full pre-purchase inspection before I commit myself." Roger was cautious. "But if it's as good as it seems then yes, I think that would be a fair price."

"Johann," I said, "let me tell you how we got our first aircraft..." and, over the next few minutes, I gave an account of 'The Quiet Hour' and how - with much prayer - finance had come in over six months until, just two weeks before the 'deadline', the aeroplane had been paid off.

There was a hush before Johann spoke. "Doc, I'd like you to tell me a bit more about this Flying Mission. When did it begin? Who all is involved? What exactly does it do? I may have to tell the folks back in Jo'burg who it is that is interested in buying this 'plane."

There followed a potted history of Flying Mission from the days when Gudrun and I had travelled the Kalahari on the back of a truck with the Scottish Livingston Hospital medical teams, right to the present when the decision had been made by the Mission Executive to look for a Cessna 206.

Again there was a hush.

"Doc, it's interesting." Johann reached for his coffee mug and held it toward Gudrun. "Mrs. McArthur, may I have another mug of your delicious coffee?"

"Of course... But please call me 'Gudrun'."

"All right, I will. And let me tell you folk something now." Then, with the mug refilled, Johann held us spell bound as he shared his story. He and his wife had been nominal Christians all their lives but, for various reasons, had begun to feel dissatisfied and had begun to look for something more in life. They had started attending a home Bible study group and, only recently, they had come to submit their lives to Jesus Christ.

"So you see," Johann finished, "today, and this visit to you, I see as fitting in with the whole scheme of things. I'm beginning to see that we are all directed by an Higher Authority than most of us realise. And anyway, it is not for me to make decisions about how we can help you pay this aircraft off. You will have to talk with the National Airways Corporation (NAC) Finance Manager in Jo'burg."

A long-term friendship was begun.

*   *   *

Within a few days I found myself in Johannesburg sitting in the office of the Finance Manager of the National Airways Corporation. The story of Flying Mission was recounted again. The situation with regard to Flying Mission having no money, at present, to pay for the 206. The miraculous way that the 185 had been paid off. What would be the possibilities?

"There's no way that we can let you have that 206 until it's paid for". The Finance Manager was adamant.

"What about you keeping it in your hangar here until we've paid it off?"

"Hmm. That's not a good idea. A 'plane is meant to be used. If it sits around in a hangar it suffers. The oils congeal and it may get bumped and damaged. No. Why don't you go to your bank and see if they will lend you the money?"

It looked as if we had reached the end of the road. I could not possibly imagine any reason why the bank would lend us money to buy an aircraft. Somewhat sadly I returned to Gaborone.

At the next Flying Mission Executive Committee meeting I reported all that had happened.

"It's a real pity." Roger looked despondent. "That would have been just the 'plane for us. And it was a beaut."

There was a quiet moment.

"Well." Ngaire with her ideas again. "You were told to go to the bank and see if they would lend us the money. I think that's what you should do."

"But we've never borrowed money for anything before." I countered. "Surely if God wants us to have that 'plane He will provide what is needed."

"That's right." Ngaire was firm. "The bank might give us a loan. Perhaps even free of interest. If you were told to do that then that's what you should do."

So, a few days later, and feeling very stupid, I entered the bank manager's office.

"Doctor McArthur... What can we do for you?"

I had the distinct impression of a lion, looking cuddly but waiting to pounce and tear me apart.

"Er... well... I'm wondering if you can lend us some money?"

"Yes. How much?"

"Well, sixty-five thousand Rand."

"Tell me what you have in mind." The manager pulled a writing pad toward himself. "Here, sit down. Would you like tea or coffee?"

"Well, you see, we want to buy a 'plane." I felt a real fool. But there is, in the Bible, a verse about 'being fools for Christ'.

After a somewhat shaky start and, realising that I had not immediately been thrown out as I had imagined I would be, I explained the whole situation along with the background of the 185 purchase and where we were now. "So you see, we need an aircraft with easier loading capabilities and better handling for smoother travel for patients.

"Let's think." The manager's chair tilted back and he gazed toward the ceiling.

That really stupid feeling swept over me again. Who was I to be sitting here asking for such an outrageous sum of money? But... it was a miracle situation. And God loves a situation... where only He can work a miracle for His children.

The chair snapped forward. "It's not an unreasonable request. It's really just a matter of how we work out the details." He pressed a button on his desk and after a moment a door opened and a neatly dressed clerk came in. "Julia... Please get me the files for the Flying Mission."

It took only a minute or two and then came the decision... "Yes... Look... I can offer you an overdraft facility for one year. And we'll make it for sixty-eight thousand because you will have insurance and maintenance and so forth to think about." He scribbled notes while I gaped. "The aircraft will have to be bonded to the bank and registered in the bank's name until it's paid for. But that's just a formality. Is there anything else?"

"Er... no I don't think so. I mean... yes... Yes there is... Thank you. That's tremendous!"

*   *   *

Everyone was delighted. Roger got the inspection done and pronounced his verdict... "A perfect aircraft." Johann enjoyed more coffee. The money was transferred to the National Airways Corporation who, incidentally, generously dropped the asking price to fifty-nine thousand Rand. Bob Hampshire made out the Department of Civil Aviation (DCA) paperwork.

That afternoon, when all was completed - and almost before the ink had dried on the DCA documents - a call came from Tshabong (550 km southwest of Gaborone) with a request to collect a woman who was in obstructed labour. Alpha Two Alpha Bravo Golf began its life of service to God and to the people of Botswana.

A2-ABG - 'Lephoi la Pula' or' Butterscotch & Toffee'

Of course we still had a big debt to pay off. But much prayer was sent up to our Heavenly Father with regard to finance. It was exciting. Every time I went to the post box to collect the mail it seemed that there was a letter with a cheque, or a postal order, from someone who had heard that Flying Mission was buying a second 'plane... and "here is something to help." As with the 185, many of the folk who sent gifts I had never heard of before. It was a humbling experience.

With Divine provision, and perfect timing, just two weeks before the termination of the one-year overdraft arrangement with the bank, Alpha Two Alpha Bravo Golf was paid off. Shortly after that Flying Mission held a dedication service for the aircraft and it was named 'Lephoi la Pula'... 'Dove of Blessing.'

*　　*　　*

121

Ancient & modern forms of transport (Photo: J Calhoon)

That little 'plane did much hard work in the Botswana skies for 23 years. It carried patients from all the remote corners of the land, with every conceivable injury and illness, to hospitals in Maun, Gaborone, Francistown, and some even to Johannesburg. And it took the message of God's love and Christ's sacrifice to many. During those years of service it was fitted with a new engine more than once and at 5000 flight hours - as per Mission Aviation Fellowship regulations - it underwent a complete 're-build'. For this it was taken apart completely and had all its parts checked for damage, or stress fatigue, before being reassembled and sent back to the flight line for further duty.

Butterscotch and Toffee... Lephoi la Pula... Dove of Blessing. It certainly was a great blessing... and a wonderful example of God's care and faithfulness.

"Thank you Lord."

-oOo-

Lephoi la Pula - Dove of Blessing - on the salt pan at Zutsha

A frequent dilemma

The last post. Ngaire scribbles a hasty note to be taken for posting in Gaborone

CHAPTER 5
TRAINING

-Δ-

'Practice makes perfect' is a well know proverb.

Regular training soon became an integral part of the Flying Mission pilot's schedule and we were helped in this by Mission Aviation Fellowship (MAF) who had been in the business of mission flying for many years and in varied locations around the world and who had a wealth of experience to share.

With the help of visits from Terry Hibbs, who was serving with Mission Aviation Fellowship in Lesotho, and others, we began having regular flight checks and were given exercises to sharpen flying skills. Many of our pilots visited Mission Aviation Fellowship's Lesotho programme, which was very different from what Flying Mission was doing in Botswana. Botswana is more or less 'pancake flat' while the mountains of the Drakensburg in Lesotho provide enormous challenges to a pilot in other ways.

Roger Schultz - seconded to Flying Mission by the Africa Evangelical Fellowship (AEF) - had been adamant from his early days, that the Mission pilots should all have a Commercial Pilot's Licence and, ideally, an Instrument Rating and a Night Rating. He encouraged us to practise instrument flying 'under the hood' (with himself acting as safety pilot in the right seat!) and this quickly brought home to us how much we still had to learn.

These 'nudges' toward perfection eventually bore fruit, and a Policy Manual was also compiled which has gone far in raising the standard of flying in the Mission, and helping to avoid major problems, by laying down clear directives concerning staying within safe limits.

*   *   *

Down & Locked?

I thought him rather stupid at first. On my yearly instrument check ride his question on short finals was always the same...

"Checked wheels down and locked?"

"But Sir." He was after all the Examiner for the Department of Civil Aviation. "This is a Cessna 206!"

"On **BOTH SIDES**?"

"But..." I would protest, "This is an aircraft with fixed gear that is carefully maintained."

"Yes..."

Then would follow his story of losing a wheel in the Alaskan tundra whilst taking off in an aircraft overloaded with reindeer meat. Somewhere in dim history.

"One day..." He would smile, knowing I suppose that he was casting a pearl before a swine, "you might just be able to save yourself an unexpected shock."

He was right. And if I had had sense I would have applied his teaching much more liberally.

*   *   *

On a later occasion, a routine practice and safety check were going well. My steep turns were smooth and co-ordinated and slow flight expertly performed.

The sky was clear and free from other flying debris. The weather was perfection.

"You just stay under that hood and fly the 'plane straight and level." Roger Weaver, our American Chief Pilot, drawled. "I'll play around with the flaps and see how you get on. Keep your airspeed below 100 knots and maintain altitude. This is a great exercise for sharpening skills on the yoke and throttle."

If you've never done it, and if you have someone in the right seat to operate the flap selector lever, give it a try. It's worth the flight time.

I soon got on top of things and Roger's hankering for coffee was never far away so, pretty soon, it was "OK. Let's get back to the pattern and have a soft field touch and go."

Most of the strips in Botswana are sandy and it's easy to get bogged down. Not so much on landing, but certainly when taxiing and trying to make a tight turn to avoid a cow or a donkey.

A short while later, our tyres caressed the concrete at the Sir Seretse Khama International Airport at Gaborone, Botswana's capital city. We touched down daintily and were off again with minimum fuss. Roger was satisfied.

"OK. Go around and now let's have a short field full stop."

Coffee clarifying in my imagination also, I applied power, climbed away, and turned downwind. Base leg and setting up on final were professional.

"Bit high this time." I murmured as I tweaked the flap lever to 20 and then 40 degrees and eased the yoke forward.

"Also a bit fast..." Roger drawled.

"Hey... what's wrong with this aircraft?" I wrestled impotently.

Alpha Echo Papa crossed the threshold far too high and floated rebelliously along the runway as if we had a stiff tail wind. To my chagrin we eventually touched down well passed the second set of VASI (Visual Approach Slope Indicator) lights.

"What did you do?" I eyeballed the circuit breakers and looked at Roger accusingly. "Or did we just strike a thermal?

"I did nothing." Roger was emphatic. "And I don't remember seeing any dust devils either."

The reason was obvious when we looked round. The flaps were fully retracted. They had never extended so much as a degree.

Checking the undercarriage (Photo: J Philipsen)

No amount of playing with the flap selector lever would budge them. And when we got out to investigate further, the wing flaps were immovable.

It was the Chief Engineer who, after several hours of hard work, discovered the malfunctioning micro switch somewhere under the instrument panel. (Part Number: S1906/1.)

I was glad it was the Chief Pilot who had been playing with the flap lever! And I was also glad that the incident occurred when we had a couple of kilometres of concrete runway to land on. Over coffee we considered what might have happened if we had been coming in for real and with a heavy load on a short, sandy strip out in the Kalahari Desert. The prospect of nesting in a thorn tree is definitely for the birds.

The lesson I learnt? Why stop at wheels on both sides anyway? From now on I shall check **EVERYTHING**. And I would strongly encourage you to do the same.

Something will happen sooner or later. It's Murphy's Law. And it could be while coming into that grass patch at

Denham, or anywhere. These things don't happen only in darkest Africa.

Yes... Regular check flights are well worth having as a part of the operating routine.

Like the man said: "Save yourself an unexpected shock!"

*   *   *

Fish & Chips

"That's good Malcolm. Now maintain this heading and watch that the NDB (non-directional beacon) needle doesn't creep."

Roger Schultz - a short-term volunteer seconded to Flying Mission by the Africa Evangelical Fellowship - was acting as lookout pilot. I was practicing an 'instrument approach' using the non-directional beacon at the old Gaborone airport. This was in the days before the opening of the new Seretse Khama International Airport with its modern Instrument Landing System (ILS) approach facilities.

Roger had convinced me that some experience in instrument flying was a wise addition to the Private Pilot's Licence (PPL) that I had obtained in the days before I had begun studying medicine.

"If Flying Mission is going to get anywhere it must have well qualified pilots." Roger had been vocal on the subject since joining the Mission. "Ideally you should all have a full CPL (Commercial Pilot's Licence), with at least a Night Rating and preferably also a full Instrument Rating."

Whenever possible he would encourage us all to don the 'instrument hood', that restricts one's view to a small space on the instrument panel of the aircraft, and practice flying 'on instruments'. "You never know when you may be caught out in bad weather. It's better to be safe than sorry."

At first I could never keep the 'plane on the right heading and at the required altitude. I would concentrate on

129

keeping the heading right but then altitude control would go hay wire, or vice versa.

"Malcolm... You must learn to scan." Roger was enthusiastic and also patient. "Don't focus on just one instrument. Keep your eyes constantly moving between the artificial horizon (AH), the altimeter, the turn and bank indicator and the air speed indicator. The AH is primary. Always come back to that one before checking one of the others. That way you will pick up any changes early and you can apply a corrective action before things get out of hand."

As I battled to scan the instruments, control the aircraft and visualise exactly where we were in relation to the radio beacon and the airport runway I had my hands full. With practice it gradually became easier and, once the scanning procedure had become reflex, and I had mastered the art of keeping the paperwork and the airport Approach Plates in view on the small pad strapped to my right knee, things began to improve and confidence increased. But there could be surprises...

On one such NDB approach Roger shot the question, "Now, where exactly do you think you are?"

Under the hood I glanced at the Jeppeson Approach Chart on my lap and confidently confirmed, "We're over the Gaborone dam and about five miles out from the airport."

"Right, Malcolm. I want you to take off the hood, look up, and see where you are heading."

Removal of the restrictive hood revealed that we were indeed about five miles out... But nowhere near over the Gaborone dam. And, although the runway was lying dead ahead as I had expected, Kgale Hill filled much of the windshield!

"Ooops!"

"Not bad!" Roger was laughing. "You're about right for height, but you might have lost a wing if you had continued. You didn't allow for the wind. We've got a fair bit of a crosswind today and while you've been keeping nicely pointed to the NDB we've been drifting to port, and you failed to notice that the DG (Directional Gyro) has precessed. Remember, you need to keep checking the DG against the compass every few minutes."

To gain experience of "instrument flying"....

....pilots wear special vision-restricting headgear.

"Ooops!" (Cartoon: S Mingham)

In turbulence things can get out of kilter very fast if you don't watch carefully.

It was a good lesson that highlighted the dangers. Roger was an excellent teacher. But he was also a master at timing distractions, to try and intentionally 'rock the boat' and force one to lose concentration to sharpen skills.

On another occasion we were practising a VOR (VHF Omni-range) and Localiser approach. That is a bit simpler than the NDB form of instrument approach, but it is still an exacting procedure demanding close concentration.

We had returned from a flight to the Desert and it was late morning. All was going splendidly. We were in contact with Gaborone Tower and we had been cleared into the approach from a holding pattern over the VOR beacon.

"Hey, Malcolm. We'll be home in time for lunch." Roger suddenly came to life. "What do you think Gudrun and Ruth are cooking up for us today?"

The needle of the VOR swung across the dial as we passed overhead the beacon. We were nicely positioned for the let down and I throttled back and began the descent.

"I've no idea." I lowered ten degrees of flap and re-trimmed the aircraft for the slower airspeed.

"You know I fancy fish and chips today..." Roger chortled on.

"Gaborone Tower we are..." I gave the Tower our position report and acknowledged their instructions.

"The last time Ruth and I were in Jo'burg we had fish and chips. We found a place in Discovery..."

Our descent was going exactly as planned.

"They had such fresh and succulent fish. It was absolutely delicious!" He nudged my arm. "Malcolm, do you like fish and chips?"

"Yes Roger, but..." My scan was working well and I had checked the directional gyro a minute before.

"You must go there Malcolm. Next time you are in Jo'burg..." Another nudge came my way this one expertly timed to accompany the next call from the control tower with the latest wind report. "You would love their hake. It is so tasty!"

Roger had been in real estate for many years and he could be very pushy and persuasive.

"Gaborone Control, thank you. We are joining the Localiser."

"And the chips they do there... Malcolm you like chips don't you?" Another nudge and in his southern American drawl he continued. "They were just like Gudrun makes... crisp and lovely. And the batter...man, I can feel my mouth watering just at the thought..."

There... we're established on the Localiser. The needle is centred. Altitude check... Descent going as planned... Five hundred feet a minute...

"Gaborone Tower, Zulu Golf Bravo is established on the Localiser."

"Malcolm... Isn't your mouth watering?"

"Yes Roger."

"Alpha Two Zulu Golf Bravo is cleared to finals."

"I can't wait. Man I'm hungry! And I just have such a vision of that tender, white, juicy fish..."

"Golf Bravo, finals next."

"And I can just feel that wonderfully crisp batter between my teeth..." Nudge.

"Oh Roger!"

Check the directional gyro. And altitude... There decision height is coming up..."

"Hey, Malcolm..."

"Gaborone Tower, Zulu Golf Bravo is finals zero eight."

"They do a pretty good steak there too."

"Alpha Two Zulu Golf Bravo is cleared to land. Wind is two seven zero at ten. And please expedite. We have Air Botswana turning downwind."

"Zulu Golf Bravo."

"Well Malcolm. Take that hood off. You made it."

The hood came off and yes... There it was - at last! The touchdown zone. That bit of the grey, paved runway with all those black tyre marks on it. We really had made it,, and - for once - perfectly. In spite of the fish and chips.

"I really did my level best to distract you... But you did well. You even checked the DG." Roger was genuinely delighted.

As we pulled up at the pumps to refuel I almost punched his nose.

* * *

It did not take long to convince all the Mission pilots that the Commercial Licence and Instrument Rating idea was a good one, and certainly that move has been a factor in the good safety record of the Mission over the years. But all of us pilots also willingly acknowledge that prayer, and having a loving and caring Heavenly Father, is by far the biggest reason for that excellent safety record.

Yes, there have been the occasional incidents. A few bent propellers, and - to date - one argument with a Cape Vulture. But no fatalities or serious injuries... other than, occasionally, dented pride.

The Cape Vulture? It was permanently grounded. The aircraft as well. But that is Tim's story.

* * *

Long grass and anthills can be a problem

The Leak

In 1980 'Butterscotch & Toffee' joined 'The Quiet Hour'. The Mission fleet had doubled in size. First the Cessna 185 and now a Cessna 206 - named 'B & T' for short on account of its colour scheme. It was a smart little 'plane.

John Rempel, Frank Winters and I were using the two aircraft to travel about Botswana in the course of our duties. Air travel made a huge difference, saving us time and energy. But there were problems.

"Malcolm we need to get together and talk." Frank had just flown in from Maun where he had spent several days attending to patients with eye troubles and removing cataracts. John and I were helping him tie the 'plane down for the night.

"What's on your mind Frank?"

"Well, you know I love flying. And I know that you and John do too."

"So?"

"You must have noticed that lately the Ministry of Health has been requesting us to do a lot of 'mercy flights'. During this visit to Maun, I was asked to fly down to Ghanzi to bring in a woman with an obstructed labour. I have no problem with that. It was a necessary flight. But it messed up my operating list and I had to stay an extra day."

"You mean the emergency Caesarean 'bumped' you and it meant you couldn't finish your op list? That could happen any time." John laughed.

"No John. I think I see what Frank is getting at. We are here to do surgery and spending our time taxi driving is not what we're paid for. I've been thinking about it too. Last week I did a flight to Tshabong to bring in three badly burned folk. Their hut had caught fire. They were in a mess and it would've taken a whole day on bad roads to bring them in. But my Out Patient Clinic had to be cancelled."

"You've hit the nail on the head Malcolm." Frank leant on the wing strut and gazed out over the taxiway toward the distant veldt. "Hey guys. We are so blessed. It's such a beautiful afternoon. I love looking out at the heat haze... See how it makes the horizon ripple... Didn't our Creator do a magnificent job putting all this together?"

"There's another thing." John had become serious. "B & T, Alpha Two Alpha Bravo Golf... It's a first class 'plane. Looks super and it flies beautifully. But, I was thinking that if we took off the 'fancy pants' it would go a couple of knots faster."

"You mean take off the wheel covers?"

"Yes."

"It wouldn't look so good. But, on the other hand it would stop us collecting grass and sticks on some of the bush strips we fly into. Last time I was at Hukuntsi, I had to clear a lot of grass out to free the wheels."

The chitchat covered a multitude of subjects and eventually settled on the subject of maintenance. A recent bill for a minor repair job had not been insignificant.

"It's a pity we can't do some of the maintenance ourselves." Frank looked thoughtful. "An oil change is not such a big job."

"Mmm! You mean we should do mechanical work on our taxis as well as drive them?" John giggled. "I wonder what the Permanent Secretary in the Ministry of Health would think about that!"

Yes, there were problems. But the 'Boss' had a solution...

*   *   *

"Hey John. Where's Frank. I have some news."

"Frank? I last saw him in Sister Dikeledi's office in theatre."

"Perfect... Let's go..."

Soon the kettle was bubbling and John was spooning the instant coffee into three cups.

"OK you two. What's it all about?" Frank took off his glasses and wiped them on his green cotton theatre shirt.

"Malcolm says he's got some important news." John poured steaming fluid into each cup and added milk.

"Yes I have. Listen to this. You know what we were talking about the other day... You remember - us being taxi drivers. Well now... Sister Mary, are there no fat cakes today?"

"Ao Ngaka! First you take over my office and you want to make my office into a conference room... And now you expect room service too! Frederick..." Sister Dikeledi pushed back her chair and, as if by magic, Frederick appeared at the door holding a brown paper bag with large grease stains on it. "Ee Mma. I have them here." The Head Theatre Porter was grinning from ear to ear. "I saw the Dr Rempel and Doctor McArthur coming and I sent Betty to get some 'magunya'."

"Sister... You run this operating theatre wonderfully... It is such a real delight to work here!"

"Ngaka! You are so cheeky. And Doctor Rempel is no better. But here in Botswana... Hey, we just have to take what we can get. Just remember that those greasy fat cakes will give you coronary heart disease very fast." Sister Mary Lucy Dikeledi had trained at the Scottish Livingstone Hospital, Molepolole, from 1956 to 1960, and qualified as a general nurse and midwife. Then, from 1971 to 1972 she had done further training in operating theatre nursing at the Victoria Infirmary in Glasgow. The Princess Marina Hospital operating theatres were her 'empire' and she ran them expertly, with smooth efficiency, yet maintaining a happy atmosphere for both patients and medical staff. Later she was to become Matron and, later still, would be absorbed into the ivory towers of the Ministry of Health to assist in directing the Nursing Services for the whole country.

"Aw Sister... You look so upset... But that smile... It's beautiful!"

"It's all right. You are welcome to use my office." Sister Dikeledi laughed. "Doctor Winters, please see that these two young boys leave this place tidy. I have to go to the Nursing Council for a meeting with the Chief Nursing Officer."

The door closed behind her and, over the coffee and fat cakes, Frank and John looked at me expectantly.

"It's exciting. I met with Ed and Irene Weaver yesterday. Ed is the head of the Mennonite Ministries here in Botswana."

"And?'

"Well, some time ago I spoke with Ed about our situation and the need for a full time pilot for Flying Mission. Ed said he would look into it and he made the suggestion that

Mennonite Ministries might be able to find a Pilot/Mechanic who could be seconded to Flying Mission."

"Wow. That'd be great." John's eyes lit up.

"Now then... " Frank was chewing a mouthful of fat cake. When could this happen?"

"Ed has spoke to the Mennonite Ministries Director, Larry Fisher, and he was very positive. Larry's is going to contact his folk in the USA and he thinks they could find someone be very soon... That's if you all agree to the idea."

"Agree! Why shouldn't we agree?"

"Great. I'll tell Ed that we're all in favour. And by the way, 'Bravo Golf' is out of the hangar. The hundred hour inspection went fine."

"Super. Is it OK if I do some circuits in it this afternoon?"

"Sure, John. And if you can refuel it after you've finished then it'll be all ready for whatever."

Fat cakes demolished, and the table cleared, the 'meeting' was closed and we left Frank to finish writing up his operation notes.

Later, as I was sitting at my desk at home, I heard John doing his circuits. 'B & T' had a loud hum on take off compared to the trumpet like blast of 'The Quiet Hour'.

Ed's proposition was a wonderful offer. Maintenance was being done for us by Kalahari Air Services & Charter. However, they ran their own charter business and their own aircraft, of course, took priority and they were always busy and under pressure.

Around half past five the telephone rang. It was John.

"You'll never guess what happened." He sounded serious

"Not another dose of 'P Factor' I hope. Tell me."

"No, not that this time. Today it is 'L Factor'... a leak, and a big one."

"Go on. Has that fuel cell that was oozing a little really come apart now?"

"No, not that. I collected the 206 and did my circuits. Everything seemed perfect and it was a beautiful afternoon... Not much turbulence. Anyway, after my last landing I taxied to the pumps and got out to refuel and as I was standing talking to the BP pump attendant suddenly there was a click and oil just gushed out of the engine! Yes. The whole sump emptied right onto the tarmac and when we opened the cowling the oil filter had come loose. Why it didn't happen while I was flying I don't know!"

"Ouch! That would have been a nasty experience."

"You're telling me. I've pushed the 'plane back to the Kalahari Air Services hangar. They're looking at it."

"Mmm. Thank The Lord it happened when it did and not ten minutes earlier. And imagine what would have happened on some bush airstrip or, worse, while in flight somewhere over the Kalahari."

"The sooner we get our own Mission Pilot/Mechanic the better."

'The Boss' thought so too.

*   *   *

The talks between Ed Weaver and Larry Fisher bore fruit quickly and it was only a matter of a few months before Jay Aeschliman, and his wife Cynthia, arrived in Botswana to serve with Flying Mission. A firm link was forged between Flying Mission and Mennonite Ministries that was to be beneficial to both organisations for many years to come.

-oOo-

The Botswana National Assembly Building in Gaborone

Dr Alfred Musgrave Merriweather
CBE, POH, MD, FRCPE, DTM&H

Dr Alfred M. Merriweather graduated in Edinburgh in 1941 and arrived in Botswana in 1944 where he held positions of Superintendent of the Scottish Livingstone Hospital in Molepolole, and then of the Princess Marina Hospital in Gaborone. He was appointed the first Speaker of the Botswana National Assembly at Independence in 1966, and also served as physician to the President of Botswana, Sir Seretse Khama. He was a Minister of the United Free Church of Scotland and was made a Moderator of that Church in 1979. He always took a keen interest in the Flying Mission and he became the first Patron of the Mission.

140

CHAPTER 6
HEADING

-Δ-

Once airborne it makes sense to get onto the heading to one's destination as soon as possible. However, if the take off run has had to be into a direction opposite to that of the required route because of the prevailing wind, a few gentle turns may be indicated, and, any instructions that come from the control tower have to be followed also.

On one flight, as I was making a gentle turn to achieve our required heading, the passenger sitting in the right seat next to me leant over and, with a cheeky smile, commented "Is not the shortest distance between two points a straight line?"

Roger Schultz, as you have read, was obsessed with the compass and the directional gyro (DG), and rightly so. It's hard to reach one's destination if one does not know the direction in which to fly, and it's worth checking regularly that one is 'on track', especially in areas like the Kalahari Desert with few easily recognisable landmarks.

On one flight to Kuruman Dr Merriweather was convinced that we were heading in the wrong direction. "Malcolm, surely this is the wrong direction. Should we not be going that way?"

Many things can pull one off course. Variation in wind speed and direction. Turbulence. A poorly trimmed aircraft. Distracting conversations about fish and chips.

A directional gyro is affected by gyroscopic 'precession' and needs regular re-setting to the compass heading. The compass itself needs to be 'swung' and adjusted to work

141

accurately in the aircraft in which it is installed, and, even when correctly installed, its function may be interfered with by placing metal objects too close to it. Some areas of the earth's surface may affect compass behaviour because of high iron content in the earth's crust, and the pilot must also be aware of magnetic variation - the difference between 'magnetic' and 'true' north - that affects flight differently in different regions of the globe. In turbulence the compass may be hard to read on account of its mobility and for that reason, of course, the directional gyro, that tends to be more stable, was invented.

What was to be the 'destination' of Flying Mission and what was the 'route' to be flown?

Frank, John and I were committed Christians and it was our aim to share the Christian Gospel and extend Christ's Kingdom in all that we did and those became the aims of Flying Mission. It followed, naturally, that Jesus became the 'compass' pointing the direction in which we should move forward, and The Bible was the equivalent of the Pilot's Operating Handbook or POH.

*　　*　　*

Aims & a Motto - 'Go, Preach, Heal.'

"Malcolm, it's time Flying Mission had some headed paper." Roger Schultz, the Africa Evangelical Fellowship volunteer from the USA, had got another bee in his bonnet.

"Headed paper?" I wondered what was coming now. "What for? We've managed fine with plain paper till now." My Scottish heritage tended to resist anything that might lead to any further expense.

"Well, we're now beginning to correspond with all kinds of folk." Roger's American drawl continued. "It would give a much better impression if FM (Flying Mission) had its own headed paper, and even a logo."

Roger had a point, as usual, and a few days later I mentioned it to Gudrun who, to my surprise, was all for the idea. "You could ask Liesel and Uli to draw something for a logo."

"Liesel and Uli?"

"Yes, they're 'arty' and Uli will probably give us some good ideas too. Let's see what they come up with. And let's get Verena in on it too."

"Well, for a motto what about taking the title of the United Free Church of Scotland film... the one that they made about Molepolole?"

"You Mean 'Go, Preach, Heal'?"

"Yes... that's it. We've had close links all along with the United Free folk and that was in any case taken from Jesus' great commission to His disciples. And I think there should somehow be a cross in the logo. We want FM to be a Christian Mission and the primary aim should be the extension of Christ's Kingdom. Is that not so?"

"Definitely."

After the idea was put to Liesel and Uli and Verena it was not long before they came up with a logo...

"You wanted a cross at the centre and something representing flight." Uli - a retired Swiss engineer - held up their submission. "And we thought that the medical aspect of Flying Mission needed to be included so we put a snake in around the cross."

"Ao, Uli. That looks good... But the Batswana are fearful of snakes. That bit definitely needs to come out!"

"Those words GO PREACH HEAL look super in that black ring but it's all a bit severe looking." Gudrun had reservations. "What about putting some colour somewhere? And shouldn't the name FLYING MISSION be included?"

A short while later, Verena had added a blue background and the logo was complete to everyone's satisfaction.

"There. Super. And we've managed to include the Botswana colours - black for the Batswana majority, blue for the sky and water, and white for the small number of Europeans. Excellent!"

"And that 'bird' thing that's behind the cross that looks a bit like the old British Overseas Airways Corporation sign can be representing the Holy Spirit - always there in the background directing the Mission. I like it."

Uli promptly brought out his mouth organ and burst into a jaunty Swiss tune.

Roger approved heartily and, within days, had somehow managed to produce a fine draft of proposed headed paper for the Mission with the new logo enlarged, printed faintly, and almost filling the A4 size sheet.

"Fantastic... It looks great."

"Let's do it!"

And that logo and motto have, for years, reminded us of the primary aim of the Mission - to extend Christ's Kingdom in a wonderful country, and a unique nation.

*   *   *

The Little White Cloud - References

It was only a little one. But I learnt a lesson from it that I have never forgotten.

A2-ZHV was a lovely machine. It was a Cessna 172 with a pleasant green and white livery. I had hired it for some reason that I have now forgotten. Indeed, just why I was by myself, and tootling along flying westward a little to the north of Sekgoma Pan, also escapes me.

Departing Gaborone that afternoon, I had flown directly to Kanye and then turned right to follow the road that would eventually take me to Kang. It was a simple route that I was perfectly familiar with, having followed it several times. The Meteorological Office had reported weather as 'fine with about three octas of cumulus at around seven thousand feet with winds light and variable and no sig' (no significant change expected.) It was a great day to add flight hours to the total in my Pilot's Log Book, a total that stood at nearly 250 hours as Pilot in Command.

"Johannesburg, Alpha Two Zulu Hotel Victor."

144

'That little white cloud...'

"Alpha Two Zulu Hotel Victor this is Johannesburg. Go ahead." The voice was clear today. Sometimes static could be a real problem with the Short Wave communication.

"Johannesburg, Alpha Two Zulu Hotel Victor is operations normal and coming up abeam Sekgoma Pan."

"Alpha Two Zulu Hotel Victor... Thank you. Report again destination in sight."

"Johannesburg, Alpha Two Zulu Hotel Victor - roger."

I switched to the VHF and set it to the en route frequency of 125.5 MHz. "VFR traffic this is Alpha Two Zulu Hotel Victor, a Cessna 172, Gaborone to Kang." I gave details of my position, altitude and an estimate of the arrival time in Kang and ended up with what sounded a rather forlorn "Does anyone copy?"

There was no response. I had the airspace over the Desert entirely to myself.

With that chore out of the way, and having made an entry in my flight log, I could relax and enjoy the scenery.

Far below me, the flat Kalahari landscape stretched in every direction like an unending sheet of crumpled brown paper with an occasional dark splodge where the shadow of a cloud lingered. The white, bean shaped salt pan at Sekgoma was sliding past under the port wing with the minute looking, round huts of the village dotted sparsely around the northern edge of the pan. The pale yellow ribbon of the sandy Desert road divided just before the village, and the road to Werda and Tshabong veered off to the south to disappear in the haze of a rather indistinct horizon.

The altimeter read 6,500 feet. And yes, there were the few fluffy white cumulus clouds around me and at an altitude of not more than a few hundred feet above me. One was directly in front but still some way off.

That little white cloud set the grey cells in my brain jiggling. Isn't it odd how a bit of stupidity - or just plain sin - can look so attractive?

Now... if I advance the throttle and re-trim to a gentle climb...

The dye was set. It was only a small cloud. Who was to know? I had the Desert to myself, didn't I? And I was now an experienced pilot with well over 200 hours of Pilot in Command time... No, I'd never flown in cloud before - except as a passenger. No, I did not have an instrument rating, but I'd done a little 'partial panel' stuff during my flight training - all those years ago, out of Denham, in G-AGVJ, that fabric covered Auster that I did my first shaky solo flight in. This was a great opportunity to try flying blind in cloud. Anyway, I'd be out of that cloud before I knew it. It was only a small one.

That little white cloud was now dead ahead. The altimeter was steady at 7,100 feet. My hand tightened on the yoke. It was getting closer... right in front... and getting bigger each second, as was the excitement.

Bam! Suddenly the world became white and completely blank.

There was nothing different to feel. The engine was still humming in front of me. I could not detect any strange movements. But the horizon was gone. In an instant the Desert had been rubbed out. All visual references had been swallowed up in whiteness. It never occurred to me to look at the artificial horizon. My gaze was fixed through the windshield waiting for the vanished world to return.

Exactly how long I was flying in that blind state, boring lunatic-like along a path I could not see, in that 'little white cloud', I do not know. I was completely unaware of the potential and horrific dangers that lurked in the escapade I was indulging in. At the time, it all seemed such fun and so harmless. It cannot have been more than ten seconds at the very most. It was exciting. And I was doing it so well!

How foolish can one be? An inexperienced Visual Flight Rules pilot dabbling in Instrument Flight Conditions flying is one of the worst sins in the aviation world. Thankfully - with the exception of my personal Guardian Angel - I was alone in that airspace. And, thankfully, there were no Vultures or Bateleur Eagles in the vicinity. It was a few years later before I got to see the damage that could occur in a collision between one of those birds and an aircraft.

The white veil parted as dramatically as it had closed in about me and as I came hurtling out of that cloud there, before me, was the brown, crumpled looking surface of the Kalahari. It filled almost the entire windshield. A further rapid investigation revealed an indistinct horizon off the end of the port wing tip. But it was at a most odd angle. More vertical than horizontal.

A glance at the altimeter showed the needle moving rapidly in an anticlockwise direction.

Jolted back to reality, I became suddenly aware of a loud rushing noise. Further investigation revealed that the airspeed indicator needle had risen alarmingly to near that ominous red mark on the dial that signifies that the manufacturer's guarantee of the structural integrity of the airframe was about to be put to the test.

It was the moment for an immediate application of the principals and wisdom to be found in the Pilot's Operating Handbook - a copy of which was tucked into the pocket of the cabin door at my side. However, this was no time for a speedy read. There was an acute need for instant and effective action and, with the outside world again in view, and some quick adjustments to the throttle, ailerons and elevators, it did not take too long to bring life back to a degree of normality. My pulse rate took considerably longer to settle.

It was a salutary lesson, lasting a total of only about 30 seconds, and it demonstrated with incredible clarity just how easy it is to lose one's bearings totally in a very short space of time, and the potentially disastrous effects.

Firstly, it helped me to decide very quickly that it would be well worth while getting some proper instrument training and, in the interim, I would not, under any circumstances, tangle with any more of that white stuff, however tempting it might be.

Looking back this was definitely one of my better decisions. Now, with over 2000 hours as Pilot In Command (PIC) and full Instrument and Night Ratings, I have come to believe firmly that it's much better to keep one's visual references and be able to see exactly where one is going all of the time.

Then, on thinking further about it later, that 30-second event offered some much deeper lessons on life.

One can be cruising through life on an even keel with all the trims set and everything nicely balanced. But just one little sin and everything can go disastrously wrong very fast.

The Bible makes it clear that sin can rapidly result in confusion with a loss of control, disorientation and, subsequently, violence, pain and, ultimately, death.

Yes, no question about it. Sin can rapidly cause a loss of balance, a distraction from purpose, a loss of direction, and set one on a path toward rapid, violent destruction.

Is this not something we see going on all around us in this world all the time - a blatant disregard for God's laws with catastrophic results? Are we not constantly meeting with confused, hurting people who are doing their own thing in their own way having lost - or deliberately abandoned - the important and vital details and reference points that are provided by our Creator in His book of instructions?

What is the answer?

Consult the Pilot's Operating Handbook. The Manufacturer's Handbook. The instruction document that so often we ignore in our excitement to get started. Even better, have the content of that document fixed firmly in the mind ready for instant and immediate retrieval and application. There could not be a better encouragement to keep satisfactory reference points by regular study of the Maker's Handbook - The Bible.

The remainder of that flight was uneventful. I had done quite enough experimenting for one afternoon and I think my voice was back to normal tones when I made my next call...

"Johannesburg Control Alpha Two Zulu Hotel Victor has destination Kang in sight."

"Alpha Two Zulu Hotel Victor, call again airborne."

"Thank you. Alpha Two Zulu Hotel Victor."

Would that sin was always so painlessly resolved.

It's a lesson for all of us. If we want to get to the destination safely then we must study the Handbook carefully - before we get into difficulty. It may seem a waste of time but it really does make life simpler.

Thank You, Lord, for teaching me a lesson and, for once, the easy way.

*   *   *

Lost

It was a perfect day. A brilliant, blue, cloudless sky. Visibility was unlimited and I was flying low level along a road that I knew well. So how could I possibly get lost? Very easily - as I was to learn.

The distance, as the crow flies, from Kang to Hukuntsi is only about 60 kilometres. The road in those days was a deep sand track, sometimes two tracks, where the sand was really deep and vehicles were often getting stuck. The trip by road would usually take about three hours. Longer, if one had a problem - like the two Danish medical students who were doing their 'electives' for a period at the clinic in Hukuntsi. They had had to take an emergency patient to Lobatse and were driving back to Hukuntsi after dark. Tired, and anxious to get back to the clinic, they were traveling too fast and hit a wildebeest. The poor animal was killed outright and ended up draped over the buckled bonnet of the Landcruiser that they were in. The vehicle's radiator was badly damaged and the two

149

aspiring medics were stranded. They were in for more excitement than they had ever imagined possible. The scent of fresh blood does not go unnoticed in the Kalahari.

The first arrivals at the scene of the accident had been the usual clean up team - some hyenas. However, these soon retreated to a safe distance once the big boys moved in. Two lion took over the dinner at about two in the morning.

The medical team had a night they would never forget and plenty of time to make resolutions never again to drive at speed after dark in the Kalahari. Fortunately, the lion were content with the meat of the wildebeest. It could have been a different story. The windscreen of a Landcruiser does not offer much protection and it was not until some time after sun up, when another vehicle came along, that the two Danes were rescued. They had plenty to talk about.

By air, the trip takes fifteen to twenty minutes depending on the aircraft type, the altitude to which it climbs, the power settings at cruise, and, which particular crow one happens to follow. Crows seldom fly direct. The Flying Mission Cessna 185 had plenty of 'punch' and could cruise fast. But I was in no hurry... a bit like the average crow.

"Ooo! Malcolm," I thought to myself, "you're on your own!"

The Desert was mine to muck about in and do as I pleased.

"There, that's the pre-flight checks done. Let's get going." I climbed into the pilot's seat and closed the door. "Now - throttle open, mixture rich, magnetos on and check the propeller is clear." As soon as the starter button was pushed the six cylinders jumped to life and settled down to a companionable rumble.

"No donkeys, cows or people on the strip. The windsock's standing out a little. We'll need to taxi to the other end for our take-off." I eased the throttle forward and, after an initial effort to start moving in the deep sand, we were rolling forward. "Controls free and movement full... Check the magnetos while we're moving so as to minimise damage to the propeller from flying stones. RPM drops normal. Flaps - moving freely and set to twenty degrees for take-off. Cowl flaps

150

set to open. Radios on, and set, and a quick call to check if anyone might be in the circuit..."

The only person likely to be around Kang in a 'plane was Heine Strumpher, the trader. No one answered my call.

"So... Let's go. Alpha Two Zulu Golf Bravo... You are cleared for take-off... And to Hukuntsi."

The motor roared. The world outside picked up speed and the hot, Desert sand sank away. The village of Kang shrank. Some small boys waved as we passed over them and banked right towards the big, white Kang salt pan.

The airspeed came up to 110 knots. The throttle was brought back to bring RPM down to 2,400. Wing flaps were retracted slowly to ten degrees... then to the fully retracted position. Airspeed came up to 130 knots. RPM was brought back to 2,200 and engine cowl flaps closed for cruise.

As the big round, white salt pan passed below me I was high enough to see the Hukuntsi road to my right and I altered course towards it. Once over it, I positioned the aircraft so that the road was below me on my left. That way I could see it easily. I was not going to waste time and fuel to climb up high.

The flight was only about twenty minutes at most. Anyway, it was much more interesting being low. There may have been game to see. Perhaps even a lion. It was a bit bumpier, but I thought it felt a bit like being in a sailing boat. Also, when one is just above treetop level, one is more perceptive of the horizon and it's easy to pick up changes in trim and bank and respond accordingly.

"Ah. There's Dinokwe pan." Dinokwe is a large grass covered pan a little to the north of the road and it often had game on it. "Let's go over and have a closer look."

Yes... there were some springbok...

"Now, Malcolm, remember what Milton taught you. You are flying west along the road and turning north to have a look at the game on that pan. When you've finished you'll have to turn south and just fly until you pick up the road again." Easy.

I checked and re-set the directional gyro against the compass first to make life easier still. There now, the nose was brought round, power settings adjusted. I put on ten degrees of wing flaps to slow the 'plane a bit, and...

"Wonderful! There must be a good fifty springbok down there... And hey, even four or five hartebeest. Lovely."

As I skimmed over the pan, banking gently, springbok darted in all directions, leaping and prancing to show their white haunches. I circled slowly enjoying the view.

"Oh... Look... There's another largish pan over there. And that one has got some game on it too... Let's go over and have a peek..."

After the game viewing I turned south, re-established cruise settings and waited for the Hukuntsi road to appear.

It didn't.

"Well that's odd. What's happened to that road? Mmm. Well, I'll give it another three minutes."

The three minutes became five minutes. And there was no sign of the road. No sign of any road for that matter.

The Kalahari is a big area. Landmarks are few. The Desert is an enormous flat region covered with clumps of grasses, thorn bushes and thorn trees. Yes, there are 'wrinkles' here and there. And there are salt pans. Some of them are large, and some have a recognisable outline, like the bean shaped pans at Sekgoma and Tshane. Don Horst, who became one of our best Flying Mission pilots, after he had been taken for his first orientation flight over the Kalahari, wrote home that he had 'flown for over two hours and had not seen anything that he would be able to recognize again as a landmark!' Of course, as one builds experience flying over the Desert, one does learn to recognize features and patterns and the different villages and scattered settlements. But that takes time and, even then, there are vast tracts where there is little of note except flat sand and grasses and thorn bush.

It was just such an area that I was over. There was absolutely nothing recognisable in sight.

"Well, Malcolm. You are lost."

"Rubbish... A pilot is never lost. Merely a little uncertain of the position... "

"Malcolm. You are lost."

"All right... But..."

"Malcolm. You are lost."

Navigation in the featureless Kalahari Desert...

.... can be a problem.

"Malcolm. You are lost." (Cartoon: S Mingham)

What does one do in such a situation? Well, one assesses all the geographical options and, remembering that most of Botswana lies to the west of the railway line, the sensible thing to do is to fly east until one reaches the steel tracks and then make a decision to turn either north or south until one finds a recognisable landmark. But, from where I was, that railway line was a good two hours away.

Then there are the fuel options and the daylight options to consider.

My various flying instructors had taught me well, that the two useless things on any flight are the runway and the fuel left behind on take-off. The runway was long gone. The Cessna 185 was fitted with long-range tanks and fuel - at this point - was not a problem.

Daylight, too, was not a problem as it was late morning and the sun was not about to depart suddenly. Nevertheless, my pulse rate did go up a notch.

The obvious thing to do was to get myself off the treetops and climb to a height where I might be able to see some feature that I might recognise.

The time had also come to ask direction from 'above' in a short prayer.

" Lord... Please... help..."

"Ah. At long last you have realised that it would be a good idea to communicate, and to get a bit closer to Me. Excellent! Come along... up higher..."

"Throttle fully open." I recited the checklist. "Engine cowl flaps open to keep the motor cool and comfortable. Raise the nose and trim for climb. There, that was easy. A piece of cake. Now... let's see what we can find."

"Five thousand feet..." As the little 'plane climbed higher the view improved... But it only emphasised the barren uniformity of the surface of the Desert that was gradually falling away below me and, with every minute that passed, my pulse edged upward also.

Six thousand... Six thousand five hundred... Seven thousand feet...

"Lord, there must be something going to come into sight soon."

There was still nothing I could see that gave me any clue as to where I might be and it was at last beginning to dawn on me just how far 'off course' I was.

The motor purred smoothly. "Mmm. An engine failure. That's something I do not want at this point, Lord!"

Eight thousand... Eight thousand five hundred... Nine thousand feet. The altimeter needle wound steadily up.

"Lord, I still don't see anything remotely helpful... And if one is above ten thousand feet for any length of time one is supposed to use oxygen. And yes, Lord, I know I did try that one time to see just how high this 'plane can fly, and I did manage to coax it up to seventeen thousand feet before it refused to climb any further... even at full throttle. But it made me decidedly light headed and You know that I had to get down fast. Anyway, I don't have oxygen with me today."

"I know. I am watching you."

The motor continued to hum in a disinterested sort of way. My ears popped.

"Well, we're at nine thousand five hundred feet and still climbing Lord." The Cessna 185 was well established in a smooth climbing turn that gave me the opportunity to scan the ground out to the horizon as it moved slowly around my field of view. I thought, as I so often have, how similar the Desert looked to a sheet of brown paper that had been crumpled up into a ball and then spread out again. Just a flat, lifeless looking, brown surface with occasional patches and streaks and bare areas carved by the passing of a bush fire in some past and forgotten moment of time.

"Aha... There, away to the northwest... a shimmer of white. Let's head toward that... about 285 degrees."

After five minutes, the white shimmer had clarified into a bean shaped salt pan and another two round salt pans had been coaxed out of the hazy horizon.

"Aha... Thank You, Lord. That's Tshane Pan and to the right Diphofu Pan, and that farthest one is Hukuntsi Pan. And there is my lost road coming in to the north of me! Now how did that happen?"

On reflection, it was obvious. While 'buzzing' the first salt pan at Dinokwe to look at the game I must have turned south without realising it. Then, seeing the second pan ahead with more game on it, I had not noticed the road passing beneath me when I had my attention focused on all those beautiful buck skipping about.

"Yes... That was a silly mistake."

"Yes it was!"

Minutes later, the Hukuntsi airstrip was below me and, at the end of a routine circuit to check for potholes, donkeys and other animals it was good to, again, feel the soft Desert sand beneath the balloon tyres of the Cessna 185.

Hmm. How easy it is to be distracted and led astray.

"Thank You, Lord, for keeping me out of major trouble that day - and, also, on the many occasions in life before, and since, when I have allowed myself to be 'distracted' from what is really important in life."

"It was a pleasure. And, remember, the sooner you call on Me for help the better. In fact, it's a good idea to stay in close communication with Me ALL the time. After all, I am always available!"

"I'll try and remember that in future, Lord."

"It could save you a lot of hassles."

"Thank You, Lord."

-oOo-

155

An aerial view of the settlement of Xade. Some places could be hard to find

'Lephpoi la Pula' on the airstrip on Zutswa salt pan

CHAPTER 7
CONTROL

-Δ-

"Alpha Two Alpha Bravo Golf is cleared to Flight Level seven zero. Turn right to heading two six zero. Report overhead the Golf Bravo Victor."

Instructions given by a controller are rapid and precise and are to be put into effect immediately or safety may quickly be compromised in busy airspace and under Instrument Meteorological Conditions (IMC) when visibility may be severely reduced.

When flying on instrument it is a wonderful feeling to know that someone on the ground is monitoring one's situation and giving clear directions that keep traffic well separated, ensuring the well being of all concerned.

However, the benefits of radar, distance measuring equipment (DME) and radio beacons are all useless unless communication is good and a pilot is ready and willing to follow the controller's advice and instructions.

In the Christian life it can be similar. Waiting for instructions from the 'Heavenly Controller' can test both one's patience and one's willingness to comply with the instructions received. It is also wonderful to know that our 'Heavenly Controller' has everyone's ultimate well being in mind at all times.

A pilot is actually heavily dependent on many people. The aircraft designer and manufacturer, maintenance teams, administration folk, cleaners, secretaries, and a host of other personnel who are in the back ground but who provide key back up energy and expertise that make flights safe and useful.

*   *   *

Back Up

With our fulltime pilot, Jay Aeschliman, coming 'on board' and the increasing number of flights for the Ministry of Health, a number of issues surfaced that needed attention. The development of Flying Mission became a 'growing process', and that has continued over the years as the Mission has sought to serve both the missions and churches in Botswana and also the Ministry of Health. The servant must adapt to the needs of those being served and in a way that can offer the best service possible. And, when necessary, the servant needs back up and also protection.

The following pages highlight some of the developments, and why and how they were made.

Looking back it has amazed us just how wonderfully needs have always been provided for and how both personnel, passengers and aircraft have all been 'protected' over the years.

*   *   *

Once he got stuck in to the work, Jay was full of ideas...

"You know, Malcolm, several things stand out that could do with looking at seriously." Jay wiped his oily hands on a piece of rag and eased himself out from under the engine of 'The Quiet Hour' where he had been attending to a small oil leak.

"Don't let me interrupt the good work."

"No problem... we're both busy and it's not often we get a chance to talk, so let's take this opportunity. I could do with a little fresh air. Mind your head on that wing tip."

We dodged our way through, and out, of the Kalahari Air Services hangar and onto the tarmac. A light breeze was fiddling with the orange windsock.

"I was thinking about the radios installed in the clinics the other day, and the thought came to me that it would be great if we could set up a flight following programme for Flying Mission."

"What exactly do you have in mind?"

"Well, once we are out of range of the Gaborone Control Tower VHF radio we often have problems talking with Jo'burg. Could we not perhaps get a radio like those in the clinics and have someone keep a listening watch for us when we are flying? I was talking with Cynthia about it and she would be happy to be involved. It would cost a bit, but we could have a mast put up at our house and Cynthia could listen to it as she does her housework."

"That sounds an excellent idea. I'm sure we can fix that."

In the 1970s the Johannesburg Control Centre monitored flights over the Kalahari Desert. This was accomplished using short wave, high frequency (HF), radio transmissions that were often unreliable due to the distances involved. However, once the quality of Single Side Band (SSB) radio equipment had been improved and their usefulness discovered, Flying Mission set up a flight-following system to keep track of flights. Flight following soon became a happy occupation for wives in the Mission and, eventually, we employed a full time person to keep a flight following watch on all Flying Mission aircraft in the air. Mission pilots would call in every 30 minutes reporting the estimated position of the aircraft, and any other relevant information, until the destination was reached. It was a safety measure that was well worth the effort and it was greatly appreciated by those on the ground as well as those in the air.

Eventually all the Flying Mission aircraft radios were also fitted with the necessary 'crystals' to enable them to speak directly with clinics, District Medical Officers and the referral hospitals, a real boon for checking on local weather conditions during emergency mercy flights and for arranging an ambulance to meet an aircraft on its arrival back in Gaborone with a patient needing a quick and smooth transfer to the hospital.

There is no doubt that on many occasions good communication between a Flying Mission pilot and those on the ground has been a lifesaver.

And is a prayer sent to our heavenly Father not the same thing but using infinitely simpler technology? On how many occasions have we received answers to our prayers that can only have come from a heavenly Father who is intimately concerned for His children?

Since the early days of Flying Mission, it has been customary to meet in the home of one of the personnel every Thursday evening for a time of sharing experiences and placing requests before God and asking for guidance and help where these have been needed. Thursday evenings were often exciting times when 'the FM family' could laugh and joke and also be serious together looking back over the week's efforts and events and praying about needs and problems that required a solution. The quip that 'a family that prays together stays together' has much truth in it.

As an extension to the Thursday evening prayer meetings, days were eventually set aside monthly for periods of reflection and prayer, usually led by a 'speaker' who gave a short devotional Bible study that was followed by a time of prayer for Flying Mission and personnel.

These times of sharing and prayer together have been a wonderful blessing and a great encouragement on many occasions. We continually thank our Lord for His abundant provision for all our needs and for His loving protection at all times.

*　　　*　　　*

Jay and I strolled to the spot where we usually tied down the aircraft.

"And these 50 litre tie down weights..." Jay placed his foot on one. "They're OK, but if the wind really gets up it can easily flip a small airplane over onto its back."

"I suppose we could find some larger cans somewhere. We made those things by just filling a paraffin tin with cement and embedding a steel loop in the top."

"Even that would not be enough if a real big dust devil came through. Also, and I've been meaning to speak about this for some time, when we park the aircraft here it sits in the direct sun all day and even with the heat shields we stick up the temperature inside the cabin gets mighty hot."

"Yes, but it cools off quickly enough when one gets the windows open and the prop spinning,"

"That's true. But for a whole day sometimes these radios in the panel are being fried and it doesn't do them any good."

"Have you got any ideas?"

We watched the Air Botswana flight slowly pick up speed and depart off runway 08 for Johannesburg before Jay answered.

"Well... we do put up the reflective sunscreens on the insides of the airplane windows and that helps a bit. But I think we can do better."

"So?"

Jay looked round at the Kalahari Air Services & Charter (KASAC) hangar. "Noel Fitzgerald is a super guy and he's helped with the maintenance on the 185 before I came. I know he loves that aircraft."

"What are you trying to tell me?"

"That KASAC hangar is often full to busting with aircraft that he is working on for his customers." Jay squinted at me. "I was thinking - wouldn't it be great if we could have our own hangar? That way we'd have a place to work out of the sun without bothering Noel, and we'd also have a place to keep our aircraft protected from high temperatures and gusting winds."

"Aha... I thought you had something up your sleeve!"

"I'm serious."

"Yes I know you are... Let's have a think. Would the Department of Civil Aviation (DCA) approve? And where are you thinking it might be located?

"Well... actually..." Jay was smiling, "I spoke with folks in the DCA the other day to sound them out. It seems that we could have a plot the other side of the control tower. They were quite positive about it."

"Great. But now... how much would such a thing cost and where would we find the money?"

"You'll have to give me a little time to work out a cost. We could have just a shell, but if we're going to build our own place it would be good to have a small office and a place for spare parts." Jay laughed. "And I knew you'd ask about the cash side of things! But you are always quoting Hudson Taylor to us - 'God's work done in God's way will not lack His supply...' If it's the right thing for FM then 'The Boss' will supply all that's needed. Isn't that so?"

I had no answer for that and, when Roger Schultz heard about the idea, he took to it like a wild boar to truffles.

There is a saying that "Ideas have legs."

And a hangar?

When the time was right.... everything fell into place perfectly.

*   *   *

The Hangar

"Malcolm, this is great. At long last. Imagine what that will save in repair bills for our radios." Jay was delighted when the decision was made to go forward with the hangar project. "I'm sure that there are many folk out there who would love to help finance such a project. I know there's a Rotary Club and the Lion's Club and there must be many more."

Roger with his background in real estate in the USA was a builder at heart. Any such project was a delight to him, and sure enough, as we prayed about it, doors began to open.

"I've got a guy with a bulldozer who will come and level that patch in no time at all..." Roger's enthusiasm was wonderful to see. "And there's a building company that has a steel structure that the Lion's Club think they can get for us. Then we just have to find some cladding... and I think I know where we might get two sliding hangar doors in Jo'burg..."

Sure enough the Lion's Club raised some money, and it arranged to buy the steel framework that Wade Adams, a local construction company, was selling.

A lot of time, effort and prayer went into the Flying Mission hangar project... but for some reason it would not move forward as we wanted it to. There were constant delays and problems. Days became weeks. Weeks became months. Roger was often frustrated in the extreme. However, eventually, the bulldozer did a fine job and the plot was levelled beautifully. The following Saturday, all available hands turned out and, with much effort, under a roasting sun, and with Roger supervising, the foundation for the steel framework was measured out and steel marker pins driven into the red earth.

A few days later - again with much sweat - the bases for the steel framework were poured, and then the great day came when we were to set the first of the high tensile, steel bolts into the cement bases. By the end of the day, with Roger's watchful eye constantly checking the alignments, the first set of the threaded bolts projected up in exactly the right places.

It was a finicky job and I think we were all happy when we were able to go home and wash off the sweat thinking that now, at last, things were progressing satisfactorily.

For various reasons the setting of more of the high tensile bolts had to be delayed. Patience was again tested. But then we realised there was a purpose behind the delays...

"Malcolm, guess what!" Roger had a peculiar glint in his eyes.

"Tell me."

"I went to the DCA this morning to get my US licence validated." Roger was smiling. "I learnt something new."

"Well. Go on."

"I'm beginning to see why our hangar project has been going so slowly."

"Ehe... Why?"

"Today I discovered that there are big plans..." he paused and his smile widened. "We've been running ahead of The Lord."

"In what way?"

Fundraising for the hangar
(Cartoon: S Mingham)

"The folks at the Department of Civil Aviation tell me that there's going to be a new airport. They say this airport that we are using is too close to the town and the new one is going to be located 15 kilometres north and well outside Gaborone. And it sounds like it's going to be **BIG**. They hope to have it up and running as quickly as possible and then the plan is to close the present airport."

"Aha! So that's why things have been dragging with our hangar project..."

"I asked what would happen to this airport. I was thinking of our hangar of course." Roger paused. "They told me that anything we build here will have to be moved out to the new airport as the land that this airport is on will be allocated to either the University of Botswana, or the Central Transport Organisation. I asked about a plot at the new airport and they said 'No problem... Just apply.' So we had better do that fast." Roger threw his head back and laughed loudly. "Our 'Boss' had a better idea... as usual. And I was just too impatient to get things moving!"

164

And a better idea it certainly was. A plot was allocated at the new airport site, and once we had adjusted our thinking to be in line with the Divine planning, then things began to move forward. Donations came from the Netherlands and Germany. The original plans were extended to accommodate offices, an air-conditioned storeroom for parts, a paint store, and also rooms for pilots for flight planning and preparation, along with toilets and washing and showering facilities and a small kitchen.

On the 15th of August 1988 the contractor officially handed the keys of the new building to David Gallacher, the Flying Mission Administrator. The hangar was larger and more practical than we had ever envisaged at first, and it was the first of the 'private' hangar facilities to be completed at the new Gaborone Sir Seretse Khama International Airport.

Interestingly... many years later... another even larger structure has been erected immediately next door to the Flying Mission hangar. It houses the jet aircraft of the President of Botswana, Ian Khama, the eldest son of Seretse and Ruth Khama, and I am sure that both parents are delighted with both structures and the work carried on in each them. 'God moves in mysterious way...'

*　　　*　　　*

Certification

The message was short. A two line e-mail from Dan Cutler in the Flying Mission hangar in Botswana. It read: "Successfully completed the Botswana Department of Civil Aviation Engineer Certificate examinations."

"Praise The Lord, Dan!" That was indeed wonderful news. Dan had been working for that examination for some time and, having got it behind him, meant that he was now officially recognised by the Botswana Government and qualified to work in the hangar in Gaborone and to 'sign off' Botswana registered aircraft as fit to fly after maintenance work had been done on them.

The contractor officially handing over the hangar keys to David Gallacher

Dan came to Flying Mission as a 'short termer'. His story was unusual. He was a 'Missionary Kid'. But with a difference. His family in America had all become Christians within the space of about 2 months, and it was soon decided that to be a Christian meant to be a missionary. Suitcases were packed and tickets obtained to travel to Pakistan. A major change indeed for any family.

Dan had found himself in school in Pakistan where he made a number of Pakistani friends and picked up Urdu, the local language, and also learnt much about Pakistani culture and religions. Much later, after returning to the USA, Dan finished schooling and trained as an aircraft mechanic. However, he felt the Lord calling him back to mission work overseas, and it was a joy to welcome him to the Flying Mission hangar in Botswana. After a year of service, he returned to the USA, entered Bible College and then came back to Botswana and was seconded to Flying Mission by the Africa Evangelical Fellowship.

Now... why should the Lord take a young boy to Pakistan to learn Urdu and pick up information about cultures? Obviously - to send him later to Botswana where the African people speak Setswana! The ways of the Lord are perfect, and, if one waits a while one sometimes comes to understand what is going on. Although there seemed to have been a mix up, that was not the case. An earlier e-mail had contained this paragraph... "I have made friends with a Pakistani family here in Gaborone! I'm even helping the children with their school home work."

Yes, God had brought a licensed aviation engineer from America, who was fluent in Urdu, to befriend a Pakistani family in Botswana. Quite amazing!

-oOo-

167

John Calhoon works at a paint job (Photo: M Spicer)

Mark Fuglestad inspects a fuel tank

CHAPTER 8
CLEAN UP

-Δ-

After taking off in an aeroplane with retractable landing gear, the landing gear and wing flaps are raised as soon as it is safe to do so and, once an aircraft has reached its allotted cruising altitude, a number of cockpit chores need attention.

The motor, which has been working at maximum power for take off and climb, is throttled back to a more sedate level to reduce wear and tear and noise. On an aircraft with a propeller of an adjustable pitch, the RPM is reduced, by coarsening the propeller pitch, to gain better efficiency for the faster air speed of cruise configuration. The mixture is leaned to peak EGT (Exhaust Gas Temperature) and set slightly on the rich side of peak. The cowl flaps that have been open to help cool the hard working power plant are now closed to improve streamlining. Trims are readjusted and, once the airspeed has settled, forward estimates are made of the expected arrival times at designated reporting points along the route and the controller is informed accordingly.

A sharp look out is maintained at all times for other users of the airspace and the engine instruments and fuel gauges are closely monitored as well as the flight instruments and the directional gyro and compass.

Once Flying Mission had settled into 'cruise configuration', there were details that demanded attention if problems were to be avoided and smooth onward flight maintained.

This chapter has been written in response to specific questions from Flying Mission personnel as to how, and why, things were set up and done in the way they were. I trust that the chapter will be informative, and helpful to those having to make similar choices and decisions that may have important and long lasting effects, as well as being of interest to other readers.

*   *   *

Housing

Housing was a part of the Mission administration that was particularly blessed from the beginning.

When Flying Mission started, I was in the post of Specialist Surgeon to the Botswana Government. This was a posting that was partly funded by the British Government's Overseas Development Administration. Gudrun and I had first come to Botswana in 1968 to serve as mission personnel under the United Free Church of Scotland at the Scottish Livingstone Hospital in Molepolole. In 1975, the mission hospital had been handed over to the Government and we had opted to enter Government service. After a few months, we were requested to transfer to the Princess Marina Hospital, in Gaborone, and, in December - with heavy hearts - we moved and were allocated a new 'type 2' house that had recently been completed in Gaborone Village.

"Welcome to Government Service." Dr Simon Moeti, who was in charge of Government medical personnel, adjusted his thick glasses. "Come and meet Dr David Sebina. He's really your chief here at the Ministry of Health." He eased himself out from behind his desk, picked up a file and took me along the corridor to another office door that bore the sign 'Permanent Secretary'. He knocked briefly and we entered.

"Aha. Good morning. Dr McArthur." Dr Sebina stood up. He was tall and slim.

"Good morning, Sir!"

"Dr McArthur - Malcolm isn't it? Come and sit down."

"Yes, Sir."

"And you're married? Gudrun..." he looked down at the papers in my file that Dr Moeti and placed before him. "That's a German name, isn't it?"

"Yes, Sir."

"Good. But hey," he leaned back in his chair, "we must always remember that a wife is the neck that turns the head!" The comment was delivered with a wide smile.

My new 'chiefs' proved helpful and they became life-long friends.

"Now, Malcolm. You're new to Government. Here's a copy of the General Orders. It will tell you everything you need to know as far as the administration goes. Housing allowances, holiday entitlements, travel allowances, sickness benefits, compassionate leave... You name it, it's all in here." Dr Moeti handed me the green, hard cover publication that was to make fascinating reading and would make clear how I was to breathe, eat, sleep and work for the next few years. "Dr John Moor is the Hospital Superintendent at the Princess Marina Hospital. He'll get you organised there. And here's a letter to the Government Housing Department. They'll sort out your accommodation."

And sort us out they did... with a colonial efficiency.

"Honey... We've got a completely new house."

"Wow! Three bedrooms. Super..."

"And look... it's all fully furnished..."

Yes... A newly painted home all ready to occupy. Even a garden... Although, we were to discover that our new 'plot' - number 5249 - had been the site for the building contractor's concrete mixing plant and much of its production was still lying about. No matter. Gudrun pitched in and created a wonderful home and, eventually, lovely garden with several productive citrus trees and a guava tree as well as colourful flowerbeds and even a strawberry patch. It quickly became 'home from home' and, looking back, it was a big influence in determining later Flying Mission housing policies as were the Botswana Government's General Orders.

"In the old days, missionaries were sent out with a Bible, a spoon and a begging bowl. No longer!" Gudrun was adamant that if folk came to Flying Mission as volunteers and were going to do a good job then they would be looked after and have a place to call home from home. It would be a place to relax in after a hard day's work and a place where a family could be happy and contented. And, when Gudrun later became the Mission's Housing Officer, she stuck to her beliefs and was acknowledged by all as having done a splendid job when she eventually handed over her duties to two of the younger Flying Mission wives many years later.

When Flying Mission began, it was set up to serve the missions, churches and the Ministry of Health in any way that it was needed. Drs Winters, Rempel and McArthur were all involved in working at the Princess Marina Hospital and our duties also required us to visit outlying hospitals. Once the Mission was established, the Cessna 185 was in demand for such trips as - in those days - roads were not good and travel could be slow and tedious. In addition, all of us were quite happy to help out when a request came for a 'mercy flight' to bring in a patient from some remote clinic. Since we were Government Officers, Dr Moeti felt it appropriate that, when the opportunity arose and the Mission needed housing for its personnel, he was justified in recommending that Government housing be made available to Flying Mission. That was a wonderful provision, for the Housing Department not only provided housing that was fully furnished with items from the Government Stores, but - and this was an enormous help - the rent was also subsidised.

As Flying Mission became increasingly involved later with flying District Medical Officers round their clinics in remote areas, Flying Mission became seen as an integral and important part of the Health Service.

Government housing was an enormous help in the early days. However, the time eventually did come when such accommodation was no longer available.

While initially Flying Mission did not need to provide housing (we three pilots were all catered for as we were Government Officers) once Mennonite Ministries offered to second a full time pilot/mechanic to the Mission, there was a realisation that houses might not, indeed would not, always be available from the Government and alternatives were sought. The Africa Evangelical Fellowship offered a building plot that they had no use for and Roger Schulz, with his experience in real estate, undertook the project and Flying Mission built its first dwelling house.

"Malcolm... I've researched all the options and there is no doubt in my mind that we should go for a 'prefab'."

"But Roger... No-one wants to live in a 'prefab'..."

"Don't you believe it." Roger was in his element. "They're the most cost effective way to go and that wife of yours will work wonders. I guarantee that, when it's finished, you'll want to live in it yourself. The ceilings are well insulated. The walls too. We'll install ceiling fans... You won't believe how comfortable a 'prefab' can be. I've lived in one myself!"

House No 7959 was the first building to be erected in the new Gaborone district of Broadhurst. The work took 6 weeks from start to finish.

It was a fine 3 bed room 'prefab'. Gudrun worked wonders with the décor. Roger and his wife Ruth were the first occupants and Jay and Cynthia Aeschliman - Flying Mission's first full time pilot/mechanic and his wife - moved in when they arrived.

The property has been the home of several families since and is still in use and as good as new. We were quickly converted to 'prefabs'.

*　　　*　　　*

As the Mission grew and funds accumulated, opportunities presented that enabled property to be bought, or built, with obvious savings in rent outlays. This policy was pursued where possible with the thought that it was better to invest cash in property rather than keep it in a savings account or pay out rents. With judicious handling - and perhaps also some Scottish sense thrown in - but, above all, with much Divine blessing, the Mission grew and developed in a most amazing way.

Tiffany MacLeod (L) and Michelle Royce (R) took over from Gudrun as Mission Housing Officers.

By 2001 Flying Mission was operating 7 aircraft, two of which were twin-engine aeroplanes. The Mission was running its own hangar and maintenance programme and, in addition, and at the request of the Department of Civil Aviation, a commercial maintenance service was being offered to other aircraft owners and operators. By 2001, homes were being provided for around 14 families and single folk who were, by that time, serving with the Mission.

*   *   *

'Hire or Reward'

In 1980 Flying Mission was registered as a Charity with the Registrar of Societies. It had a Constitution and an Executive Committee and a bank account and one aircraft.

"There's one thing that bothers me." From the sound of Roger's voice he was about to say something that would be worth hearing. "It may be nothing... Or it may open a can of worms."

"What's the problem?"

Roger slurped his fruit juice thoughtfully. He had 'discovered' the litre packets of fruit juice offered in the local supermarket. "My, this stuff is good! And so healthy." He put his glass down and leant back in his chair. "You know, we used to drink nothing but coffee and then I realised that I was just too stressed out. All the time. But since Ruth and I have switched to these fruit juices we've felt so much better. And they're so tasty and the variety is fantastic... Grape... Strawberry... Peach... Apple... Banana... You name it. And they're cheap too."

"Mmm. So what's bothering you about the fruit juices?"

"Oh, it's not the juices. They're all fantastic."

"Well what is it?" The day was moving along. Letters were waiting to be answered. Lindah - our Motswana office receptionist or 'gofer' as Roger used to describe her - would soon be going to the post office and returning with even more correspondence to be attended to. My patience was wearing thin and my mind was drifting beyond fruit farms.

"Malcolm... I have a nasty little bell ringing in the back of my head and it won't stop." Roger leant forward to command my full attention. "FM - Flying Mission - is registered as a non-profit making Charity with the Registrar of Societies but at the Department of Civil Aviation we are registered as a Private organisation. The aircraft is registered in the Private Category. We pilots all hold Private Pilot Licences."

"Yes. That's all clear. So what?"

"I'll tell you what." Roger had a keen look. "FM is also insured as a 'Private' organisation. Now, tell me. What happens if we load up that 185 with some church folk who want to go hold a service in some remote village... and perhaps a patient goes along who needs to get home?"

"Yes...?"

"For the sake of argument, let's say the weather clamps down. We don't have Instrument Ratings so we have to stay low and in sight of good ol' Terra Firma. The cloud base lowers... Then, suddenly, bam! No visibility. We're in the soup... In more ways than one. The next day they come along and pick up the wreckage. 6 people killed. Can you imagine the scenario? I've seen it. Frank will confirm it. The lawyers will be everywhere looking for dollars - or Pulas - by the billion. The insurance people will be dodging round like mad and looking for every excuse not to pay up a single Thebe. Relatives will be shrieking for compensation." (Botswana currency: 100 Thebe = 1 Pula.)

"Mmm..."

"You can sit there and say 'Mmm...' But I tell you it would be a **real** mess. And there's something else. It's then discovered that a cheque was written by the pastor of the church folk, who we were flying, to put toward the cost of the flight." He paused. "In the Private Category we are not supposed to fly for 'hire or reward.' I tell you this could get mighty sticky."

"Yes, I see what you mean."

"We need to think very carefully. Of course, we could all get ourselves Instrument Ratings, and even Commercial Pilot Licences, but that would take time... and money. But perhaps we need to consider that option."

The matter was put to the Executive Committee at the next meeting. It provoked much thought and discussion, prayer, and, eventually, a possible solution.

"The answer is, perhaps, to create a 'Friends' section in the Mission. We currently have 'Members' who have certain responsibilities and from whom we elect the Executive. But we could have 'Friends' who can have an interest in the Mission but not have any responsibility for the administration, or running. They would be under the Mission 'umbrella' and would benefit from access to flights without being further involved in any way. They could commit themselves to being

176

concerned for the welfare of the Mission, pray for it and perhaps pay an annual subscription and help with funding if they felt led. As a part of the Mission they would be chargeable for flights that they make in the same way as the Members."

"Yes, and, other Mission organisations could also be 'Friends' and their own members would then qualify too for flights and perhaps other privileges. That way payments made toward flight expenses would all be 'in house'."

"That's an excellent idea."

"What about Ministry of Health personnel such as District Medical Officers, nurses and patients?"

"I've thought of that. The Ministry of Health (MOH) and the Department of Civil Aviation (DCA) are both Botswana Government institutions. When I spoke with the folk at DCA, they more or less told me that if other Government Departments want to use Flying Mission and pay for the flight costs then it's no problem. DCA licenses us and Government therefore know what we are doing and by using us they agree with what we are doing."

The arrangement of having Friends and Members worked well, at least for a few years. Later it became obvious that, with the increase in the transport of Government folk who had no interest at all in Christian Mission work, and with the likely commencement of full commercial charter flying by the Mission, a change to pilot requirements, and the aircraft registration, and the way we did things, was needed.

Once the Department of Civil Aviation saw the excellent record of the Flying Mission hangar maintenance, it put the proposition that Flying Mission open its doors to provide maintenance to other operators on a commercial basis. The suggestion that Mission aircraft be available for charter work, when not in use for Mission purposes, followed soon after.

"What does it matter whether we fly illiterate rural area dwellers, or a Government Minister? Surely they all need to hear the Christian message. It's for everyone. John's Gospel, chapter 3 and verse 16, makes that very clear. 'God so loved the world that He gave His only Son that whosoever believes in Him may not perish but have eternal life'. It's absolutely clear. It's intended for everyone."

"Yes, that's true. And if a 'plane is not needed for an FM flight, and a request comes in for a commercial flight, then let's take it. It's better for a 'plane to be used rather than letting it sit on the ground, standing in the hot sun doing nothing, when it could be generating some income for the Mission."

"Yes. And we do keep tracts and Christian literature in all the seat pockets along with 'sick sacs'. I think it's a wonderful opportunity for Christian ministry."

It took a while, but it soon became a requirement that Flying Mission pilots should hold a Commercial Pilot Licence as well as Night and Instrument Ratings. We were glad to have made these decisions, for it was not long afterward that the Department of Civil Aviation also brought in a requirement of its own that any pilot flying in Botswana air space outside the prescribed air corridors should have at least 500 hours as PIC (Pilot in Command). Much of the Mission flying was just that.

As a Mission, we did our best to stay well within the law and ahead of any Government regulations. It was a policy that paid great dividends and earned Flying Mission respect from all the other aircraft operators and from the Department of Civil Aviation. It also helped contribute to the excellent safety record of the Mission, although we recognise a Divine Hand and continually thank God for His constant watching over us and His careful protection.

*　　*　　*

Finances

Finances, perhaps not surprisingly, would often provoke a lively debate. However, it was wonderful to see how the final outcome was always acceptable to everyone and, looking back, there is no question in my mind that Flying Mission was greatly blessed financially and in many other ways too. The reason, I believe, was because we always endeavoured to follow Biblical principles when it came to using the money that came in.

The Bible makes it clear that God will supply what is needed to accomplish what He wants done. We often quoted the great missionary to China, Hudson Taylor, who always maintained, "God's work done in God's way would never lack God's supply." That was proved true time and again in Flying Mission. When we had a need we would ask God to provide what was needed... and He would. Although often not in the way we expected - or wanted! But there was always enough for what was needed, and often more. Occasionally, so much more, that we wondered why, until we came to see the reason and how to act accordingly.

It became a 'policy' that - in general - we did not ask for money, and it was soon discovered that if one shared with folk what the Mission was doing and how God was blessing the work, then donations and gifts poured in. Yes, we would make a need known, and, if asked, would provide detailed information about the estimated cost of a project such as the acquisition of an aeroplane. In certain instances, application was made to a sources of finance that we knew might be interested in assisting. However, that was only for large projects such as for an aircraft, or the hangar.

Day to day running costs were paid for from the general account, into which account was paid any contribution toward expenses that were incurred and, also, any undesignated gifts that came in, that is, those not given for some specific purpose.

It very soon became clear that Flying Mission, or 'FM', was 'taking off' and - looking back - thankfully, The Lord had made His preparations and had His chosen key people in place. Doctors Frank Winters and John Rempel - both Christian colleagues working at the Princess Marina Hospital - had pilot's licences and a wealth of flying experience. Don Genheimer, the current Field Director of the Africa Evangelical Fellowship, had wide experience of setting up and running a mission organisation. Roger Schultz brought with him a great entrepreneurial spirit and much lateral thinking and constructive ideas.

"Malcolm, now that we have the FM account up and running you need to keep a record of the account..." Don was invaluable... "Here, I got you this ledger."

"Ledger? What's a ledger for?"

Don & Eileen Genheimer (Africa Evangelical Fellowship)

David & Mamie Gallacher (Administration)

Les & Pauline French (Accounts)

Lindah Mauwane (Secretary)

The Accounts Office

Debbie Lawson (Short Term Volunteer)

Ann Hunter (Office Supervisor & Prayer Co-ordinator)

Debbie Spicer (Secretary)

Onica Kobedi (Secretary)

Some of the administration & office personnel

"I'll show you..." Patiently, Don instructed me in the basics of 'income and expenditure'. "Now label the next column 'Bank'. That's for all your banking entries, income, expenditures and interest. Then should come 'general expenses' followed by..."

Frank, who had himself owned an aircraft back in the US, was immensely knowledgeable about the expenses involved in running and maintaining an aeroplane.

"Now, Malcolm. It's great to have an aircraft, but just remember, it needs avgas and oil to run on, and there will also be maintenance, One Hundred Hour Inspections and the Certificate of Airworthiness inspections. And, an engine has only a limited life - a couple of thousand hours. We need to have money set aside for replacement of such things when the time comes."

"Yes... And don't forget insurance." Roger had many tales to add colour and emphasis to his suggestions, but also much sound advice. "I think it would be good to work out the hourly cost of flying that 185. And I suggest that we work in the same way MAF (Mission Aviation Fellowship) does and, to start with, let's reckon that the running cost is about double the cost of the fuel and oil. That will give us a ball park figure that we can assess and check from time to time."

The columns in the ledger began to take on significance. For every hour the 185 was flown, we set a figure to be 'charged' as expenses to the user. From this 'income' we set aside a figure for the day to day running costs for the aircraft, as well as for engine overhauls and, eventually, for engine, and even aircraft, replacement. After some years, these set aside funds had accumulated considerably and, where it was deemed right, periodic 'loans' were made from these funds to, for instance, put toward the purchase of a property. However, this was with the clear understanding that, should the need arise, the capital would be made available for the use for which it had been set aside. The rationale being that it was obviously better to use such set aside funds rather than to take a loan for which interest would be payable.

As the organisation and the financial figures grew, the benefits and many advantages of having registered Flying Mission as a non-profit making charity became clear.

HOURS					
Type of Flight	1981	1982	1983	1984	1985
Ministry of Health	98.1	216.7	321.5	453.1	525.0
Christoffel Blindenmission	37.4	58.9	76.1	77.8	100.6
Mercy Flights	65.1	83.6	156.6	178.7	185.5
Mission Flights	102.4	247.8	451.9	542.2	700.6
Check/Training Flights, etc.	44.1	23.6	67.5	122.4	125.4
	347.1	**630.6**	**1073.6**	**1374.2**	**1637.1**

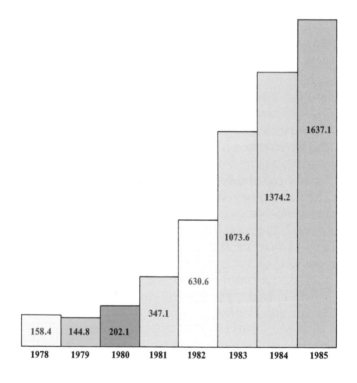

'*...the organisation and the financial figures grew...*'

Somehow, it all came together. One thing led to another... It was a steep learning curve.

As a Christian organisation, and wanting to do things according to Bible principles, at first I paid all bills 'on the nail' when they were received. That soon annoyed the accountants in the group, who believed that invoices should be paid monthly. I learnt that there was wisdom and method in that approach when faced with keeping accurate track of high cash flows!

Of course, the subject of loans came up early on in the life of the Mission.

"If The Lord has promised to provide all we need to do the job, then surely we don't need to take out loans? After all, when we decided to buy the 185 it was agreed that we could pay it off over 6 months as, and when, money came in."

"That's right. But, the aircraft remained the property of the Seventh Day Adventist Mission. So... technically they were loaning us the aeroplane until it was paid off."

"Yes... And now, with this suggestion of a Cessna 206, the bank is offering us an overdraft facility for one year, but it will take ownership of the aircraft until it's paid off. Only then will the ownership be transferred to FM."

There were occasions, however, when we had a project that we desperately wanted to go ahead with and money just did not come in. The hangar was one such project and the delays frustrated everyone. It was not that we had not prayed about the hangar project and carefully considered every aspect. And it all seemed so right and necessary. However, money had not materialised and a considerable amount was needed. Such a building would be modest and yet sufficient for our requirements. It had definitely seemed the right way to go, but the finance was slow in coming.

As was often the case, our 'Boss' had other ideas. We had to learn that God's timing is **ALWAYS** perfect.

The hangar - and many other projects - when eventually completed, were well worth waiting for.

*　　　*　　　*

183

Appreciation

It would not be right to leave out of this volume a "Thank You" to the many Donors who have given so generously over the years to assist Flying Mission.

Your gifts have been greatly appreciated by all of the Flying Mission personnel, and by many others who have been helped because aircraft and facilities have been made possible by your generosity. I would like to make it clear that you have been a part of the growth and service of the Flying Mission and, without your willing involvement, much would not have come to pass... and many hours of pain and suffering could never have been avoided for many sick or injured people.

Thank you

Assets & Salaries

As Flying Mission grew there was in increasing need for accommodation for personnel. Initially rented accommodation was used but it was quickly realised that to purchase properties was a much better option and, where possible, accumulated funds that had been set aside for such things as aircraft engine overhauls, were invested in property rather than kept in savings accounts. Roger Schultz, with his experience, was invaluable in planning a safe path forward.

"Malcolm, we need to think about Flying Mission's assets." Roger's tone meant I had to listen carefully.

"Go on."

"Think about that worst scenario. A major disaster with some of the passengers killed. You cannot imagine how fast the lawyers would be on us?" He ran his fingers through his hair. "In that kind of situation all sorts of relatives and other folk appear demanding hard cash for compensation. The bills can be horrendous. The Mission could be wiped out overnight! Now, we need to come up with a plan that will protect Flying Mission's assets."

"What do you suggest?"

"Well, I think what we should do is set up a 'non-profit company'. Call it what you like. Flying Mission Aviation perhaps. And here's the point. This 'company' should hold **NO** assets whatsoever. All the assets of the Mission should be in the name of Flying Mission, the registered charity. And the 'company' should rent, or lease the property, or aircraft that it uses, from the Mission. If any profit is made then rents, or lease payments to the Mission, can be adjusted to even out the balance and to maintain the 'non-profit' status of the company. That way, if there is a disaster, any come-back ends at the company level and the Mission and it's assets are protected."

"Mmm. I see."

"Also, if the company is registered as "non-profit' it will not be lialble to pay taxes and any income that is generated can be paid to the Mission and be used for Mission projects."

"That would certainly be a big advantage."

"And, while we're talking cash," Roger went on, "and with FM growing the way it is doing, the day will come when we have to think about employing more folk. We have Lindah as a secretary now but later on we may need perhaps an assistant to wash down the aircraft. As things develop we'll need to think some day about having to pay many salaries."

"That's no big problem. We're all volunteers. Salaries don't come into it."

"Now Malcolm. Use your head! Can you see any Motswana ever volunteering for a job? After all we expatriot personnel are all supported by a home church or mission agency. None of the Batswana I know would be able to raise support for themselves like that."

"True. But here's an idea. If ever we have to pay people we could base salaries on the Government's General Orders and salary levels."

"Yes. However, let me make a suggestion. We want to attract folk who want to do the job because they want to do it. Many employees just want the cash. But, if someone really wants to do a job, the money is secondary. I suggest that, if we employ someone, we offer say 80% of the Government salary, or perhaps even less. That way we will only get people who really want to work for FM."

*   *   *

Looking back Roger's words of wisdom were just that. When the time came to take on employees those taken on have proved to be worth their weight in gold.

Patrick Tsheko has been a faithful hangar assistant for more than 20 years and his ready smile and willing hands have been an encouragement to many a pilot and mechanic. During this time he has become a specialist in the art of welding and, at the recent 30 year anniversary celebration of Flying Mission he was presented with his dream tool - a welding machine. There were tears in several eyes at that moment.

Neo Thipe, who came from Mathubudukwane and who, sadly, passed on in 1995, and Kgomotso Khasa, from Kanye, have also been long term employees of the Mission.

*Patrick Tsheko touching up
paint on a propeller
Patrick has been a faithful
Hangar Assistant for more
than 20 years*

Neo Thipe

*Neo and Kgomotso have also
been long term employees of
the Mission*

Kgomotso Kgasa

With their clear voices and quick wit, Neo and then Kgomotso, have given splendid service manning the hangar telephones and operating radios for flight following.

*   *   *

In time the Executive Committee considered setting up a 'not-profit' company, and, when Les and Pauline French joined the Mission in 1993, the proposal was approved. Les, with his experience in accounting, and after discussions with the Mission's auditors, worked out the details and, around 1996, 'Flying Mission Services Proprietary Limited' (FMS (PTY.)Ltd.) was started. This move enabled Flying Mission to lease both the hangar and aircraft to FMS (PTY.) Ltd. and the arrangement proved well worth while practically as well as financially.

The Ministry of Health, and later, commercial customers, paid FMS (PTY.) Ltd. for services provided. FMS (PTY.) Ltd. made no profit and therefore paid no tax and Flying Mission, being a charity, was exempt from tax. The arrangement worked well and Flying Mission was able to 'pay its way' and keep administration costs to a minimum. Donors, who were always keen that their money to be used for 'mission projects' and not for general running expenses, and the Government Tax and other departments were all happy with the system and viewed it positively.

*   *   *

Over the years the Mission has sought to keep in mind the teaching of our Lord that... "You cannot serve God and mammon." It is all too easy to be carried away by bank balances and budgets and cash flows, all of which are certainly important, but they should not be the main directing factor in decision making. The Mission has at all times endeavoured to be 'transparent' and accountable in financial matters and I believe that this policy has paid big dividends. Money should be a 'tool' and not a 'master'.

*   *   *

The Mission Outreach Account

Then came the question of tithing the Flying Mission 'income'. But how to agree on the technicalities?

The Executive Committee that was formed for Flying Mission was a wonderful bunch of super and patient people. Each Member had great talent in his, or her, chosen field.

As Christians we were unanimous that to tithe - to set aside a tenth of one's income for God's use - was a Biblical principle that should be followed.

"You know that our minister at our home church in London, Westminster Chapel, is R T Kendall. He wrote a book about tithing. I don't remember all of it, but one story sticks in my mind. R T was visiting a friend of his who was pastoring a church and R T asked this friend if the members of his church tithed. The response was in the affirmative. R T then enquired what percentage of the church members tithed, to which his friend responded without any hesitation 'Oh 100%'. R T was somewhat amazed and sought further confirmation of this somewhat unusual fact."

"Well?

"The response was that his friend knew very well that some of his congregation tithed, and, with a broad wink, he then informed R T that he also knew that some of his congregation did not voluntarily tithe - but he had noticed that The Lord took it from them anyway!"

"Aha... Well, right then, the next point is, should one's tithe be 10% of the net income, or, 10% of the gross income?"

"Mmm... and what about donations received for a specific purpose? If we are going to tithe the donations from ICCO and EZE (abbreviations for the names of Dutch and German donor organisations - see the Glossary) that have been given for aircraft or - when it comes - for the building of the hangar we'll have nothing left in the kitty."

"Not only that, but we could be regarded by some folk as being dishonest. If money is given for a specific purpose it would surely be only right to use it for purpose for which it has been given."

Discussions were lively with everyone putting his, or her, ideas and views and sharing experiences.

"Well, we need to make a decision." The Chairman shuffled his papers. "I believe we are all in agreement that to tithe is the right thing to do. FM is a Christian organisation and we should aim to follow God's laws. The Bible is clear that one should set aside a tenth of one's income for The Lord. So, let's begin as from today by setting aside one tenth of all income and placing it into a new and separate account that we can call the "Mission Outreach Account". This will be from gross income and that will include general donations but not gifts of money given for specific projects. Money that accumulates in the MOA will not be used for Flying Mission expenses. It will be for specific mission outreach projects such the purchase of Bibles for patients in hospital at Christmas."

"What about someone who comes with some specific need, such as urgent medical expenses, or a hut that's collapsed, or something?"

"Well, such cases should be considered. And, if a case of hardship like that does come to our notice we may allocate some funding to assist those in need."

The Mission Outreach Account was born. And, eventually, a Committee was formed to administer the fund and consider all applications for mission outreach projects and any requests that were made for financial assistance.

The Mission Outreach Account became one of the most exciting parts of the Mission and it brought blessings to many. Yes, Bibles were bought and distributed to patients who had to spend Christmas in hospital, and other folk too. On one Christmas distribution - in a year when Botswana had given asylum to many refugees - it was amazing to see how many of the recipients came from distant parts of the African continent.

Often there were requests by nursing staff and orderlies - and even the occasional doctor - for a Bible. These requests were met with a polite suggestion that, because the applicant was working and receiving a good salary, they should go to the Lesedi Christian Bookshop located not far from the Princess Marina Hospital gate. A supply of discount vouchers offering a 50% discount on any Bible purchased, within a certain reasonable time frame, was given to such applicants.

Helping to build the church in Zutswa by transporting tools & personnel

Bibles, Christian books, & other items for the bookshop, often filled the cargo pods of Flying Mission aircraft going to Kang

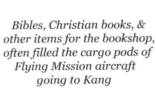

Mission outreach projects in the Kalahari

It was interesting that over the years the number of folk who actually took advantage of that offer were remarkably few!

*   *   *

The Mission Outreach Account fund grew rapidly and was also used to subsidise flights for churches and other mission organsisations whose funds were limited, and it was a delight to see that, as the Mission Outreach Account accumulated, so did the subsidy that could be offered. What began as a 10% subsidy for missions and church organisations eventually was increased to a subsidy of around 60%.

Yes. The Maker's handbook is well worth following - even when it comes to matters of finance. Our ways are often not God's ways, but, if we can learn to follow His directions and go at His pace, incredible things happen.

-oOo-

Helping to put up a new church at Digawana
(Photo: D Spicer))

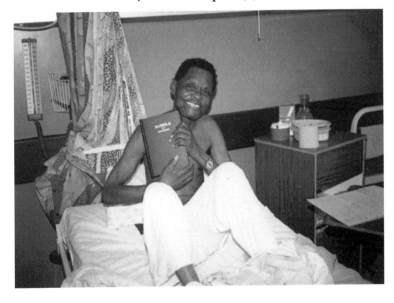

A grateful patient

Good News
(Photo: D Spicer)

CHAPTER 9
CRUISE

-Δ-

Once at altitude and on course with the trims and general tidy up and adjustments made, a pilot has moments of peace to appreciate passengers and perhaps share a joke together. On a long flight, listening to the BBC World Service on the HF Radio is an option. Some passengers snooze.

On one occasion during a long haul in a big jet travelling between London and Johannesburg, at around three o'clock in the morning, being unable to sleep, I asked the airhostess if I might be allowed to visit the flight deck. This was in the days before hijackers made such things impossible.

"Sure," she smiled, "I'll go forward and ask the Captain if that's all right. I'm sure he will be happy to have you visit."

After a short while, when I saw her returning, I unbuckled my seat belt in happy anticipation of some moments of pleasant diversion with the crew up front.

The young lady came and bent over me looking rather sheepish.

"I'm so sorry," she said. "I went to speak with the Captain... but they're all sleeping up there. But don't worry. I'll try again for you a bit later."

She received a wide smile and I told her that I had no problem with that, and sure enough, around five o'clock, she returned and took me forward to the nerve centre of the big aircraft where I had a great time, learning about flying such an enormous machine, joking with the crew, and enjoying the magnificent sunrise.

Some moments during the cruise segment of a flight can be entertaining... but one has to be prepared for sudden changes and be ready to think and act accordingly. Life is always interesting and it can also become exciting.

*   *   *

Storms, Lightning and a Rainbow

It was another of those unusual wet days. Two Hoopoes - smart, bright brown birds with black and white markings and long curving bills - were probing the lawn for insects in a half-hearted manner under the overcast sky as I set off for the hospital where my operating list progressed much as usual until...

*   *   *

"Ngaka, switchboard say that Tshabong is calling for you on the radio." Mary Lucy Dikeledi, the Matron of the Operating Theatres at the Princess Marina Hospital, had popped her head round the door of the office where I was writing up notes and enjoying coffee with Doctor Grazyna Bate our Polish anaesthetist.

"You are an important man today." Grazyna lifted the telephone from its place on Matron's desk and placed it beside my coffee cup on the table between us. "You had better see what they want. It's a good thing that we finished the list already."

I dialed the switchboard and asked what the problem was.

"The Sister at the Tshabong Health Centre says that last night there was a big storm and a hut was struck by lightning and caught fire. She says that they have three patients with severe burns and she's asking if you can go and bring them back here to Marina."

It was almost noon. There was just enough time for me to grab a sandwich and head for the airport.

196

Kalahari lightning

To get to Tshabong would take just under two hours flying. If all went well we should get back well before sunset.

"Can you ask her what the Tshabong weather is like?"

A few moments later confirmation came that the Desert weather now was fine. The storm that caused the trouble had moved on and the skies were clear again. It would be no problem once we got there but there might be weather to cope with on the way.

"Please ask her to keep the radio on and say that we should be there in about two and a half hours."

"And if they have not already done so then they should please start some intra-venous fluids." Grazyna, expecting the worst, was thinking ahead.

The requests were passed.

"One day you must take me in this 'plane of yours. You always get all the excitement and I have to stay here." Grazyna eyes twinkled mischievously. "You know I have never, ever been in a small 'plane."

"I don't think you would like it today. It was raining earlier." I moved the telephone back to Sister Dikeledi's desk.

"If you have any problems while I'm away John Rempel will be around." I headed for the locker room to change out of my green, surgical theatre clothes, popping into theatre number two on the way. My colleague John, an experienced surgeon, and also a keen pilot, was finishing his operating list and I filled him on the situation.

"No problem." He waved an artery forceps in my direction. "You're getting all the flying these days. But I hope to get to Maun next week. Enjoy the flight."

*   *   *

"Alpha Two Zulu Golf Bravo is cleared for take off zero eight for Tshabong. Wind is zero niner zero at ten knots. After take off turn left. Report on track."

"Alpha Two Zulu Golf Bravo is rolling zero eight for Tshabong with a left turn out. On track next."

The red throttle knob was pushed forward. The engine roared and the sleek Cessna 185 aircraft gathered speed quickly. Slight pressure on the left rudder pedal counteracted the swing to the right. The tail came up. The ground began to sink away. Four hundred feet... Five hundred feet... Flaps were brought back to ten degrees and the throttle back to adjust the RPM to twenty-five hundred for the climb. Trims were set. I checked that all was clear to the left before placing the aircraft into a rate one turn... holding it until rolling out on track for Tshabong.

"Gaborone Tower, Alpha Two Zulu Golf Bravo is on track Tshabong and climbing through five five for eight five."

"Golf Bravo contact Approach now on one one eight decimal niner."

"Gaborone Tower, roger. To Approach on one one eight niner, and thank you."

I twisted the radio knobs to change frequencies. "Approach, Alpha Two Zulu Golf Bravo, Charlie one eight five with you on one one eight niner. We're on track Tshabong, through six five for eight five. We estimate the boundary out at one two one five."

"Golf Bravo report reaching level eight five."

"Zulu Golf Bravo, roger. Report reaching eight five next."

The village of Mmankgodi passed beneath the port wing. There was a patch of rain over towards Kanye, the capital of the Bangwaketse people of the Southern District. I diverted a little to the south and passed over the few dwellings of Ranaka huddled against the foot of the escarpment. That way I was sure of passing well clear of the high ground around Kanye. Once over the lands south of Kanye it was flat all the way to Tshabong and if I had had to dodge under cloud I would have had the big, dry bed of the Molopo River as a good landmark to follow as far as Werda, then the road on to Tshabong.

"Gaborone Approach, Golf Bravo."

"Zulu Golf Bravo, Approach. Go ahead."

"Approach I'm not going to make eight five. The cloud base is at about seven thousand feet. Request level change to stay at six five." Rain was beginning to streak over the windshield in fine beads.

"That's approved. Change now to one two five decimal five. Call again when in range. Have a good trip."

"Approach, Alpha Two Zulu Golf Bravo. Changing to one two five decimal five. Thank you sir."

With the radio work out of the way I settled to keeping out of the worst weather and finding my way to the Molopo. The rain over Kanye was only the beginning. Masses of dark cloud had begun piling high above me and this forced me to fly lower. The wide, sandy riverbed came into view, a curving gash in the landscape. It was no longer dry but had large puddles from a recent downpour. The cloud base came down to five thousand feet leaving me with a clear airspace of two thousand feet. Comfortable enough as I could see that it was clearing up ahead.

*　　　*　　　*

One hour and forty-five minutes after departing Gaborone, we were nosing our way down to the sandy surface of the airstrip at Tshabong. It had been a good flight although

I'd had to make two quite large detours to avoid localised thunderstorms.

When we got to the parking area the Tshabong Police truck was waiting.

Switches and fuel were turned off. The control lock inserted into the yoke. Something else needed attention but in the rush of the moment I did not follow the checklist. It would later result in a major problem. I opened the side window.

"Dumela Ngaka." The Police driver stepped forward. "Sister asked me to collect you. I'll take you to the Health Centre."

"Thank you Rra." I climbed out and stretched. "Let's go."

The short trip took less than five minutes and the Sister was waiting. "Dumela Ngaka. Thank you for coming." There was relief in her voice. "I kept the patients at the Health Centre until you had seen them. We've got drips going. They are not a pretty sight. One looks like sixty percent. The other two are not so bad, probably about thirty to forty percent. It happened last night."

"All right Sister, let's go and have a look."

The situation was worse than expected. All three patients had severe and extensive burns. The Sister's estimate of surface involvement was conservative. The prognosis was not good. "You've done well to get drips up. These burns are terrible. I'd estimate between fifty and sixty percent on these two patients and about eighty percent on the third. They'll need lots of fluid. The sooner we can get them to Marina the better."

After a rapid assessment we lost no time in loading the three patients into the ambulance and immediately returned to the aeroplane. Speed was important. The Police truck followed the ambulance.

The Cessna 185 is a narrow aircraft and we had to get two men into the middle seats and the third one into the co-pilot's seat. They were under the influence of strong medication and drowsy. However, we managed... somehow.

"All right Sister. Thank you. We'll be on our way."

"Thank you, Ngaka, for coming. It would have taken many hours by road."

I climbed in and pulled the door closed. The Sister and the two drivers stood clear. After priming the engine I pressed the starter button.

Nothing happened.

After scanning the dials and banks of circuit breakers I found that the switch for the red beacon light on the tail of the aircraft had been left on. Leaving the beacon light on is an easy mistake to make and it can flatten a battery in no time at all. It had.

What to do?

Seeing that there was a problem in starting the helpful Police driver came over and asked what the matter was.

"Rra, I have a flat battery."

"No problem Ngaka," he beamed. "We'll give you a push start."

"That's a great idea, but I'm afraid it won't work Rra.... But do you have any jump leads I wonder?"

"Ee Rra. I'll get them."

Those jump leads saved the day. I silently thanked The Lord for them. Once I had the luggage compartment opened up it was a simple matter to take the cover off the battery bay and clip the two large crocodile clamps to the battery terminals. The engine roared into life at the first touch of the starter and a few minutes later, after removing the cables and waving my attendants 'good bye', we were soon climbing to altitude and turning for home.

However, more problems lay ahead. The flight was not smooth sailing by any stretch of the imagination. The thunderstorms that I had detoured round on the outward trip had developed significantly. At one point our path was blocked by a roiling mass of dark, threatening, grey-green cloud that was down to ground level and extending far too high for me to attempt to climb above even if the aircraft had had the power to do so. My lack of experience in instrument flying meant that I had to stay within Visual Flight Rules (VFR) to be able to see where I was going.

At one point I remember looking round at my patients. All three of them were huddled in blankets, eyes closed and looking for all the world like corpses. I wondered if that was going to be the end result for all of us on this flight.

Of course I should have resorted to it much earlier. I prayed. And, almost immediately, a rainbow appeared directly ahead. A gap opened up and, somehow, we wiggled through into clearer air on the other side of that bank of towering cloud. The cloud base soon lifted and, after a while, the Kanye hills appeared to port. From that point on it was plain sailing.

That day I learned two valuable lessons. One was to remember the problem with the beacon light and, in future, always use the checklist. And the other lesson? Don't wait until the last minute to pray!

*   *   *

After their shattering experience, followed by that hair-raising flight all three of those patients deserved to survive. Sadly, in spite of putting up a hard battle, they did not.

There was no specialised burn unit in Botswana in those days and patients with extensive burns did not do at all well although we could always make them more comfortable. Not all prayers are answered in the way we want, or expect. Somehow that is an inescapable fact of life, as we know it.

*   *   *

The Bushwoman

The brown, oblong patch of skin measured ten by twenty centimetres. The remainder of the little Bushwoman was covered by green surgical drapes. Her form lay still with the exception of the rhythmic rise and fall of her chest as anaesthetic gases ebbed and flowed along the tube placed in her trachea. Her story flickered through my mind as the big, shadow less operating theatre lamp was focused on the incision site.

*   *   *

Ncojane is a small village some 700 km west of Gaborone, far out in the Kalahari Desert. It has a clinic run by a staff nurse. The doctor visits once or twice a month. Between visits the lifeline of this community is three-fold. A rough sandy road leads north to the village of Mamuno and then east to Ghanzi, about a seven hour drive. A pole at one corner of the white-washed clinic building supports a flimsy length of wire in a drooping inverted "V" and, with the small grey box at the end of the wire, this radio is truly a "voice crying in the wilderness", and often unheard because of static. Finally, the third tenuous strand of the lifeline is a rough, stony airstrip running north/south beside the clinic building. Work in such surroundings and isolation demands either a combination of dedication and courage, or the blank acceptance and contentment of madness.

*　　*　　*

The night had been long. The boy of twelve with epilepsy had required heavy sedation to control his fitting. His tongue was raw and bleeding from unconscious biting. But now he slept. The tired staff nurse rose from the floor where she had been kneeling beside the boy who lay on a mattress. She adjusted the paraffin lamp and yawned. Her shadow in the golden lamplight ran up the wall and over the ceiling as she stretched her stiff body.

She smoothed the front of her white uniform and moved to the maternity wing to check on the small Bushwoman who had come in the afternoon before in a long and slow labour. The little patient had a young face, brown and with high cheekbones. But now it was tired and expressionless. Labour was obstructed and her pain was eased only by the strong narcotic injections, which had been given at intervals since she had arrived at the clinic and the staff nurse had assessed her condition. That had been 3 pm yesterday. It had been one of those impossible moments. There had been no available road transport. The doctor was not expected for two weeks. The radio had produced nothing but the crackles and clickings of the dry, turbulent Kalahari atmosphere. The nurse had patiently called for help until 4 pm and had then decided that it was too late to summon an aircraft anyway and she must make the best of her awful situation. The patient would probably die. However, she had set up an intravenous infusion and had done what she could to ease the excruciating pain of the spasmodic uterine activity, and, with much care, the little Bushwoman was now holding her own although the baby's heart, which had been irregular since 6 pm, had finally stopped beating shortly after midnight.

The dawn had brought a new day and a cool clear morning with the possibility of better radio reception. At 7 am the staff nurse had again clamped the connections to the 12-volt, truck battery and her hopes were rewarded by the sound of the Flying Mission base station in Gaborone asking if anyone needed help.

The yellow Desert flowers springing from the red earth outside the clinic window had suddenly seemed to stand up and become brighter, and to wave excitedly, as she called in and requested assistance, and, it was with relief, that she stretched out on an examination couch a few moments later to snatch a little sleep before government working hours began and patients started arriving for their injections and dressings. She was glad that the child welfare clinic with its hundred or so babies had been held the day before and that the new day was scheduled to be fairly quiet.

*　　*　　*

The small green and white Cessna 185 landed in a cloud of dust at three minutes past eleven. Some thirty five minutes later the staff nurse stood shading her eyes as the engine again sprang to life and the plane swung into the wind for take-off. She enjoyed these visits although they were brief. The Flying Mission pilots were good folk and always helpful. One had once climbed to the top of the radio mast to re-thread the pulley for the antenna - a job no one else had dared to do! And the pilots often brought a small quantity of fresh fruit or other supplies. Today she had been given - and accepted gladly - a copy of the Gospel of Mark in Setswana. As she watched the wheels of the little 'plane bounce down the strip over the sharp calcrete stones, she wondered if aeroplane wheels ever became punctured.

Moments later, the hornet like buzzing stilled, and all that remained was the distant bleating of goats, the rustle of wind in the thorn tree beside the clinic, and a column of brown dust rising and fading in the cloudless blue sky.

*   *   *

The scalpel cut easily into the brown skin and the yellow fat tinged immediately to orange as the cut blood vessels spilled their life-giving contents. I thought of the small plane. It would have been an uncomfortable flight. The Desert thermals reach maximum intensity at about 2 pm making the up draughts and down draughts strong and the pilot's job exacting. At times, the tiny aircraft would have been tossed up 1,000 feet or more and then have dropped, like a wounded bird, in the afternoon turbulence. Holding course and altitude in such conditions would have been tiring and demanding. The intravenous infusion probably gave trouble with the formation of bubbles in the tubing due to the reduced atmospheric pressure. The two patients would have been cramped in the small space available. An epileptic fit in such a situation could have meant the end for the small boy and a nasty incident for the pilot. However, the drugs had worked perfectly and the two patients had been oblivious to flying through the air at 250 km/hour in their aluminium shell - a small speck in a vast expanse of blue, far above the dry, brown Desert bushes.

The pilot would have reported to Johannesburg Flight Information Region Control from time to time. The only other noise would have been the steady drone from the six cylinders in the Continental engine, rhythmically pumping power to the two black and curving blades of the propeller. How many things could go wrong on such a flight? A wire work loose? A fuel line chaff and leak? A particle of dirt block a fuel jet? The flight took two hours and thirty-five minutes and passed over only one main road and two small villages until it arrived within one hundred kilometres of Gaborone.

*   *   *

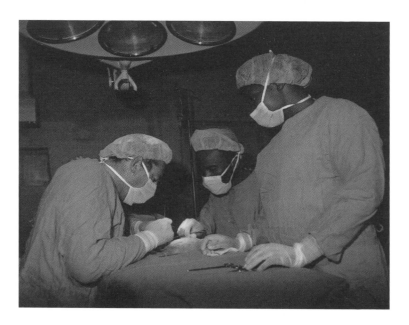

The Princess Marina Hospital operating theatre
(Photo: P Tladi, Government Information Service)

Three hours later, after much hard work, the final skin sutures were placed, after unravelling a mass of sepsis that had necessitated transplanting a damaged and leaking ureter. Even so, the operation had been easy compared with the surgery that had been performed when this little patient had first arrived in hospital.

The small body had been weak. Infection of the pelvic organs had set in. The baby had long been dead with the skull jammed tightly into the unyielding pelvic ring. The stink of rotting flesh had filled the operating theatre and the following weeks had been stormy. The Bushwoman's life had hung precariously balanced on the edge of a sandy, Desert grave.

Gradually, however, the raging fever had subsided, and strength had returned, and with it the realisation that urine was trickling steadily and continuously onto the sheets - soaking, smelling, excoriating skin and bringing looks of disgust from patients in adjacent beds.

Today's surgery had dealt with this problem and she would now enjoy a dry bed when she awoke, and a normal life again following removal of the drainage tubes after two weeks. Normal? How can life be normal for one who can no longer hope for children? Would her husband understand? Would neighbours jeer at her?

I saw her periodically after surgery and always her cheeky face looked at me with the hint of a smile. Fat returned to her thin body and her voice became stronger, and, toward the end of her hospital stay, she would wave to me from her bed in the corner by the window.

*   *   *

The wheels lifted uncertainly from the asphalt. The propeller seemed to scratch the air and then began to nibble and bite and the ground fell away. The corrugated iron roofs of Broadhurst shrank to small glinting squares and oblongs. The bright blue swimming pools of the Gaborone residential districts flashed in the sun. The old Cessna 207 pointed its nose northwest and laboured up to 8,500 feet. After ten minutes, I called the Gaborone tower and reported "November 42472 is boundary out at 85 and on track Ghanzi".

"Roger 472. Contact Johannesburg on HF. Good day!" came the reply.

I took off the headphones, settled down for the long flight and glanced back. She sat behind me with eyes wide, nervously holding her seat belt. But the cheeky face broke into a smile and she relaxed when I twisted round and patted her knee.

At Ghanzi we were met by the Toyota Land Cruiser Ambulance and driven to the health centre. In my broken Setswana, I told her that we would fly to Ncojane in the morning and that she would be put up in the Health Centre overnight, but she shook her head and indicated that she wished to stay in Ghanzi, for her husband worked in Ghanzi, and she wanted to find him before returning home. The cheeky face again broke into smiles. No words of thanks passed her lips but her dark eyes sparkled their gratitude.

She walked away lightly on the sand carrying her blanket and a yellow plastic bag with what few belongings she had - back to the hot, red sands, the bleating goats, the thorn bushes.

By rights, she should have died.

*   *   *

Joy - Part 1

"You know..." John Calhoon from the USA, who was one day to take over the Flying Mission hangar and Maintenance Department, drawled... "What we really need is a Cessna 210."

"Oh, why?" I was interested to hear his views. "We've had the 206 models for several years and they're doing well. I've always thought the 185 and the 206 were ideal for us."

"Yes... The 206 is a good airplane." John ran his fingers through his thinning hair. "But a 210 is faster and more economical. You see it's a retractable. The landing gear tucks up inside it and that increases airspeed considerably."

"That's true... But..." Fride Thorsen, from Norway, who had flown for a number of years as a mission pilot in Liberia, chipped in. "I've always felt that the fixed gear of the 206 was an advantage. It's one less thing to remember when you come in to land."

"Yes, and the maintenance is simpler on fixed gear." Joel Bolthouse was with Flying Mission as an aircraft engineer, but was working toward getting his pilot's licence. Joel was the son of American missionaries working in Zambia and as a small boy he had lived much of his life in Africa. Some years later he was to become a key person in starting up the Flying Mission programme when it opened in Zambia in 2005.

"Ach... the maintenance is no big deal." John was an experienced aviation engineer as well as a pilot, and when he made up his mind it was definitely made up.

"The smaller wheels wouldn't be good for sand strips. The 206's balloon tires are a blessing in such circumstances." My mind went back to my experience in Bokspits when I had sustained two fractured ribs.

"Yes... I know what you're thinking..." John was smiling. "I do agree that the smaller wheel size might be a problem in a place like Bokspits where the sand is deep. However, these days, with the Department of Civil Aviation improving the airstrips all over the country, and with many of our flights being long ones, it would make a lot of sense to make the next aircraft a 210." John had his reasons, and yes, many of the flights that the Mission was now being asked to make were indeed often over two hours in length.

"Well... Let's think about it." I was not yet fully convinced.

"You know..." It was Reg Epp's turn to comment. "Mission Aviation Fellowship are gradually switching to the Cessna 210 model where it can." He cleared his throat and we all looked expectantly at him. "It's a good aircraft and certainly faster and more economical than the 206. But you can't fit a cargo pod under it and many of the mission folk we fly - like Ngaire and Miss Lueling - always like to make use of every available space. A 210 would not be popular with them. But I'm sure both those ladies would be very happy with a DC3..." He paused and smiled widely. "And I've always wanted to fly a DC3!"

Over the following days, the debate was tossed back and forth. Those pilots keen on the idea would scan the pages of 'Trade a Plane' magazine and other aviation publications to seek out suitable advertisements. From time to time I would get another nudge...

"Malcolm... Here's a good offer... This one is a 'low time' machine and the avionics look great. It's got a glide slope for instrument approaches..."

"Yes... But it's in the USA!" I would feign negativity. "Just think... We'd have to get it ferried over. That's big money. Either it has to be taken to pieces and crated and then re-assembled here... Or one has got to fit extra fuel tanks and then find some lunatic who wants to fly a single engine aircraft across the Atlantic. How would you feel, sitting over a raging sea listening to a spluttering motor as darkness descends? I've heard that 'automatic rough' always kicks in about an hour out of Gander!"

"I wouldn't volunteer for that sort of flight." Fride was adamant. "I am perfectly happy over African bush but not over an ocean."

"OK you guys... I've heard most of this before. But I think that if The Lord really wants us to get a 210 then, surely, He can have one for us that we don't have to fly all the way from the 'good ol'e US of A'. I'm sure God's economy would ensure that we could find one either here in Botswana, or, at the very farthest, in South Africa."

"Mmm... You might have a point there. The 'Quiet Hour' and 'Bravo Golf' both came from within Botswana. It would be a big saving."

"Well, let's pray for a 210 and see what happens."

A short while later, and with the approval of the Executive Committee, I began to communicate with EZE, in Germany, about the possibility of obtaining funding for such an aircraft. The Evangelische Zentralstelle fuer Entwicklungshilfe - EZE for short - had been helpful with funding projects in the past and I was hopeful that they might again be interested in helping with yet another project. They were. But such things take time and demand much paperwork and patience. Donor organizations do things in their own way and at their own pace and will not be rushed.

However, one day, things began to fall into place... And, when the Divine Hand moves, it can be amazing how fast things happen...

*   *   *

"I'd like to back up a little." John Calhoon emitted the dreaded phrase in his Eastern American accent. It was a sentence that often resulted in a long diversion that, however, was usually worthwhile in the end.

The other members of the Executive Committee tried hard to concentrate. It had been a long meeting. More than once we had had to "back up a little" and reconsider something in the light of a new inspiration, or a fact that had not been remembered during earlier discussion.

"About this Cessna 210 which was advertised in Trade a Plane," John plunged in enthusiastically recalling the advert

210

and whatever it was that had struck him anew, "I really think we should consider it seriously. It's a snip." He was at his persuasive best.

But was this really the aeroplane for us?

"Let's pray about it, John, and see if the Lord has any clear guidance for us." Keith Irvine shuffled his papers. "I know it sounds good, but it is in America and we would have to pay for extra insurance as well as messing about fitting extra fuel tanks. That would all put the price up."

We spent the next few minutes in prayer, asking our heavenly Father what His views were, and then we sat in silence.

"It's a long way to go." Keith spoke again. "Let's check locally and in Jo'burg first. "

Later, I telephoned Rob Garbett of Professional Aviation Services at Lanseria Airport in South Africa.

"Rob. Yes, it's me, Malcolm." I could visualise Rob in his smart office surrounded by glossy brochures of Cessna Citation business jets that were his usual sale items.

"Yes, Malcolm. How are you all up there? And how is Fox Mike Charlie?" Rob had been instrumental in getting us our Cessna T207, registered now as A2-FMC and named 'Morongwa wa Kagiso' (Messenger of Peace).

"Listen Rob, that 207 is wonderful. It's just what we wanted and it flies like a dream. We're really pleased with it. And it's so roomy - wonderful for stretchers. But now we're thinking of a 210. Something that will be a bit faster for long flights like up to Maun and Harare. Have you any suggestions?"

"Malcolm, give me a little while to look around." Rob rang off and I wondered what would happen.

It did not take long before I found out.

*   *   *

"Keith, Rob Garbett has just telephoned."

"Rob Garbett? Who's he?" Keith had his mind on other things.

"You remember. The gentleman at Lanseria who sold us the 207. He's just telephoned me to say that he has located

211

a 210. It sounds good and he thinks that if we are interested we should not delay getting to see it."

"Great. When do you want to go?" Keith was suddenly all agog. "I'm in Gaborone for this week, then Jo and I are off to Tshotswa again and we'll be away in the Desert for some time."

"The aircraft is at Wonderboem airport. Could we manage a trip tomorrow?"

"That would be wonderful"

Keith Irvine was a missionary with the Africa Evangelical Fellowship. He was an engineer by training. He and his wife Jo spent a total of some eight years living in different locations in the Kalahari and they had travelled widely on almost all the remote Desert tracks. They were both firm converts to travel by Flying Mission aircraft whenever it was possible for them to do so.

"It would have to be a quick trip. Down and back in one day. I have to see about some maps in Pretoria and John Calhoon wants an aircraft instrument taken in somewhere for calibrating. We can take a look at this 'plane too. Let's make an early start. If we aim to take off at six thirty we should be back by teatime."

"Ehee, Ngaka... Let's go!"

*   *   *

The next morning, Keith and I were flying low over the tops of the Magaliesburg Mountains, looking down on the rough, rocky outcrops with the lush, neat orange groves of the Rustenburg citrus farms clustered at their bases.

"Oaee..." Keith frequently lapsed into Sekgalagadi exclamations. "Just look at that mist coming off the Hartebeestpoort Dam. Isn't that just beautiful? We have a wonderful Creator!"

After a smooth flight over the dam, we reported our position over Roslyn. Minutes later, our tyres kissed the tarmac at Wonderboem Airport and the controller directed us to a suitable parking place. The trip, that by road would have taken the best part of five hours on a good tarred road, had taken us only one hour and fifteen minutes.

Wonderboem airport was its usual sleepy self and, once inside the cool terminal building, we headed for the cafeteria for some coffee before making arrangements for transport for the short trip into Pretoria.

"It'll take me a minute or so to fix a car and we'll have to find out where this 210 is."

"No problem... I need to visit the loo. I'll wait for you beside that notice board near the main entrance."

After making arrangements with Imperial for a vehicle, I found Keith standing at the designated spot with a twinkle in his eye...

"Malcolm... Is this not the Cessna 210 that we've come to look at?" He pointed to an A4 size sheet of paper pinned to the board. It read:

FOR SALE - CESSNA 210

The specifications looked right. In the photo, the 'plane looked clean enough and, after asking at Reception where the seller's office was to be found, we climbed the stairs to the first floor of the building and found a heavily made up secretary who was all smiles and oozing with helpfulness.

"Yes... We have a 210 for sale. Mr. X who owns it is out at the moment but I can take you to see it if you'd like..."

"That would be great. Thank you."

Miss Helpful led us back down the stairs... Along a corridor... Out into the brilliant sunshine... Across some grass and tarmac... And there it was, the Cessna 210, ZS-LAP. A little dusty, but a trim and sleek machine. There was no obvious damage. The paperwork seemed in order. The colour was a sort of light buff / tan. Certainly a serviceable colour in Botswana. It looked for all the world as if it was just waiting patiently for us to take it away.

"Mmm. She's beautiful." Keith let out a sigh. "And so graceful..."

"Aoaee Keith!"

"I mean the aircraft!" Keith had a dreamy look and was already seeing himself skimming the treetops of the Kalahari in this sleek aircraft. "And I'm sure Jo will love it!"

"I'm sorry, I can't tell you much about it. It does need a wash down. But if you are interested I can get Mr. X to contact you and answer your questions. I think he'd be happy to take you up for a flight in it if you wanted that. You'll have to make up your minds fast." The trim piece of Secretarial Service brought us back to earth with efficiency. "We've already had several offers."

"Yes, well... we are missionaries and it's a big decision involving a lot of money. If God wants us to have this 'plane I'm sure he will keep it for us. We have to go at His pace." Keith smiled benignly.

"Well..." The neat young lady looked dumbfounded.

What else was there to say to these two cranks from the Botswana bush?

"Anyway, we are really interested." At this Miss Helpful brightened visibly. "What we would like to do is to arrange for the aeroplane to be flown up to Gaborone for a day so that our engineers can see it."

As we walked back to the terminal building, I explained that our mechanics would have to do an inspection and, if they gave the go-ahead, then we would be in business.

I don't think Secretarial Services was too impressed. And I doubt she thought that God would ever come up with the money.

*　　　*　　　*

Joy - Part 2

As expected, John Calhoon was cautious. However, he soon warmed to the proposal and arranged to inspect the aircraft.

"Now, don't get your hopes up. This inspection may turn up snags. We'll have to do an analysis of the engine oil. That take's time, but it'll be worth it. It could save us a BIG bill down the line."

How blessed we were to have John heading up the Maintenance Department. His verdict, when it came, would not have been made lightly and an aircraft that he agreed we should buy would be a good one.

*　　　*　　　*

A couple of days later, John Calhoon and Gene Thieszen went to work on the aeroplane in the hangar, removing cover plates and cowlings, and peering into every nook and cranny to check wires and cables and control surfaces as well as checking the engine and the retractable undercarriage.

At the next Flying Mission Executive meeting, John was ready with his report. However, he kept us in suspense "I guess I have to tell you that I went through this aircraft with a fine toothed comb." He shuffled the papers in front of him importantly. "I found nothing major amiss. There were a few little things, but they can easily be put right." He paused, enjoying his moment of power, and continued with his eyes twinkling and a broad smile spreading over his face. "I would go for it. I think it's a bargain."

The talk turned to finance, and I reported details of my correspondence with EZE who, by that time, had indicated that they would approve the needed funding. Our prayers were being answered. But, there was a mountain of paperwork to work through.

"The problem is, that Mr. X has other buyers who would like the aircraft, so he wants the money 'now now'! The only solution would be for us to ask for a bridging loan from the bank."

"I'm sure they'll give it to us, But interest rates are high."

Reluctantly, the decision was made to request a bridging loan.

John communicated this decision to Mr. X and it was then agreed that, as soon the loan was secured, the aircraft would be brought to Gaborone and the cheque handed over.

All went well. The bank prepared the documents for signature. The Department of Civil Aviation paperwork was completed. I went to the airport on the appointed day with John Calhoon and met with Mr. X who came with us to the bank, where we signed the papers and handed over the cheque. John accepted the keys to the aircraft and, on our return to the airport, he happily taxied it off to the Flying Mission hangar. Mr. X departed back to South Africa. I headed back to the Mission Office in town.

It was a lovely afternoon. But I had a nagging feeling that perhaps this had all gone too smoothly.

Then it struck me. Wow! We had just signed a deal involving the payment of thousands of Pula, a vast sum of money that was going to land us heavily in overdraft. Yes, we did have an overdraft facility... but... the bridging loan was large and it was going to be costly. Had we really done the right thing? Or, had we been foolish and stupid and been in too much of hurry? God's timing is often not our own. He has eternity on His side and we mortals tend to be impatient.

As I drove I remember praying... "Lord, you know what we've done. We've prayed much about it and asked You what we should do. It all seemed so right. But there's a lot of money involved. Yes, we have applied to overseas donors and they have promised finance. But at this moment we have almost nothing in hand. And the interest payments will not be small. I'd like some confirmation that we've done the right thing."

The vehicle droned on. The white, summer butterflies continued to flit haphazardly across the road. The sun was warm.

No, there was no voice from heaven. No thunderclap.

But confirmation did come. Quickly, and in a most unexpected way that - for me at least - proved without any doubt that God had directed - and was directing - the whole project from start to finish and more. Also, that He had been making His arrangements long before we had even begun to think about getting that aircraft.

I got to the Flying Mission office at about twenty past four.

Gaone was beginning to clear her desk in preparation for shutting the office for the day. A tall, bright, young Motswana girl, she was awaiting a place at the University of Botswana. I had met her during the course of my work at the Princess Marina Hospital. In those days, if a doctor had a letter to write in connection with a patient, the doctor wrote the

Gaone Macholo

letter out 'longhand' and sent it to the Secretary Pool. It was returned with the typed letter attached. A great system... if one had legible handwriting. And disaster for such as I, whose handwriting is of an 'artistic' bent. My letters often had to be reurned, sometimes several times, before they were fit to be sent out.

Gaone had taken a job in the Secretary Pool and was one of the unfortunate girls who were faced with my scrawl. While going over corrections one day, we had found that we were both Christians and, when she had discovered that I was linked with Flying Mission, she immediately asked if she could come and work for the Mission.

In no time at all, she was installed in the Flying Mission Office and proved worth her weight in gold. (Debswana eventually took her on as Human Resources Manager for the company.) As I entered the office she stood up and held out an envelope.

"Ngaka... I checked the post box."

The envelope she held out to me had the blue markings of a registered letter. The postmark was 'Bermuda'.

"I don't know anyone living in Bermuda."

"Well, open it Ngaka. You won't know who sent it until you open it."

Inside were a letter - and a cheque.

The letter stated simply that the firm of Lartek was being dissolved and that the assets of the firm were being divided and distributed.

Flying Mission had been named as one of the beneficiaries. *It was dated a couple of months previously and had come by surface mail.*

The cheque was for US $67,000-00. It was more than enough to take care of our overdraft - and pay off a significant amount of the cost of the aircraft that we had just agreed to purchase.

Abundant provision.

"Yo... Wow..."

Perfect timing.

"Thank You, Lord!"

The following morning, that cheque made possible the cancellation of the entire bridging loan... and, that decision to liquidate the Company, and to sign that cheque, had been made months before our need for the finance. The timing was incredible.

But then... God's timing always is. Isn't it?

On the 13th of September 1990 ZS-LAP arrived back in Gaborone and joined the Flying Mission 'fleet'. The South African registration number was changed and, in Botswana, it became A2-AGG. On the 10th of January 1991, the aircraft was dedicated to the Lord's service. The name "Morongwa wa Boitumelo" (Messenger of Joy) was emblazoned on the tail fin and the aircraft began its work - bringing joy to many who have flown in her, and also to relatives who have been happy that their sick loved ones were spared many uncomfortable hours of travel by road.

*   *   *

Some time later, I had contact with John Kessler, an ex-director of Lartek, and I was able to share with him what had happened when the letter and cheque had arrived. We marvelled again at the timing, and the way God works His purposes out... even when we are completely unaware of what He is doing.

Wonderful.

*   *   *

Cessna 210, A2-AGG - 'Morongwa wa Boitumelo'
(Messenger of Joy) at the Sir Seretse Khama
International Airport, Gaborone

Mary and the Vacuum

Matron Dikeledi snapped the seat belt together with a satisfying clunk.

"Ao Mma... You are really becoming used to flying." I began to run through the pre-take off checks for our flight from Maun to Gaborone in the Flying Mission's Cessna 206. A roomier aircraft than the Cessna 185 and yet, also ideally suited to flying into and out of the Botswana bush airstrips.

"Ee Ngaka, I have to be, with all the travelling we have had to do over the past week." She settled her considerable frame more comfortably into the seat. "But it's been a good week. I think we've managed to sort out a lot of problems in all the places we have visited. I'm still upset with that clinic in Gomare. Can you imagine that they had a 'Kuenschner nail' operating pack? There is no doctor there and how the Central Medical Stores could have possible thought they knew what it was for I cannot imagine. I'm going to have words with Mr. Grecian when I see him."

"Well, we can certainly use that set back in Gaborone."

We had been with a team from the Instruments Sub-Committee of the National Standing Committee on Drugs (what a mouthful!) visiting health facilities and checking on what was available in each location and, where necessary, issuing new equipment. It had been a major job, extending over many months, to standardise equipment in the hospitals and clinics throughout Botswana. For Matron Dikeledi and myself that had meant, particularly, the surgical instruments and other Operating Theatre equipment like anaesthetic machines.

After a busy week, ending with two full and tiring days at the hospital in Maun, we were on our way back home to Gaborone.

Maun had a big, tarmac runway. We would have no problem taking off today. The wind was favourable and light. It was early morning and the air was a cool thirty degrees Celsius.

"Are you ready Mma?"

"Ee Rra. You can go. Once we are in the air I shall soon be asleep. Please do your best to avoid those tiresome bumps and get us to Gaborone in good time." She smiled and closed her eyes.

The Thamalakane River was soon passing under us as we banked toward the heading that would take us back to the capital.

*   *   *

Matron Dikeledi slept. The engine of the Cessna 206, 'Lephoi la Pula' - The Dove of Blessing - droned monotonously and the automatic direction finder (ADF) needle swung lazily with no promise of navigational help. This flight from Maun to Gaborone would take two and a half hours. I checked the instruments and gauges, fighting increasing drowsiness.

Thinking I might find someone to talk with, I switched to channel 3, the Government Health Service channel, on the Sunair ASB 100 HF, SSB transceiver. The antenna tuner behind the rear wall of the cabin thumped its way to the correct setting and the 5474 KHz band clicked into my headset. Almost immediately a voice, which I recognised, came through the background mush of the lower side band.

"Princess Marina Hospital do you copy Kang?"

I waited for the response.

"Princess Marina Hospital do you copy Kang?"

Silence. Saturday morning was not the best time to try and raise the Princess Marina Hospital. The call was repeated again with no success.

"Kang, Alpha Two Alpha Bravo Golf copies you." I chipped in. "Good morning Mary. Do you have a problem? Over."

I was unprepared for what followed.

"Oh Doctor! Is that really you?" Mary Marshall, the nurse at the Kang Clinic, poured out her expressions of relief. "I've been calling for almost an hour and...." There followed a quick summary of her problem. A woman with obstructed labour. A difficult, unproductive night. No sign of progress.

Mary had only just completed nursing training in a sophisticated teaching hospital in Johannesburg. She was

221

acting relief nurse for a couple of months while the Mission nurse, who normally ran the clinic, was taking some much needed leave. Kang was a busy clinic serving a population of about 5,000 and situated deep in the Kalahari Desert.

In my mind's eye I saw Mary's face with her ready smile and straight, dark hair. She would not be smiling now. Having tried for so long to obtain help, she would be near to tears.

We were three hours flying time away and, in any case, did not have enough fuel to reach Kang and then be able to continue on to Gaborone. It would take five hours at least for me to get home, refuel the 'plane and then fly west to Kang. From Mary's description of her patient's condition, delay was likely to be fatal for the child and probably for the mother too.

"Mary, is your patient fully dilated?" I asked.

"Yes. She's been that way for several hours. Our ambulance is not working, or I would have sent her in by road."

"All right. Mary... you should have a vacuum extractor in the clinic. Do you know where it's kept?"

"I think so." Mary's voice sounded steadier. "Let me go and see."

Orapa diamond mine was in the distance, ahead and a little to port.

"Yes, I have one here." Her voice came again across the Kalahari vastness. "But I've never used one and I don't know how it works."

The Ventouse Vacuum Extractor was designed for just such an obstetric emergency. Could I explain the procedure simply enough for an anxious and inexperienced nurse to follow the instructions?

Over the next five minutes, I told her how to carefully position the cup of the extractor on the baby's head, and how the vacuum must be allowed time to develop a suction pad on the scalp before any attempt is made to apply traction. Then how the 'pull' must be steady, and kept perpendicular to the cup at all times. I did my best to answer her questions and give her hints and tips that I thought would be of help. Mary said she would have a go. I promised to pray for her and for her patients, and for a satisfactory outcome.

Minutes droned by. The scarred earth and mounds and corrugated iron roofs of Orapa, bounded by a neat security fence, slid past slowly under the port wing. The Orapa Francistown road was a long, straight, whitish scratch veering off to the left over the dry landscape. Brown, seemingly unending, virgin veldt again stretched into the distance. Matron Dikeledi, in the co-pilot seat beside me, was fast asleep, her head leaning against the window - completely oblivious to the drama over 600 km away to the southwest.

The radio remained silent. I had visions of the small nurse struggling to pull an oversize baby from its mother's pelvis. Maternal tissues perhaps tearing. Blood beginning to trickle. The baby's head being deformed, and compressed, and the foetal heart rate rising and falling and becoming irregular with the distress.

No sound came from the radio. Had the mother died? Had the baby been stillborn?

The engine throbbed patiently. The automatic direction finder needle continued to waver uncertainly as if trying to decide between life or death.

After what was, in fact, less than 25 minutes, the Kang Clinic radio came alive.

The news? "A beautiful baby girl."

Mary's face would be beaming with joy as she spoke into the microphone far away across the thorn bushes. She would not forget this day in a hurry. The Ventouse Extractor had won another ardent supporter.

We thanked God together for a new life... and the miracle of modern radio communication.

As we began descending toward Gaborone, Matron Dikeledi stirred and opened her eyes. I smiled at her and leaning over told her the news...

"Just think. A baby girl!"

"Oh Ngaka," she stretched, "You do think up such wonderful stories, and you are always teasing me. I never know when to believe you."

*   *   *

223

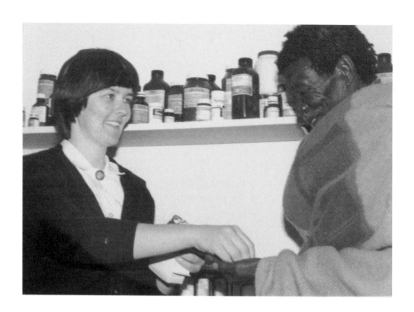

Mary with one of her patients in Kang

I don't think that Matron Dikeledi ever believed it was true. But it was no story. There was a tired but happy nurse, and mother, and a beautiful baby girl to prove it.

*   *   *

Note: Adapted from an article first published in Saving Health, Vol. 30. No. 1, March 1991. A publication of the Medical Missionary Association, London.

-oOo-

CHAPTER 10
EMERGENCIES

-Δ-

In Africa, one learns to expect the unexpected. Animals can be unpredictable. Big game can be dangerous. Venomous snakes abound. One develops an appropriate level of awareness of such things.

A pilot, similarly, must develop an awareness of potential problems and think ahead to possible solutions. After all, we human beings are not designed to fly. What goes up must, eventually, come down and, it is said that if a pilot and the passengers walk away from the aircraft after landing, then it is a happy ending to the flight.

Modern passenger jets are colossal in size and complexity, but even a small, single-engine aircraft, although simpler, may still develop problems that bring a flight to an unexpected conclusion. Nothing is like the silence after the motor quits functioning during flight in a single-engine aircraft.

Many folk think that lion or buffalo hold the prize for killing people in Africa. However, more die from the microscopic malaria parasite carried by the tiny mosquito that visits quietly during night hours to indulge its desire for a drink of fresh blood from a sleeping victim. For a pilot, the unexpected and the un-noticed can be also dangerous.

Training prepares one for some flight emergencies, but even then an unusual situation can get out of hand and go wrong fast. Flying Mission has had its share of 'pulse raisers' and accidental damage to its aircraft but, to date, nothing more than a few scratches and some dented pride has been the result for both personnel and passengers and, for that, we give thanks to our Lord and Master. The Bible teaches that God's 'everlasting arms' are under us at all times. That is a great comfort.

What follows is not a catalogue of Flying Mission's disasters but a few selected accounts of some incidents that are included for completeness to underline the fact that flying in the service of our Master still requires vigilance, training and honing of skills. Some incidents have been intentionally omitted because I was not there and could only give a poor, and perhaps inaccurate, second hand account from what I learned later. However, it is my hope that those involved might be encouraged to put pen to paper and write first hand accounts of their experiences. Gene, what about that 'Hukuntsi Rock'? Fride and Jeff... your experiences of 'Communication over a Soggy Salt pan'? And Tim... your 'Encounter With a Vulture'? Dave... your exciting moments with 'A Lame Duck'? And Rick... your 'Moments of Silence' in the Sky? You all have incredible experiences to share that everyone can benefit from. Anyway, why should I do all the hard work?

We are not guaranteed a 'smooth passage' at all times. In this life we are all on a 'learning curve'. It can be both interesting and exciting.

*   *   *

Fasten Your Seat Belts

"Alpha Two Zulu Hotel Juliet is cleared for take-off runway zero eight. Wind is calm."

"Alpha Hotel Juliet." I eased the throttle open as I pressed the button on the yoke to acknowledge the take-off clearance.

The runway shimmered in the heat. The ancient Cessna 206 that I had rented staggered forward. The Outside Air Temperature (OAT) simmered around 40 degrees

Centigrade. Density altitude, if I had troubled to think about it, was probably about 7,000 feet at this airfield situated some 3,200 feet above sea level. Lift-off was reluctant.

I had no worries. I was alone, the aircraft empty and the runway plenty long enough. The weather was fine, what is often described as 'severe' clear'.

Brimming with inexperience and low on flight time, I watched the red earth of Africa sink away below me. The sun beat hotly through the Perspex canopy above and in front of me.

After about fifteen minutes the Gaborone Tower lost interest. Probably I would have no one to speak with until I got within range of the control tower at Selebi-Phikwe, the mining town that was my destination, seventy minutes away. I set the VHF radio to 125.5 MHz. As expected, the Botswana Visual Flight Rules (VFR) channel was silent. I had the sky all to myself.

The Continental engine up front was happy. I relaxed. The minutes ticked off slowly. The Cessna 206 purred north following the main road, a seemingly unending, and straight strip of black tar 3,500 feet below. My mind dulled.

Forty-five minutes out from Gaborone, the apple I had brought along seemed the solution to defeating sleep. The reddish skin polished up nicely on my trouser leg and I plunged my teeth into the cool fruit and savoured the crisp texture and delicate flavour.

Then... it happened!

BANG... bang... **_BANG_**... **_CLATTER_**... bang... **_CLATTER_**...

A most horrendous shattering of the steady throb of disciplined cylinders.

My pulse, after missing several beats, settled around 150 per minute. My blood pressure rose some fifty millimetres of mercury. My mouth, instead of being filled with juicy apple, suddenly seemed full of dry sacking.

The first thought was to pick a spot on the road below and land. I located a likely length on the black line of tar beneath me and, struggling to take a grip on my senses, began a most disorderly emergency checklist by making sure that my seatbelt was tight.

Bang... bang... **_CLATTER... BANG..._**

The frightful disturbance continued. An erratic stream of noise hurled itself into my already numb and groping brain.

"Mixture... Fuel stopcock... Change tanks... Magnetos... Master switch..." ran through my mind and seemed a sensible way to go. Those items appeared normal. My eyes roved in near panic about the instrument panel, desperately seeking some helpful clue to the disruption of what had been a peaceful flight.

BANG... bang... **_BANG..._**

RPM was 2300, as before.

Clatter... **_CRASH..._**

Manifold pressure and fuel flow were steady at 23 inches and 14 GPH. Suction was 'in the green'. Oil pressure likewise... and steady.

Airspeed was at 110 knots. Altitude was not being lost rapidly as I had feared. In fact... it was not being lost at all!

The engine seemed to be holding together. So what was the problem? I considered the airframe. Zulu Hotel Juliet was, after all, an old aircraft.

Gingerly I gently nudged the yoke to the left... and then to the right... expecting some metallic fragment to depart one of the wings. As if by magic, peace was restored and, with it, the hope of a better life.

The respite was short-lived. Cacophony returned as suddenly as it had departed. However, this time, knowing I was not going to fall immediately from the sky, I was able to look round more slowly and carefully, but still could find nothing of note.

The 'yoke nudge manoeuvre' was, once more, successful. But, again, after an interval, the devil returned to poke fun at me. The situation did not improve. During the brief moments of serenity, I began hoping that we might just make it the remaining thirty minutes of flying time to Selebi-Phikwe.

On scanning the horizon, anxious to see the tall chimney of the Selebi-Phikwe mine rising from the brown earth, the view was only that of dry, brown veldt bisected by the straight, black line of the road.

During clatter phases I vowed I would never again take to the air in anything other than a well-insured automobile.

When the tarmac airstrip of Selebi-Phikwe at last appeared, and I began my descent, naturally there was no further trouble. The wing flaps worked as expected, and the elevator. The flare was the nicest thing imaginable. And the soft rumble of rubber on the bosom of mother earth was heavenly. I taxied to the fuel pumps and shut down, exhausted.

"Excuse me Sah." The fuel pump attendant jolted me from my thoughts.

"Oh... Hi." I tried to look in total control. "Yes, full please. Both wing tanks. Thank you."

"Yes Sah". The stocky African bent to attach the earthing lead to the exhaust pipe. Straightening up he flashed perfect teeth in a broad smile adding, "Excuse me... Sah."

"Yes?"

"Sah... You have a seat belt hanging out of the cargo door... Sah?"

"Oh. Thank you."

A seatbelt!

I was humbled - and red-faced.

Inspection confirmed the horrible truth - that the belt was indeed the culprit for the mid air crises. And, also, that during its wild and periodic oscillations, it had done a fair bit of damage chipping the surrounding paintwork. Noel, who did the maintenance on this aircraft, was not going to be happy.

If nothing else, the incident forced me to read the handbook and review emergency procedures before making the return trip. And it strengthened my resolve to practise forced landing procedures much more frequently.

Later that day, after completing a careful pre-flight - tucking away loose straps and making sure the doors were properly shut - I rediscovered the beauty and peace of a late afternoon flight... when the air is cooling and still and the golden orb of the sun is sinking slowly in the west...

No doubt about it. To fly *IS* the way to travel. Motor cars are so slow... and so tiring... And driving in traffic is such a nerve-racking business.

* * *

Headwinds

"Man!" Reg's eyes widened and he leant forward. "I only just made it..."

The Thursday evening prayer meeting was an exciting time. It was an occasion for sharing experiences of the past week, as well as placing our needs before our Lord and Master. Each week we met together in a different home and, after the leader for that evening had given a brief Bible reading and devotional, there would be a time of sharing stories and experiences and making needs known. Then would follow a time of prayer.

At this point, all eyes were glued on Reg Epp, an experienced pilot/mechanic who had been seconded to Flying Mission by the US Mission Aviation Fellowship. Reg was a valued member of the flight team and Mary, his wife, was a talented singer and musician who - soon after their arrival in Botswana - had collected a group of the Tlokweng kids and started a Sunday School under a tree near their house in Gaborone Village.

"I tell you." Reg continued. "It was last Sunday. I had been to Jo'burg that day, then to Umtata, in the Transkei. The last leg of my trip was to Maseru for the night. I was with a Mennonite family, who were not permitted to land in the Republic of South Africa. Our Flying Mission insurance prohibited us from flying over most of Lesotho, so I had to make a dog-leg around to the west and, on the last stretch, up into Maseru, I hadn't really noticed the wind - probably a cross-wind at that point." He paused.

"Go on."

"It was getting prematurely dark, due to a line of thunderstorms over towards Bloemfontien, but I was in good

VFR (Visual Flight Rules). However, none of the Maseru NavAids were operating, including the non-directional beacon. When my time came and went for Maseru, I flew 10 or 15 minutes past my estimated arrival time, and, with no Maseru in sight anywhere, I decided to head for Bloemfontien. Bloem informed me that the airport was closed due to the heavy rain, wind and lightning.

"Ehe... The plot thickens!"

"I had departed Umtata with 3 hours of fuel. The flight should have been 1.5 hours, leaving a 1.5 hour reserve. When I turned for Bloem, the DME (Distance Measuring Equipment) was indicating a 64-knot ground speed. I didn't believe this, of course, and waited for it to 'get right'. Then it hit me..."

"What hit you?"

"You won't believe this." Reg was keeping us all in suspense. "I was hardly moving!"

"What do you mean, hardly moving?"

"Well... That wind had increased to a gale. The ground speed indication went down to 60 knots and the vehicles on the road below me looked like they were going faster than I was!"

"You're joking."

"Not at all. After the DME settled down, it showed that I had 50 nautical miles to run - 50 minutes of flying! Yes, the cars on the highway below were passing me. They were probably going 120 km per hour. There was a lot of wind and rain most of that last 50 minutes."

"You should have tried leaning the mixture."

"Believe me, I tried every trick I knew. I fiddled the mixture to the leanest without running the engine rough. I ran one tank dry. By the time I got in sight of Bloem, I was seriously thinking I'd have to declare an emergency. My last fuel gauge was on almost zero. Thankfully, they cleared me for a straight in approach. I tell you, I prayed hard. And by the time I had landed and taxied to the terminus, those gauge needles had been completely flat for about ten minutes. I honestly did not think I was going to make it, but somehow The Lord got me there."

"Ouch!"

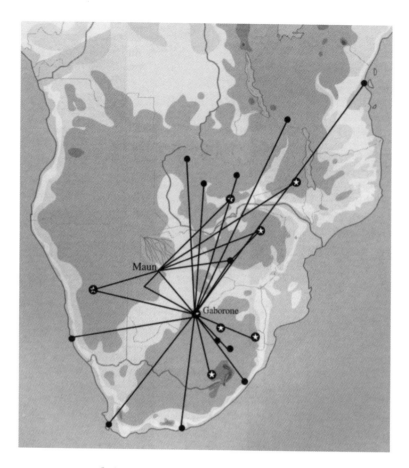

Flying Mission flight routes in 1999

"Yes, Ouch... but that's not all. Since it was dark, and with an international landing, I didn't taxi up to the pumps, but went directly to the terminal, where we were interrogated quite extensively by the Immigration Officers there."

"I can imagine there would have been some questions!"

"Yes... they fortunately accepted my explanations. And then, when I re-fuelled the next morning, the tanks took about 20 litres more fuel than we had figured these tanks can hold!"

"Ah! You see, The Good Lord was looking after you." David Gallacher was our Scottish accountant. "He knows that a few extra litres of fuel are a lot cheaper than having to replace an entire aircraft."

"I was hankering to get home so I didn't spend too long in Maseru when we eventually got there, but I learnt some interesting facts. I visited with the Mission Aviation Fellowship team in their hangar. Those guys... They told me that sometimes when they fly in the mountains they look out of the window and see a horse looking **down** at them! And hey, they fly some odd stuff. Their hangar had large piles of wood all along one side and when I asked about it they told me that whenever they have any space on one of their flights out into the mountains for the Flying Doctor Service then they pack in as much firewood as they possibly can."

"Firewood?" Dave was amazed. "Do they burn firewood in their aeroplanes?"

"No no... Lesotho has no trees up in the mountains and in winter it gets viciously cold. The firewood is to make life a little easier for the folk who live up in the remote villages. They have to collect cow dung to burn to to keep themselves warm and to cook on."

Denise, the wife of John Calhoon our Chief Engineer burst into a fit of uncontrollable giggling. "Can you... imagine... what porridge tastes like when it's cooked on cow dung?" A titter of laughter drifted around the room.

"Aw, Denise! This is supposed to be a prayer meeting you know."

"You weren't the only one with headwind problems that day." Roger Weaver chipped in. "I was coming back from Maun and it only took me an hour and a half - for what is usually a two and a half hour flight. And that was with the power setting right back as low as I could get it. I was really humming along. But I could hear the guys going the other way were having a terrible time and two of them eventually turned back to Gaborone."

"Sunday, 19th July, 1987 is a day I shall remember!" Reg smiled. "And I want to say a very '*BIG THANK YOU*' to The Lord for getting me safely back to earth."

We all echoed his thanks.

*   *   *

2001 MAINTENANCE STATISTICS

		Hours
Inspections:		
FM aircraft	914.7	46%
commercial	944.0	44%
other mission aircraft	90.5	6%
*Projects:	114.4	4%
	2063.6	**100%**

(*non-aviation-related work)

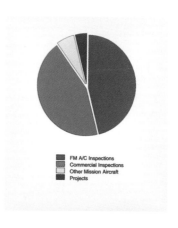

FM A/C Inspections
Commercial Inspections
Other Mission Aircraft
Projects

2001 FLIGHT STATISTICS

		Hours
*MOH – Mercy	537,9	36,9%
Mission	339,7	23,3%
Commercial	178,9	12,3%
Medical	69,7	4,8%
Personnel	67,2	4,6%
Relief	62,4	4,3%
MOH – *DMO	41,1	2,8%
FM Admin	39,1	2,7%
FM Training	36,3	2,5%
Government	36,3	2,5%
Maintenance	25,5	1,8%
Development	11,4	0,8%
Pilot Service	11,4	0,8%

*MOH – Ministry of Health
*DMO – District Medical Officer

Commercial
Development
FM Admin
FM Training
Government
Maintenance
Medical
Mission
MOH – DMO
MOH – Mercy
Personnel
Pilot Service
Relief

234

*Len McKay & Kenneth
Thlabiwa check
construction diagrams*

*'Mox' Keitshokile Marari
works on an
aircraft interior*

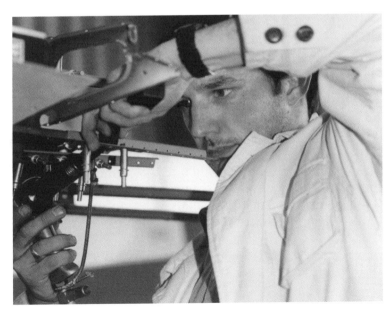

Jeff Royce works on an engine (Photos: B Wilson)

235

Great Stuff

"I have set before you life and death... Choose life..."
(Deuteronomy 30 v. 19)

Mark Spicer, our American Operations Manager, and I had been on an overnight trip to attend a meeting of Mission Aviation groups operating in Southern Africa. Mission Aviation Fellowship of South Africa hosts these meetings. Representatives come from as far afield as Angola and Zimbabwe. It's a grand time of sharing, finding out how best we can help one another in serving our Master.

After the meeting, Rae Absalom had come up to me.

"Malcolm, could you use this?" He handed me a carton. "There's a chemist in Edenvale who gives us this sort of thing. Usually it's a pile of drugs which are about to expire, but I noticed that this is well within its expiry date."

"Let's see." I opened the carton and extracted a 250 ml bottle. "Fluothane - this is a powerful general anaesthetic. And it's expensive. The mission hospitals in Botswana will love this." I carefully returned the bottle to the carton. "In 1968 when I first came to Molepolole, Jim Skinner - he's now a doctor in Tain in Scotland - taught me how to use Fluothane. Just 5 ml will put a patient to sleep in about 30 seconds. It's great stuff. This is probably enough to keep a hefty adult asleep for at least a week!"

The Lord provides in mysterious ways... Wonderful!

Without thinking, I had stowed the 4 cartons, each holding 6 bottles, into the boot of the car and had gone about the day's business. Mark had gone to collect a shipment of Bibles for the Christian Bookshop in Gaborone. We met at the airport at ten o'clock the next morning for our flight back to Botswana and, as the twin's engines began to hum and the aircraft accelerated down the runway, I felt myself pressed into my seat.

The Cessna 335 - Alpha Juliet Foxtrot - rose into the air. Johannesburg shrank behind us. In no time we were climbing through seven thousand feet for flight level one zero. Mark was trimming the aircraft for climb. The Johannesburg

Air Traffic Controllers cleared us for Gaborone, 40 minutes away.

"Pfew... 15 boxes of Bibles. That's a load." Mark was beginning to relax after the high workload of taking off from the busy airport of Lanseria. "That Customs guy couldn't believe we had so many Bibles!"

We had taken out three seats. Boxes of Bibles were stacked along the cabin wall restrained, in case of turbulence, with a green cargo net. The brown cartons boldly proclaimed: "**BIBLES, HANDLE WITH CARE**". A notice I had often pointed out to folk emphasising "**HANDLE WITH CARE**", for Bibles are life changing. How wonderful to be taking the Word of Life to Botswana.

"You should have seen the Customs Officer's face when I told him that your 4 boxes were all full of some drug." Mark grinned at the thought. "I told him we had no papers for the stuff and he just about went through the roof! But then I told him it was a gift for mission hospitals in Botswana and he... "

The rest of Marks speech was lost to me. Alarm bells were ringing in my head. Four boxes - twentyfour bottles. All full of 'some drug...' Horrors! There it was - neatly tied down behind the Bibles. With us in the cabin. 'Just 5 ml... in about 30 seconds...' The words boomed in my brain. 'Enough to keep a hefty adult asleep for at least a week!' Our predicament hit me like a sledgehammer. Alpha Juliet Foxtrot was climbing merrily through level nine five (nine thousand five hundred feet.) My ears had already popped a couple of times. The cabin pressure was reducing - rapidly. Which meant that the pressure in those bottles was rising...

"Mark!" I yelled. "Quit climbing! That Fluothane is highly volatile... and those bottles are not made to withstand undue pressure... if one of them cracks and leaks we're going to be asleep in seconds. You know what that means!"

"OK, I won't go any higher!" Mark levelled off. "We should have stowed that stuff in the cargo pods."

The printing on the cartons glared at me through the green net: "**THIS SIDE UP. FRAGILE**". It was a gross understatement. I prayed silently - and fervently. As a boy at school I had been in trouble for brewing ginger beer. The brew had tasted extra good because I had used some empty sherry bottles which had been discarded from a master's room. Disaster had come one night when, one after the other, three of the bottles had exploded leaving a pungent aroma of fermenting ginger beer, and a yeasty mess, everywhere. It was all too easy to imagine - and vividly - how that Fluothane could easily burst a bottle and envelop us in stupefying vapour. For the rest of the flight, I was planning what to do if my nose informed me that a leak had occurred, and I decided that the best thing would be to fling open the cabin door and heave that wonderful and expensive gift overboard and fast.

The Lord hears prayers. All 24 bottles remained in tact.

A silly slip up resulted in an exciting flight, but with a happy ending. Many patients will benefit and be given an extra lease of life. But, on reflection, an extra lease of life is nothing compared to the gift available thorough Jesus Christ and His atoning death at Calvary for each one of us. The labels on those boxes of Bibles, "**HANDLE WITH CARE**", also seem a gross understatement for the Word of God that contains an invitation to eternal life.

Yes, Fluothane is great stuff. But how much greater and more powerful is God's Word.

Thank you, Lord.

*   *   *

A Light to Remember

This story is a bit technical. I beg forgiveness. It is included primarily for the reader who is a pilot but I trust will be of interest to all.

In order to comply with Civil Aviation regulations, when Flying Mission became registered in the Commercial Category for carrying passengers, it became necessary for the Mission's pilots to have regular flight checks. These involved flying with the Flying Mission Chief Pilot (or, some other Department of Civil Aviation Check Pilot) to demonstrate proficiency in handling the aircraft during emergency situations and other adverse conditions. Such flights were also learning opportunities, and could be full of surprises and excitement for the pilot undergoing the flight check, and, sometimes, for the Chief Pilot (CP) as well. My turn came for a Night and Instrument Rating flight check...

"OK Malcolm... Let's go." Roger Weaver was always keen to fly. "Let's try some recoveries from unusual attitudes."

As the sun was setting, we did the pre-flight inspection of the aircraft and, as we taxied out to the runway, the first eager stars began to twinkle high above us.

At the holding point of runway zero eight the African night settled over us as I attended to the engine run-up, magneto checks and pre-takeoff cockpit routines. All went smoothly. Minutes later we were cleared for take-off and climbed into inky blackness leaving the lights of the airport and Gaborone behind us as we headed Westward to the General Flying Area (GFA) where we would have space to manoeuvre and be clear of other air traffic.

"Alpha Two Alpha Bravo Golf report reaching the GFA." The controller's voice was crisp in my headset.

"Alpha Bravo Golf, Roger."

The altimeter needle climbed steadily. All the instruments were functioning well. The motor rumbled contentedly. The air was still and, after setting the trims for the elevator the little 'plane almost flew by itself. Above us the stars were bright and there was a pale, quarter moon. Below us was blackness... with an occasional pinprick of orange light where a Motswana family was perhaps gathered around an open wood fire cooking their supper.

The red cockpit lights glowed warmly in our little bubble of a world floating in the darkness...

*   *   *

"Gaborone Tower, Alpha Bravo Golf has reached the GFA."

"Bravo Golf, Report rejoining."

"Bravo Golf, Roger."

"Right... Put the hood on and I'll give you instructions." Roger became business like and I obediently donned the hood that restricted my vision so that I could only see the flight instruments. There really wasn't much to see outside anyway. However, it was some time since I had done this sort of thing and I hoped he was not going to be too strict.

"OK, make a climbing turn to the left and level out at seven thousand five hundred feet on 275 degrees."

The aircraft responded perfectly in the still night air and I managed to level off on the desired heading.

"Right... let me have her." Roger took the yoke. "Now shut your eyes and when I tell you open them and take over again."

I sat back, closed my eyes and waited. I could feel the nose coming up and hear the airspeed falling.

"OK... You have her."

I opened my eyes. A quick scan of the dials revealed an imminent stall and nudging the yoke forward, to drop the nose, and at the same time adding power, soon had the problem sorted out. I had achieved one smooth recovery from an unusual attitude, but Roger, our Mission's Chief Pilot, was not put off lightly. I had not flown with him for six months. He put me through several more situations and then...

"All right... now... get your head right down against my shoulder." Roger's voice gave no hint of what was in store.

"What's he up to now?" I wondered. The night was clear of cloud. The quarter moon was only a faint glimmer and the stars were almost as bright. I obediently closed my eyes and bent sideways. The Cessna 206 began to complain at being heaved about. The motor wheezed.

"This is fun," Roger chortled as he continued to work the aircraft into what felt like a frenzied gyration. His shoulder was warm against my forehead. I did my best to visualise what was happening in space. Of course it was useless. And, on looking back, perhaps it made things worse.

"OK." Roger's voice was relaxed, while the engine, in contrast, shrieked and then moaned. "Now... you have her."

I brought my head up, struggled to focus my eyes and scan the instrument panel.

The artificial horizon, the turn-and-bank and the climb-and-descent indicators leered devilishly at me in the dull red glow of the panel lighting. They danced fiendishly, and seemed to change places at random. I had a vague notion that they were bent on my total destruction. As I fought to regain control, I was swept into a spinning world from which it was impossible to extricate myself. The aircraft bounced and rolled. The darkness outside gave no hint of what I should do, or how I might do it. The moon was gone.

Roger seemed to have vanished from the right seat. I felt crushed into my own seat as my body and limbs took on the specific gravity of leaden material and refused to obey my befuddled brain. The noise rose to a frightening roar. The instrument panel rotated before my eyes with increasing speed. Needles wagged at me accusingly and I was suddenly filled with an overwhelming nausea and a dizziness greater than I had ever previously experienced. The universe had gone crazy. A major crunch seemed imminent.

"I have her." A voice from somewhere far away, and with a hint of laughter, floated into my consciousness. A velvety blackness enveloped me and, as I released the controls, I thought, "This is it... Roger is good, but not good enough to get us out of this one."

I shut my eyes, content to spin earthward knowing it would soon be over. Life had been good. My will was in order. I had no big regrets. It was sad to leave this world feeling so sick and dizzy, but I would be glad to have my horrific symptoms relieved.

But there was no crunch.

Miraculously, the machinery held together and, gradually, the waves of nausea diminished. I became aware that the whistling and roaring noise had quietened. The back of my neck was hot and damp. My tongue was dry and I felt shaky. As I opened and closed my sweaty hands I heard Roger's voice again.

"All right, you caught me out that time." His American drawl was reassuring. "You can switch the lights back on now."

I tentatively opened my eyes. It made no difference. The black velvet, which surrounded us, was suffocatingly warm. My nausea and dizziness continued. With great difficulty - for I feared that opening my mouth would fill the cabin with the contents of my stomach - I did my best to communicate that I had done nothing to the lights. I was in no fit state to do much at all.

"In that case..." Roger's voice had a tighter quality than previously, "...we have a problem."

"This may help a bit." I fumbled for the torch that was strung around my neck.

To rotate the switch was a supreme effort, but it was rewarded by a pencil of light that stabbed onto the black instrument panel to illuminate the dials one by one. Somehow the effect of seeing only one dial lighted at a time reduced my nausea a little. Gradually the spinning world slowed and after a while it stopped.

Moments later we were 'straight and level' and headed for home and the twinkling lights of the city of Gaborone were beckoning out front.

"Well, now that we have a situation we may as well use it." Roger was all for making the most of every opportunity. "Let's imagine that we just passed through a thunderstorm that put the lights out, and while we're at it I'll cover the DG (directional gyro) and the AH (artificial horizon and we'll try a partial-panel NDB (non-directional beacon) approach to runway two six."

I had had more than enough. But what could I say to the Chief Pilot? And it ended up being about the best NDB approach I have ever done. But, much more importantly, I learnt some valuable lessons on that flight that I shall not forget in a hurry.

They say, in the tail wheel world that, "either you have, or you will, ground loop." I suspect it is the same with vertigo.

After my experience that night, I shall do my utmost to avoid any situation that predisposes to vertigo. I had enough that night to convince me that if I had been alone I would have met with St Peter. I was fortunate to have been struck with vertigo at a time when I was with a capable copilot.

Those pilots who have survived vertigo recommend avoiding any sudden movement in conditions of limited visibility when flying on instruments. I wholeheartedly endorse that advice.

I have heard of pilots flying under Instrument Flight Rules and reaching for approach plates on the cockpit floor. From now on I will think three times about doing that number, and, if ever I have to do it, I will go very slowly!

As a student pilot, I was taught that there are three things one leaves behind, or above, that are useless: the runway, the fuel and the sky. But I have added another thing to the list that I have come to believe is equally important: a torch.

If I was slack about it before - never again. On any flight that may end in the dark, I now make sure to include the torch in my preflight preparations. I check the batteries and keep my torch strung around my neck where I can reach it with minimum fuss. I discovered that night that it's a lifesaver.

And... having a trick like that around one's neck when the lights go out makes a great impression on the CP.

*　　*　　*

Note: Adapted from an article that was published in the September 1988 issue of 'Pilot' magazine (ISSN 030-1695) Page 57 and entitled 'I learned about flying from that'.

*　　*　　*

A Wing or a Prayer?

The telephone demanded attention. Operations Manager, Mark Spicer, put down his pen and picked up the receiver.

"Yes, this is Flying Mission. How can we help?"

"This is the radio control room at Medical Rescue International (MRI) with a request."

"Yes, what can we do for you?" Mark reached for some paper to take details. He mentally geared up to organise a mercy flight to some distant corner of the country.

MRI often requests the use of a Flying Mission aircraft. It's a splendid partnership. FM provides a pilot and a 'plane and MRI sends along one, or two, well trained and well equipped paramedics as the need may dictate. Calls come in to collect patients from as far away as Kasane in the North of Botswana. Flights often end up going through to

243

Mark Spicer
Ops. Manager

Johannesburg, depending on the condition and requirements of the individual patient. But today was a little different...

"We had a call," the Control Room Operator explained, "to collect a baby."

"No problem. Where do we have to fly to?"

"No, it's not a flight that we want." The voice at the other end was a little hesitant. "The address is here in Gaborone. It's for a baby who was injured somehow in an accident."

"Yes. Go on." Mark, who used to fly for the airlines in the USA, settled into his chair and gazed at the poster size picture on his office wall - of a Boeing 747 flight deck.

"Well, when our team got to the home we found the baby was already dead. The police had been called and they want to take the body to the hospital for a post-mortem examination." The Operator cleared her throat. "The parents of the baby are asking if someone could come and pray with them before the baby is taken away. Can you help - please?"

"Sure Mma. Just tell me where to find the house and I'll arrange for someone to come right away." After noting the location, Mark replaced the receiver and called the pastor of the Africa Evangelical Church in Gaborone.

An unexpected disaster and an unexpected request, with the opportunity to bring comfort and a message of hope to two desolated parents.

No wings needed this time. Just love and prayer.

-oOo-

CHAPTER 11
HEADING CHANGES

-Δ-

One thing in life seems certain and that is that sooner or later there will be a change.

Often during a flight, it is necessary to make a change in the aircraft's heading. A developing side wind may push the aeroplane off course and a suitable correction must be made if the destination is not to be by-passed.

Instructions may come from the control centre to make a heading change in order to maintain traffic separation and avoid a collision between two aircraft on converging flight paths.

Some changes can be expected and planned for. Others come 'out of the blue' and may need some rapid thinking and decision-making. Flying Mission has had its share of both.

Gifts of imagination and inventiveness do not allow their owners to be idle. There is always the possibility of a better way to do something, or a better route to one's destination, or a better use of resources.

It was not long before the original Cessna 185 was joined by the Cessna 206 model simply because the 206 was more spacious and better suited to carrying sick passengers. Both these aircraft were already sophisticated machines with adjustable pitch propellers and high-class communication radios and navigation avionics. However, discussions soon began about speed and the idea of a retractable landing gear aeroplane and even the possibility of pressurisation. The

Cessna 210 was a logical progression. Then came the suggestion of a twin-engine machine.

"It would be much faster and, if pressurised, could fly above turbulent weather." Mark Spicer was a visionary as well as being a pilot with many hours in his logbook of commercial flying in the airlines.

"Yeah, but having two engines more than doubles maintenance costs."

"That's true, but in the not too distant future the South African Government is going to bring in regulations that will require night and instrument flying to be done in twins. Single engine night and instrument flying will be a 'no no'." Bill Scott was an advisor to the Department of Civil Aviation and operated his own Cessna 210.

"Yo! Is that true?"

"Yes. And just think of the number of mercy flights we've done in the last year to take seriously ill patients to Jo'burg." Mark was persuasive. "Many of those have been at night and in bad weather."

Yes, over the years situations changed, as did equipment and also the needs of those that Flying Mission served. The Botswana roads network which, in 1968, had been largely non-existent, or at best a series of terrible tracks demanding 4-wheel drive vehicles, had been greatly improved by 1990. Even many of the rural airstrips all over the country had been up-graded and officially registered under the Department of Civil Aviation. Botswana was no longer an underdeveloped country.

"Well, we don't have the cash to buy a 'twin'."

"No. But I've seen one that is being offered for rental."

"That would certainly be a good way to 'test the waters' before we plunge in and get out of our depth. Let's pray about it."

The Executive Committee of the Mission was rightly cautious. The step up from 'singles' to 'twins' was a big one. However, it proved to be the right decision. And there were many other big heading changes to come.

*   *   *

The Okavango Delta is very different to the Kalahari Desert

No donkeys here... but other obstructions! (Photo: D Lott)

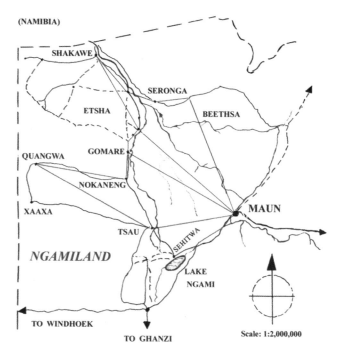

The Northwest District and Ngamiland. Waters from Angolan highlands in the northwest enter the Okavango Delta and flow into the Thamalakane river north of Maun

Maun & Ghanzi

In 1988 it became apparent that it would be more efficient to base a pilot and an aircraft in Maun. Flying in the Okavango region had increased considerably and requests for 'mercy flights' from the clinics scattered around the Okavango Delta were demanding long, two and a half hour, hauls from Gaborone to Maun in order to bring emergency patients in to the Maun hospital.

Roger Weaver and his wife Jolene became 'pioneer missionaries' moving to Maun and, initially, living in a tent, along with their growing family, until better accommodation could be found.

248

Okavango sunset (Photo: M Merriweather)

  The Maun programme grew fast and proved a big saving for Ministry of Health and to the District Medical Offciers of the region, as well as being a great blessing for the the sick folk who were flown in from the outlying areas saving them a long road trip around the Delta.

  Likewise, in 2000 a decision was made to place a pilot and an aircraft in Ghanzi, and Markus and Evelyne Breuninger and their family, moved out to begin this service. However, the flying was not as much as expected and eventually the Ghanzi operation was shut down and flights taken over by the Maun personnel.

*   *   *

Another Newcomer - OCB

Initially, Flying Mission operated only 'singles'. However, around 1996, the Mission leased a Cessna 335 for a trial period to see if operating a twin-engine aircraft was a feasible proposition. This aircraft was soon so much in demand that, early in 1997, we had to consider operating a second 'twin'. And so it was that Mark Spicer, our Operations Manager, John Calhoon, our Chief Engineer, and I, found ourselves lunching at the home of Keith Irwin and his family in Johannesburg.

"Some ten years ago," Keith looked a bit sheepish, "the Lord called me into mission aviation."

"Hmm. That's interesting. So, why," I sensed this called for a direct approach, "are you not a mission pilot?"

"Er... well..." Keith smiled broadly as he sliced into a piece of quiche, "I got side-tracked!"

We had met to discuss a lease agreement for 'Zulu Sierra Oscar Charlie Bravo', Keith's Cessna 421 'Golden Eagle'. While talking, we had discovered that Keith was a Christian and was running his own business, a combination of computer work and charter flying. By the end of lunch we had an agreement worked out and had also learned that Christine, Keith's wife, came from Hampshire and that their young daughters, Amanda and Janine, were both keen 'co-pilots' for their Dad. In addition, Keith was beginning to think of joining Flying Mission himself as a pilot. The Lord moves in mysterious ways.

'OCB' - an eight seat aircraft - was later flown to Gaborone. Standing in the Flying Mission hangar it looked magnificent - and enormous. But then the 'fun' began. Once officially removed from the South African Civil Aviation (ZS) list, it required an inspection to satisfy the Botswana Department of Civil Aviation that it was airworthy. Only then would it be re-registered in Botswana (A2) and be able to begin service.

John Calhoon and 'the team' removed the engine cowlings and opened all the inspection covers. Such an inspection has to look closely at engines, electrical and hydraulic systems, landing gear, the wings and empennage and all the control wires and pulleys. In fact, everything that can be checked is checked in minute detail. It's a job for a specialist. And... guess what? Lukas Weiss - the pilot / mechanic who had just finished his orientation with FM was a specialist in Cessna 421 maintenance! He had worked for two years in a company flying these aircraft. Yes... The Lord's timing is **ALWAYS** perfect!

In a few days 'OCB' - now registered as 'Alfa Two Oscar Charlie Bravo'- would join the Flying Mission fleet to serve the Lord in the African skies.

*　　　*　　　*

When it arrived in Botswana, the Cessna 421 Golden Eagle, 'Oscar Charlie Bravo' had just come from a workshop in Johannesburg where some major work had been done on the engines. However, during the pre-registration inspection, after removing the engine cowlings some interesting things were discovered...

"What's this... Joel, come and have a look." Jens Philipsen, an engineer seconded to Flying Mission by Missionary Aviation Fellowship in Germany, ran his fingers through his close-cropped, fair hair. "See... on the bolts at the front of the engine block. Just behind the propeller. It looks like red sealing wax."

"That's silicone sealant." Joel Bolthouse, an experienced mechanic who had served in Ecuador with Missionary Aviation Fellowship, was definite. "That's been put on because the engine bolts weren't torqued down properly when it was assembled. It's used to try and stop oil leaks. Actually, it's useless. It works its way into the engine and ends up blocking oil filters. We had better check the filters."

"Here's a worse problem." Joel poked his finger at a drop of blue fluid. "Look, this fuel pump is leaking." He sniffed at it. "No question... this pump should have been replaced. Just imagine what would happen if avgas began dripping onto a hot part of the engine in flight. A pilot's nightmare!"

It was not long before it became horrifyingly apparent that much of the work that had been done on this aircraft in the Johannesburg workshop was far below standard. Indeed 'the team' had to work hard to get the aircraft safe and flyable.

When OCB came to our hangar it had looked magnificent - white paint, sleek lines, aerodynamic curves. A beautiful product of modern science and technology combined into an efficient, fast, reliable mode of transport. But the moment those engine cowlings came off it was a different story... and the red silicone sealant was only the beginning. The trained eyes of our engineers began to see fuel lines that had been unacceptably bent, hosepipes damaged and left un-repaired, and a host of other faults.

The good news? The 'work', which had been done previously, was under guarantee. It meant delays, but soon - after much hard effort - the aircraft really did come to live up to the maker's specifications and proved itself to be a most useful workhorse in God's service.

*   *   *

All this is a wonderful reminder that The Lord looks on the heart. And don't we have here a vivid picture of what Jesus does for us? We try and look good. But when we come into the presence of The Lord He sees all our defects. The list is often long. But, thankfully, Jesus can take us apart, clean us up and put us back together again making us 'new' and useful and powerful tools ready for His service. That is really Good News.

*   *   *

Cessna 421 Golden Eagle, ZS-OCB, on its way to Gaborone to serve the Lord in Botswana

Note: Adapted from two articles - 'In the Air... From Botswana's Flying Mission', and 'Another Newcomer - OCB' (Parts 1 & 2), first published in STEDFAST

Dave Lott - Chief Pilot - at the controls of A2-OCB

Collecting a road accident victim in Francistown

Care Ministries

The care ministries of Flying Mission really began with Gudrun's 'street kids'.

Soon after our move to Gaborone in 1976, Gudrun had collected a group of orphaned, or outcast, 'street kids' who roamed the centre of town begging bread or money to buy glue to sniff.

The group of around 27 boys quickly learnt that, when her green VW beetle came to the shopping mall, they could get some bread and milk. After a short while they were all persuaded to try school where at least they benefited from one good meal a day even if academic matters made little impression on many of them. Most of these street kids spent their nights in culverts or under bridges and it was obvious that there were orphans and vulnerable children in the town who needed help. It was the start of 'care ministries'.

"I am so fed up!" There were moments when Gudrun wondered what she had taken on. "That Bashi... He's such a bright boy. He was top of the class last term and Mrs. Kasai, the Headmistress, was so enthusiastic about him and now he's just gone off. His younger brother Siene tells me he's back on the streets because he just doesn't like sitting in a class room."

"Honey, if only one of those kids does well it will have been worth it." Gudrun needed encouragement.

*   *   *

By the late 1900s, the HIV/AIDS virus had invaded Botswana and very soon almost every family was affected somehow. Everyone seemed to have a sibling or relative affected by the disease. The young adult section of the population was hit the hardest, with the result that parents were succumbing to the infection and leaving their children behind. Orphan numbers began to rise rapidly and the Government's response was to encourage the establishment of Day Care Centres. It was a step in the right direction, but it still left children vulnerable when out of school and during night hours.

HIV/AIDS affects the whole family

'... don't get fried!'

After my retirement from Government Service, it became possible to devote more time and energy to Flying Mission and, eventually, I found myself in the Director's hot seat. The organisation grew steadily, as did the opportunities to be more involved in care ministries.

Some of Gudrun's original 'street kids' managed to complete schooling and found work that led to better things.

However, there was often a need for a helping hand to cope with some problem or difficulty.

Siene asked to be allowed to be our 'garden boy' and proved quick to learn and hard working. He settled at the edge of Tlokweng village and put together what he called 'a plastic'... a shelter composed of stakes covered with black plastic sheeting scrounged from the Gaborone rubbish dumps. Eventually, he acquired the title of Flying Mission 'Estates Manager' as he took on a number of the Flying Mission property gardens and kept them neat and tidy for the occupants. Along the way, he acquired a wife and four children and, with some assistance from Flying Mission and the Daniel Helston Memorial Fund, he managed to upgrade to a 'two roomed flat'. (A 'flat' on account of the corrugated iron roof as opposed to the traditional conical thatched roof.)

Daniel Helston and his wife Shauna were planning to come to serve with Flying Mission in 1993 but an accident ended Daniel's life and Shauna set up the Fund in his memory and to benefit needy folk in Botswana. Later still, Siene was able to build a small additional 'flat' to rent out to tenants in order to boost the family's income.

Before long, Bashi, Siene's elder brother, succumbed to HIV/AIDS leaving his wife with a small child to be looked after. Such stories became commonplace. Undertaking services flourished throughout the country.

However, there were some successes.

*   *   *

HIV/AIDS

With the arrival of the HIV/AIDS virus life changed for many people.

To effectively combat this epidemic a major effort had to be made in the field of education, both of the young and the old, and with particular attention to life style and morals. This has been a battle of enormous proportions in the whole of southern Africa and it is clear that the only way that the virus will be irradicated is by a focus on the young, HIV negative section, of the population and the instillation into them of a determination to change the habits and traditional teachings of many generations with regard to responsible relatonships.

Stuart Mingham produced a series of some 35 'flash cards' with which to teach youngsters. These have proved highly effective both in schools and also in adult meetings.

Flying Mission took on the production of sets of these flash cards and they have been used widely in Botswana and will hopefully be of help in future Schools Outreach programmes of the Mission.

Healthy life styles...

...immune systems

Viruses & disease...

...discrimination

Healthy relationships...

Some of Stuart Mingham's Flash Cards for education about AIDS & a healthy life style

259

Tanki

It must have been about 1999... When we had good rains...

"Honey, all this rain has turned our driveway into a muddy mess."

"Yes, I know, and I've been thinking that if we could perhaps get some of the red bricks that they make down at the Gaborone dam..."

"Ouch... That would probably cost the earth. But I suppose we could take the Hilux and see what we can find."

The next free afternoon we headed for the Gaborone dam.

"Wow. I'm glad we came in the truck. This road is much worse than it used to be." The twelve-year-old vehicle was rocking violently and complaining bitterly. "Here, I think this is where one turns to find the brick makers." And, a short way along the rough track... "There's one of the brick piles made up ready for firing. Let's ask."

I pulled up and opened the door.

A sweaty face, wrinkled with a broad grin, appeared around the pile of stacked mud awaiting a firing.

"Ehee! Mmangaka! (Yes! Mrs. Doctor!)."

Gudrun looked puzzled.

"Mmangaka. Don't you remember me? I am Tanki. You used to buy me bread and milk, and you sent me to school."

"Tanki! What are you doing here?"

"Ao, Mmangaka. This is my business. I make bricks. There are many people here making bricks, but this is my area."

"Tanki, that's wonderful!"

"Eee, Mma. And this is where I get my mud from the river, and here are my wooden forming trays. I put the mud in these trays and let it dry and then empty the trays and, after a few days, the bricks are ready to put in the fire. I stack them with the wood and they burn for about three days. And then... here are my bricks ready for selling."

"Tanki, that is Six Five!"

(Six Five refers to the thumbs of the right and left hands... i.e.: two 'thumbs up'. The Batswana count on their fingers from the left to the right looking at the backs of their hands. The left little finger is one. The right little finger indicates ten. A woman with 7 children, when asked how many children she has, will often simply hold up her right hand with the thumb and index finger extended.)

Once we had discovered Tanki and his bricks, we were happy to pave the drive and give a little support to 'local labour', and Tanki was delighted to oblige.

*   *   *

The years continued to roll by and, although Tanki's red bricks looked great they did suffer a little from the continual wear and tear of the vehicles coming and going on the drive. By 2005, a couple of spots needed repair and I again headed along the rough track to Tanki's patch.

"Dumela Ngaka!" Tanki was still there, large as life. But, this time, propped on top of a pile of ready made bricks, was a sign bearing the name 'TANKI - Cell 72684093'. Business was good. Tanki had moved up to having a cell phone. But in the course of loading the Hilux I learned more...

"Ngaka... You must please tell Mmangaka that I am now married." Tanki had a broad smile. "Eee Ngaka. Her name is Kabelo and she is from Molepolole."

"Oaee Tanki, that's wonderful!"

"Yes. We were married last year in October... And we now have four children!"

"Tjo tjo tjo tjo!"

Between the clunking noises of loading the bricks onto the truck he continued... "I have not yet paid the eight cows for her, but I am saving for them. And two of the children, they are in the school already. And, Ngaka, I would like to bring them all to see Mmangaka. When can we come?"

"Tanki... I think the best is for me to ask Mmangaka and then I'll 'phone you."

"Go siame (All right) Ngaka. That will be good. I shall wait for your 'phone call."

Tanki's
brickworks
near the
Gaborone dam

Tanki, Kabelo and the family
in front of their room in
Old Naledi

One of the street kids that did well... it was worth it!

And so... A few days later, in the afternoon, when schools had stopped for the day, we were treated to a visit. Tanki and Kabelo and all four children, scrubbed clean and dressed in their best, appeared at the kitchen door.

"It's wonderful that you could come and bring your children. Come and sit. I've got some cake for you." Gudrun brought out the cake, handed it round and sat down herself.

"Oh Mmangaka." Tanki smiled broadly and the eyes of the children were sparkling and wide with excitement.

Well... Enjoy it! There's plenty more in the kitchen." Gudrun was about to pop a piece of the delicious baking in her own mouth... but there was a polite hesitation and an expectant silence.

"Mmangaka..." Kabelo looked askance. "We cannot eat this without first thanking God for such lovely food."

"Ehee... Of course!"

Grace was duly pronounced and as the afternoon tea continued, the young couple told us of the small church that they attend in Old Naledi... founded by two folk from Kenya.

We had a great time and when I took the family back to their one room in Old Naledi - a trip that took us round some of the back 'streets' - Kabelo proudly showed me her 'semausu' - her small shop - constructed with some of Tanki's bricks and a few old planks, where she sold some of the basic essentials to the folk of the district.

Old Naledi is the slum area of Gaborone. To get home I had to drive cautiously along a wide drain to find my way back to the main road.

"Well Honey," I reflected later, "Tanki was one of your boys who has done really well. I take back my negative comments about 'your boys'. Your efforts have been well worthwhile. Those two are wonderful parents."

"Yes, and Mmatloganolo ('a blessing'), Tshegofatsho (also 'a blessing'), Margaret and little Matthew are all lovely kids. I am absolutely delighted."

"Mmm... I suspect our family has just been extended..."

*   *   *

Car Care

Care ministries took various forms over the years and almost everyone who came to be involved with Flying Mission was drawn into some kind of care ministry sooner or later.

One of the more unusual ministires was the 'car care' ministry.

In the early days it was often hard to find reliable vehicle maintenance services and when Manuel Ferreirra offered to 'look after' the Mission's vehicles the offer was accepted with alacrity.

Manuel was a diligent worker and a first class mechainc. Ema - his wife - was a good cook and also had become expert in granding valves! They were a tremendous assest and would turn out at any time of the day or night to rescue any stranded mission driver. Their services were greatly appreciated, and not just by the vehicle owners.

Manuel and an 'apprentice' recoditioning an engine

Mogoditsane
9-16-1997

Dear Mr Ferreira,

When I start to work with you 10-12-1996 I was nothing more than a poor garden boy. Today after one year I am very gratgeful to you because I can do a regular service on most of vehicles. I can now replace points, condensers, rear and front brakes, replace CV joints, shocked-absorbers, remove and fit gearbox's and fit engines. I am now on my 33 years of age and most of time my wife have to support me. Now I know it I have to leave you for some reasons. I have a chance a find a job.

But the very immediate thing is that you show me that Jesus is very important on one's life because out of Jesus nothing can be done.

And thank you for Mrs Ferriera for the tea and the bread that she give me every morning.

Yours sincerely

M K

In addition to the splendid service that Manuel and Ema provided they were devoted teachers and this was of great benefit to a number of your men who were taken on as 'apprentices' and were able to learn with 'hands on' experience under Manuel's watchful eye.

*   *   *

New Directors

By 2000, Flying Mission had developed far beyond the management ability of a simple general surgeon and I was on the look out for someone with greater skills who could handle the growing challenges and increasing number of personnel coming to serve with the Mission. I notified the Board that we should be looking for a replacement for me. Not much happened for a few months, and then we rceived a newsletter.

"Honey... here, read this." The communication that came from John and Yvonne Lubbe stated that they were coming to the end of their current positions as Directors of the Swiss Mission Fellowship and were considering what God wanted of them in the future.

"Wow. Are you thinking what I am thinking?"

"Yes. Those two have had ten years working with Africa Evangelical Fellowship in Namibia and now they're finishing ten years at the head of the Swiss Mission Fellowship. They seconded Lukas and Brigitte Weiss and Dan Fahrni to FM."

In 2002, the Director's baton was handed to John and Yvonne Lubbe. The handover to the new Directors took 6 months to complete and went smoothly. John and Yvonne with their experience in the African townships in Namibia quickly saw many more opportunities for useful mission service beyond the sphere of aviation. Saralee Molodi was appointed to be in charge of the Flying Mission Care Ministries that rapidly became involved in volunteer work in Day Care Centres in Old Naledi and Kumakwane,as well as in the SOS Children's Village in Tlokweng.

266

John & Yvonne Lubbe with Nathania, Samara, and Matthew

This was certainly a heading change for the Mission that had, until then, been focussed mainly on aviation.

Over the years since then, other avenues of service have been entered. For example, just recently it has been exciting to see Flying Mission taking part in Schools Outreach, a ministry focusing on students in Primary Schools and through to Secondary Schools, with the aim of teaching children of the hazards of HIV/AIDS and how to avoid the infection by the application of Christian principles. This has become a wonderful opportunity for mission work all over Botswana, with potential to shape the future of the nation in a really positive way.

More 'heading changes' lay ahead.

*　　*　　*

Flying Mission short term volunteer Andrew Williamson
helps prepare a midday meal for children at the Open Baptist
Day Care Centre, Tlamelong, in Old Naledi

Isobel

The letter was written in a clear handwriting and stated... 'I am marginally over 21 years of age...' and, it continued, expressing the writer's desire to come to work with Flying Mission to help with the care of orphans in Botswana. It was signed by Isobel.

Further correspondence resulted, eventually, in the arrival of one of the most outstanding volunteers that Flying Mission has had.

Isobel came from Glasgow and, once she was over the 12-hour flight from London, she was put through the Flying Mission's orientation programme for its new volunteers. For Isobel this involved a period living with an elderly lady in a thatched rondavel in Tonota, a village in the north of Botswana, to get used to life without electricity, or running water. To learn how to collect water in a bucket at the village standpipe along with the other women, and to wash with water heated over an open wood fire. To make, and eat, the thick Botswana sorghum porridge, and enjoy it. To pick up some basic Setswana phrases to enable her to at least greet folk she met during the course of the day. To learn to live in the dust and noise of a Botswana village and to have contact with Batswana culture with its fun and laughter and stories, as well as such things as the fear of witchcraft and keeping the ancestors contented. Isobel learned the proper way to address the Kgosi (Chief) at his Kgotla in the shade of the big morula tree, where the old men would gather to discuss politics and scandals, and occasionally, to discipline the young who would not listen to their parents.

After finishing her orientation in Tonota, Isobel was taken to Molepolole to help at a school for disabled children and other Orphans and Vulnerable Children (OVC).

Over the following months, Isobel had the 'time of her life'... as she herself described it. She spent many hours every day bathing, feeding, playing with and teaching Batswana children in the Day Care Centre at Molepolole. She applied dressings to the wounded. She cuddled the lonely. She encouraged the weak and withdrawn to enjoy a more out-going and lively life. She massaged aching limbs. She washed heads. She taught songs and joined in rhythmic, African dancing with the other Batswana helpers. She administered tender love and care to all.

At night, she would often fall into bed exhausted, and sleep soundly until the local roosters shouted their daily wake-up calls.

*   *   *

Now... I have a question. What about you? Is God asking you to 'step out of your comfort zone' for a while and do something a little different?

"Ah yes," you say, "but Isobel was a little over 21 years old, and I am retired."

If I tell you that Isobel - who described herself as 'marginally over 21' - turned out to be in her late fifties... and was a widow, who had also lost one son in an accident when he was young, and who had a grown up daughter who had left home to find a job... would you be surprised?

Yes... Isobel had requested 6 months off from her own secure position as the busy administrator of a large school in Glasgow, to spend some time looking after disabled and orphaned children in Botswana.

And let me remind you too... that Moses was eighty years old when God asked him to lead the Children of Israel out of Egypt and to 'the promised land', and, in the book of Exodus we read an interesting question. God asked Moses... "What is that in your hand?" It was, of course a simple stick. But, that simple stick was the means by which Moses, under God's direction, performed miracles.

We have all been given different gifting. Ability in information technology, medical or nursing skills and training, a gifting in languages. One can teach, another can fly - or maintain - an aeroplane, or perhaps is good at cooking. Whatever gift you may have, I believe that God is waiting to do something wonderful with that gift if it is used under His direction. So what's keeping you?

*   *   *

"...Anyone who will not receive the kingdom of God like a little child will never enter it." (Mark 10:15)
(Photo: P French)

The Tender Board

"Good morning Malcolm." Mark Spicer, now the Manager of Flying Mission Services (PTY) Ltd, greeted me with a serious expression.

"Hi Mark. What's up?"

"Come and I'll tell you." Mark led the way through the hangar. "Mind your head on that wing tip. The hangar is full today. Alpha India Charlie over there is in for an inspection. Oscar Charlie Bravo needs an oil change and we need that aircraft for a Ministry of Health flight tomorrow and I've just had to sub-contract a mercy flight out to Kalahari Air Services because Jeff Royce is already doing a flight to Maun."

"Wow. Sounds like you are busy."

"John Calhoon used to say that he spent all his time 'putting out fires' and I'm learning what he meant."

"Mmm. I remember that. Dumela Patrick." As we made our way toward the large sliding hangar doors we passed Patrick preparing his toolbox for the day's work.

"Dumela Ngaka. A o tsogile?" (Have you risen well?)

"Ee Rra. Le wena?" (Yes Sir. And you?)

"Patrick, make sure that Mox gets that patch of oil cleaned off the floor please. We don't want our Patron slipping and banging his head!"

"Ee Rra. I shall tell him."

"Please. And when you go for the magunya please get some extra. Ngaka likes fat cakes!"

"Ee Rra. Go siame. (OK)" Patrick smiled broadly and Mark and I moved outside onto the parking area.

"Yes, we have a problem." Mark squinted in the bright sunlight. "I've just received a letter from the Ministry of Health to say that there are some changes coming."

"Don't tell me they want jets now."

"Not yet. But I'm sure that will come one day. No," he paused, watching the Air Botswana flight from Johannesburg landing. Its tyres squeaked as they touched the tarmac.

"You know we've been flying for the Ministry of Health for a long time now, and I believe we've given them good service and they've had good value for their money."

272

"I agree. So what's the problem?"

"Well, the Government has made a new ruling that contracts must be put out to tender. A Tender Board now has to vet applications and choose which they think is the best."

"Well with our record that shouldn't be a problem."

"No. But it's a bunch of paperwork that I could do without." Mark grimaced. "And I suspect that some of the other charter companies would very much like to have the flying that we have been doing."

"I can see all of that, but does not Flying Mission Services charge the Ministry of Health much less that the charter companies would?"

"We do. But I think there are some people out there who feel we get too much of the cake and that we are taking it from them. I'm working on the application papers. They've got to be in by the end of next week. But I think it's a prayer item. If we did happen to lose the tender, we'd have a lot of personnel and equipment just sitting about and that costs."

"Yes, I can understand that. Thanks for letting me know and please, keep me informed. You've told John Lubbe about this?"

"He's on his way out to the hangar now. Let's go to my office. Patrick should soon have those magunya and I'll ask Kgomotso to bring us some coffee. "

Over coffee and fat cakes, the situation was discussed in detail and, later, at the Thursday evening prayer meeting, John made the members of Flying Mission aware of the need for prayer.

*   *   *

The Divine Planner often does not reveal His plans until the last moment, and then there can be some big surprises.

"John, has Mark heard yet from the Tender Board?"

"Not yet. I've asked him to let me know as soon as he hears anything." John waved me to a seat. "Come and sit down for a moment. I know you've only looked in to collect your post, but I've got Bryan Wilson with me here in my office. He's got some questions. I'd like to hear your reactions."

"Oh, hi Bryan. I thought you were on holiday in Zambia."

"Hello, Ngaka. I was in Zambia. I just got back. It was a good trip apart from some delay at the Kazungula Ferry crossing."

"John says you've got some questions."

"Yes Bryan, tell Malcolm what you found up there. It could be exciting one day."

"Well, I met up with a number of mission folk. You'll remember Don Amborski. He has been running Africa Evangelical Fellowship's flying programme up there. But he's due for leave soon and he's looking for someone to stand in while he's away. He's planning to be gone for long leave. Six months or so."

"I see. Do you want John to have Mark lend you to AEF for a while?

"That thought had occurred to me," Bryan laughed. "But wait a moment. I also met with a number of other mission folk. There's at least one mission up there that has an aircraft but no pilot, and they're all complaining about the roads, or lack of them. In the rainy season, getting around in Zambia can be a real hassle. Sometimes vehicles get stuck for days. Those guys are pleading for help."

"Bryan is suggesting, and I think it's an excellent suggestion, that we might send one, or perhaps two, of our pilots up to Zambia to serve the missions up there." John leant back in his chair. "You know we've been having some discussions among the pilots in Flying Mission, and I think you are aware that there is feeling amongst them that they came here to do 'mission flying' and now much of our flying is for the Ministry of Health and for commercial charters. I've done my best to emphasise to some of them that the commercial work we do brings in revenue that enables us to put cash into mission work. We subsidise mission flights heavily and we also put money into the new 'care ministries' of Flying Mission. However, some of the pilots feel strongly that they have come to serve in Flying Mission voluntarily and that, because they are being supported by their home church and friends, they should be involved in more 'mission' type flying."

The Trans Kalahari Highway in 2000

"The trouble is," Bryan stroked his chin thoughtfully, "since Botswana's road network has been upgraded, mission and church folk here in Botswana are travelling less by air and much more by road."

"Well, as you say, that Zambia idea could be exciting. And yes, I do know that some of our pilots are having a problem with the commercial flights that Flying Mission does. I find it rather sad. The cash for the AVGAS (aviation fuel) we use has to be paid for, and if we can ease the burden on our supporters at home who give toward the work of Flying Mission, then I think that's a good thing. Gudrun always says - and I agree - that if non-mission folk are being carried in Flying Mission aeroplanes then that's a great opportunity for mission work. What about the Zambian regulations? Can our pilots fly up in Zambia without taking flight law exams and flight checks like they make us do here in Botswana?"

"Our pilots would certainly have to get their licences validated for flying Zambian registered aircraft, but I think that because we are all in the SADC (Southern African Development Community) region together the fact that a pilot is legal to fly in Botswana will make it acceptable for him to fly there. I'll look into it."

"John, I am so glad that you and Yvonne stepped into the breach and took Flying Mission over when you did! I don't think I could handle all the complex developments that have taken place since I handed FM over to you."

"Well, the challenges were some of the reasons that Yvonne and I believed it was right to come." John smiled. "We prayed much about coming as you know. And God brought us here. Yes, it's hard work, but we are enjoying it greatly and I'm sure we are in the right place."

*   *   *

The Tender Board deliberated longer than usual. It was, after all, the first time that the flying for the Ministry of Health had been on their agenda. The general feeling in the Mission was that Flying Mission would undoubtedly be awarded the tender and there was nothing to worry about.

'The Boss' had other plans.

*   *   *

Other Plans - Zambia

"Malcolm," John Lubbe's voice was sombre. "It has happened."

"Oh. What has happened?"

"Mark has just 'phoned to tell me that the Tender Board has awarded the contract for the Ministry of Health flying to someone else."

"Ooo... Ouch!"

"Yes. And I'm thinking we should arrange a Day of Prayer to ask The Lord what He has in mind, and talk over the whole situation with everyone present."

"Mmm. Yes. I think that's the way to go."

It was an interesting meeting. John booked a large room at the Maharaja Conference Centre and all the Flying

Mission personnel who could manage it came. The meeting went on for most of the day.

Bob Genheimer had been asked to prepare a short message and he recounted a trip he had made by road from Johannesburg to Gaborone in a VW Kombi. One disaster had followed another, ending with a breakdown due to a fire in the engine compartment. At each point Bob had questioned, 'Well what if I do this...? Or that...?' But ultimately he had realised that rather than asking 'What if I do this... Or that?' The question should rather have been "Well, what now Lord?' Once the right question was asked, a whole series of miraculous events had occurred that got him, and the disabled vehicle, home in record time.

Discussion ranged over many aspects of the situation. Had the application not been complete? No, Mark had done a first class job of the paperwork. Was the Ministry of Health dissatisfied with our service? Well, there had not been any complaints or negative comments. Was this an indication that Flying Mission was not fulfilling what it was supposed to be doing adequately? Had we been doing something wrong? Was God showing His dissatisfaction over some point we had missed seeing? Were we focusing on wrong objectives?

There followed a time of prayer asking 'What Now Lord?'

There were no flashes of lightning or peals of thunder. However, Bryan Wilson had brought along a visitor, Gertjan Van Stam. He was a Dutch missionary from Macha, in Zambia, where a mission hospital and school were being run and also a laboratory researching the problem of malaria in Zambia. To cut a long story short, Gertjan was enthusiastic that we send any redundant personnel and aircraft to Zambia and open a base at Macha.

It was the start of Flying Mission Zambia and we quickly discovered that our 'Boss' had things worked out far ahead of us.

Divine planning had prepared a farm - with an airstrip on it - that was offered to Flying Mission to purchase at a reasonable price and, after further prayer, the Mission Board accepted the offer. Chilongolo is located some 15 km outside the capital city of Zambia, Lusaka. It proved an ideal spot to be able to operate into, and out of, Lusaka International Airport, without having the costs of parking fees and restrictions to building hangars and other such facilities that being located at the International Airport would have incurred.

Flying Mission took to Zambia like a crocodile to the waters of the Zambezi River. It was instantly at home. Joel Bolthouse and Bryan Wilson undertook to get the new 'project' off the ground. Personnel and aircraft were re-positioned. Flying Mission Zambia was airborne. However, Joel and Bryan will have to tell you what has happened there when they write their books.

* * *

After about 6 months, Mark received an urgent call from the Ministry of Health. The company, to whom the contract for the Ministry of Health flying had been awarded, was not performing as expected. Could Flying Mission please, *PLEASE, **PLEASE**... help?"

* * *

Looking back, we could see things from a different perspective. Flying Mission would, perhaps, never have moved into Zambia if it had not lost that tender. Getting back the flying for the Ministry of Health was 'the icing on the cake.' A sort of Divine confirmation that yes, all was going to plan after all. His plan.

"So... what now Lord?"

Zimbabwe?   Namibia?   Mozambique?   Congo? Whenever 'The Boss' decides to tell us, Flying Mission will endeavour to be ready for whatever He has in mind.

-oOo-

'... ready for whatever He has in mind.'
Blankets, distributed in association with the Lutheran
Mission, to registered destitute folk in the Kalahari Desert,
were always appreciated in the cold winter months.

279

CHAPTER 12
DESTINATION

-Δ-

Once airborne, it makes sense to get onto the heading to one's destination as soon as possible. However, if the take off run has had to be into a direction opposite to that of the required route because of the prevailing wind, a few gentle turns may be indicated, and, any instructions that come from the control tower, have to be followed also.

On one flight, as I was making a gentle turn to achieve our required heading, the passenger sitting in the right seat next to me leant over and, with a cheeky smile, commented "Is not the shortest distance between two points a straight line?"

Roger Schultz, as you have read, was obsessed with the compass and the directional gyro, and rightly so. It's hard to reach one's destination if one does not know the direction in which to fly, and it's worth checking regularly that one is 'on track', especially in areas like the Kalahari Desert with few easily recognisable landmarks.

Many things can pull one off course - variation in wind speed and direction, turbulence, a poorly trimmed aircraft, distracting conversations about fish and chips.

A directional gyro (DG) is affected by gyroscopic 'precession' and needs regular re-setting to the compass heading. The compass itself needs to be 'swung' and adjusted to work accurately in the aircraft in which it is installed, and, even when correctly installed, its function may be interfered with by placing metal objects too close to it. Some areas of the earth's surface may affect compass behaviour because of high iron content in the earth's crust and the pilot must also be aware of magnetic variation - the difference between 'magnetic' and 'true' north - that affects flight differently in different regions of the globe. In turbulence, the compass may be hard to read on account of its mobility and for that reason, of course, the DG, that tends to be more stable, was invented.

What was to be the 'destination' of Flying Mission and what was the 'route' to be flown?

Frank, John and I were committed Christians and it was our aim to share the Christian Gospel and extend Christ's Kingdom in all that we did, and those became the aims of Flying Mission. It followed naturally that Jesus became the 'compass' pointing the direction in which we should move forward, and The Bible was the equivalent of the Pilot's Operating Handbook or POH.

*   *   *

Arrival at the ultimate destination of a flight is a happy occasion. However, with Flying Mission, in a sense, there is no 'destination'. The Mission is a 'servant' organisation dedicated to serve The Master. A servant seeks to serve efficiently and in whatever way is needed. One simply gets on with the job in hand to the best of one's ability and making the best use of what is available.

Flying Mission has developed far beyond anything I could ever have imagined. It has been blessed by having wonderful and talented people of many nationalities with energy and vision who 'got stuck in and got on' under what I believe has been an overall Divine planning and management. It has been amazing to watch and be a part of.

Under the leadership of John and Yvonne Lubbe, the different 'ministries' expanded and blossomed. In 2009 the leadership was handed over to Mike and JoAnne Webb and the expansion and blossoming continues. The Schools Outreach Programme, begun by John Lawson and continued in association with the Open Baptist Church in Gaborone, is touching young lives all over the country to better prepare them for their future. The Aviation Mechanics School, begun

281

by Ken Baerg, is expanding and now has full Government recognition and approval.

Graduates are already holding good positions and have an excellent reputation. One has also become a minister in the United Congregational Church of Southern Africa!

In the early days, a small box located near the tail of the aircraft was primed to 'go off' if a force greater than a certain 'G force' was applied to it. This Emergency Location Transmitter (ELT) was designed to send a request for help, after a major jolt from a forced landing, and be able to help in guiding search and rescue aircraft to a crash site.

Today, an additional small 'black box' installed in each of the Mission's aircraft houses a 'spider'. A sophisticated bit of tracking equipment that sends a report - including the Global Positioning System coordinates - every few minutes by a satellite relay to the laptop of the Operations Manager, and other personnel, to give them the latest position coordinates of the aircraft and pertinent flight details, such as the direction flown, height and speed at which the aircraft is travelling with even a visual display of the aircraft tracking over a map of the route being flown! Communication links with the Botswana Defence Force and other emergency services ensure that if a problem occurs appropriate help is available within minutes.

How different from that 7 ton truck grinding slowly over the scorching sands of the Kalahari.

Flying Mission's progress has been a journey of discovery. Incredible, exciting, amazing at times, almost unreal. So, what is the 'destination'?

Perhaps one rather insignificant flight sums it up quite well...

*　　*　　*

First Flight - Changed Perspectives

Siene

"Ngaka."

"Eee Rra." I could feel a request coming by the tone of Siene's voice.

"Deddy..." His feet shuffled and my fears were confirmed. "It's winter and I've long finished sweeping."

Siene was a stickler for sweeping the yard and he did always keep it ship shape and Bristol fashion.

"Eee Rra." I waited patiently, steeling myself for whatever it was that might be coming. One cannot rush important speeches. There is a 'right' moment, which, if lost, is forever gone.

"I was thinking..."

A new jersey for little Bakgang, his middle son perhaps? Or was Punika - his common law wife - giving trouble?

"You know..." A leaf caught his attention and it was immediately dealt with. "I was remembering..."

Oh no! What promise had I made that was about to descend on me for fulfilment?

"You once said that I might come with you in the flying machine."

"Ehee... Of course, Siene." I had indeed suggested on one occasion that Siene might like to see his home in Tlokweng from the air. And the weather was fine. In winter, it was usually clear with not much wind and little turbulence. It would be perfect for taking some aerial photographs of the rapidly expanding town of Gaborone. "Kamoso - tomorrow - we shall go. As soon as you get here, we'll leave and you can see your house from the sky. We can take some photos too."

*   *   *

The morning was crisp and clear. No clouds... an important consideration when taking aerial photos. There is

283

nothing worse than arriving on site to find the dark blob of a cloud's shadow directly over the subject and all else in brilliant sunshine.

"First, Siene, we must check the 'plane." I pointed out to him the wheels and wings and what I was looking for... tyre pressures, aileron and flap travel.

"Ngaka... How does it go forward?"

"Well... the propeller..." There followed an explanation of the fan... and a careful check for nicks from flying stones on take off and landing. "See, here is where Jay has filed a small damage out."

"Is it really safe?"

"Eee Rra! You'll see. There, that is your seat... And here is the seat belt that must go round your waist and clip here like this."

"Oaee Deddy! I am fearful!"

"Yo! You are a man!"

I settled myself into the left hand front seat and began the pre-start checks. "Now, when we are flying, I may want to open a window to take pictures. The wind will come in and make a noise... but don't be frightened. It will be all right."

"But Ngaka... There is no wind today."

"Eee... but when we fly the propeller will make a big wind. You'll see."

Moments later, we were at the runway holding point and, after checking magnetos and RPM, we were cleared for take off. The 'plane surged forward and gathered speed.

"Oaeee... It's so fast." Siene's eyes widened and he clutched the armrest on the door. "It's like being in the truck on the bypass!"

The nose lifted and, with the engine purring, we climbed into the blue.

"Ngaka! Don't stop! You must keep going!"

As the ground sank away below us, of course, it seemed that the world was slowing down... and shrinking.

"Hey... it's like being on top of Kgale Mountain! The houses are becoming so small! And the people..."

After a few moments, we were circling Tlokweng and the 'two roomed flat' where Siene lived with his family.

It was a delight to watch, and listen, as he picked out features he recognised and kept up an excited running commentary on our progress.

We circled over the Gaborone Dam, the scruffy roofs of the Lobatse Road Industrial Site and around the Main Mall area. He marvelled at the Princess Marina Hospital buildings and the stately block of Orapa House - Debswana's diamond sorting centre near the railway station. Then the circular foundations of the new Gaborone Television Centre that was beginning to take shape, and dual carriageway of the Western Bye-pass.

"Those trucks are moving so slowly, Ngaka."

With several passes over Mogoditsane, I managed to get the photos that I wanted, and then it was time to head for home.

Mmopane village passed under the port wing and the Botswana Defence Force barracks to starboard. Siene noted everything. He had long since left off gripping the armrest and was twisting in his seat to squint at every detail that passed below.

The throttle came back and the engine noise reduced to a whisper.

As the ground came closer and the nose of the aircraft rose, he craned over the dashboard and was revelling in every moment.

Wheels touched softly on the tarmac. We were cleared to the parking area.

"Ao Deddy..." his eyes shone. "That was wonderful! And I could even see my own house. I shall dream and remember this being a bird for many days. It will be like that time we were in Maun - do you remember - and we saw that hippo child... the one that looked like a man baby... all pink and shiny. That was very bad. I dreamed of that one for many nights afterward. But this will be different... I shall be flying in my dreams... just like a vulture, or a hoopoe."

A few brief moments shared. Lasting memories. Perspectives changed.

Is that not what mission work is all about? Sharing Good News that changes perspectives and lives.

Looking down on the foundations of the new Gaborone
Television Centre

What wonderful folk the Batswana are... when one gets to know them.

What a privilege to serve The Master in a country like Botswana.

*   *   *

*A new Gaborone office block. - part of the' The Square'
shopping centre complex*

A2-MJM

On the 13th April, 2007, Flying Mission held a dedication service in their hangar at the Sir Seretse Khama International Airport for a new aircraft.

For a number of years, the Mission had been operating 'twins'. The first, as you will remember, was a Cessna 310 that was leased. This was followed by a Cessna 421, A2-OCB that was purchased by the Mission and undertook excellent service in the field of medical evacuations. A2-OCB was dedicated to The Lord's service in 1998 and it was named 'Diphuka tsa Phodiso' (Wings of Healing) in honour of the Mission's first Patron, Dr Alfred Merriweather.

Soon after this, the Ministry of Health made decisions to raise standards of care and Flying Mission was happy to encourage and comply with the changes required to improve the flying medical service. In 2006, a Beachcraft King Air was identified that previously had been a part of the fleet of the Australian Royal Flying Doctor Service. This aircraft had been fitted out especially for medical work and it was made available to Flying Mission, and, after being refurbished in the USA, it was ferried out to Botswana by John Calhoon, one of the Mission's previous Chief Engineers.

When asked if I would agree to the aircraft being registered in Botswana with the letters A2-MJM, it was with reluctance that I agreed. And it was an honour for Gudrun and me to attend the dedication of this lovely aircraft. It was indeed a memorable occasion for us, and we were delighted to be there and to share with the current Mission Personnel in what was a time of great rejoicing at the way God has blessed the work of the Mission.

*   *   *

Beachcraft King Air 90, A2-MJM

A spacious interior - ideal for stretchers

Dedication of A2-MJM
(Taken from notes made for 13/04/2007)

I was asked to say 'Thank you'... but I do have a little more to say...

Firstly, we are in Botswana and it is customary here to greet everyone... therefore...

Honourable Matron and Ex Housing Officer, Gudrun... Mr. And Mrs. Director, John and Yvonne (Lubbe)... 'Air Commodore' Bob (Patterson)... Senior Captain, Mark (Spicer)... Chief Engineer, Jeff (Royce)... 'Professor' Ken (Baerg)... Visitors from Scotland... Flying Mission Personnel... Invited Guests... Thank you all for coming today.

Secondly, this is a dedication service for an aircraft that is to bear the registration letters A2-MJM.

Usually when something is dedicated, it is dedicated to, or in memory of, someone. I think perhaps I should be lying comfortably in a wooden box with the lid well screwed down. So, I'm not sure I should really be here at all!

Mark has referred to my surgical career, and yes, it is true... I specialised in 'making holes in people'. And I always was thankful that The Lord closed the holes that I made. Without His closing of the holes that I made, things would have been very different. Mark also referred to how the Flying Mission aircraft are viewed by many Batswana and I would like to emphasise what he has said. The Flying Mission aircraft do 'fly for God'. They are God's aircraft.

You will see that this aircraft has a blue spot - the Flying Mission logo - on the tail. I am delighted to see that this aircraft has a blue spot on the tail... in fact the aircraft has a total of three blue spots on it. That's good... because the Flying Mission aircraft are known to many folk by that 'blue spot'. Even the Bushmen in the remote Kalahari will tell you 'Oh... that 'plane has a blue spot on the tail... that 'plane brings us help... doctors, nurses and folk who help us.' Flying Mission aircraft are known for their mission to bring blessings. That 'blue spot' is recognised wherever we fly.

Flying Mission was started, built up and developed on **PRAYER**. God has made wonderful **PROVISION** for all our needs. We have enjoyed His **POWER** and **PROTECTION**. This hangar has been a 'house of prayer'. The floor is kept very clean... folk have knelt in prayer on this floor. I would like this to continue in the future.

I am amazed at how FM has developed. The 'First Quarter Brochure' gives an incredible account of all that is happening. Wonderful!

Flying Mission is an incredibly talented group of people... different nationalities... many talents.

In the early days, we specialised in flying a Cessna 185. Like this one here in the corner of the hangar. This particular aircraft is the one that I was flown around Zambia in last year. Perhaps that's why it looks such a wreck at this moment... without an engine and with much of the body opened up! But that is not true. It is, of course, because it is being worked on. It was in good shape last year and it performed wonderfully during the whole of our trip.

In the early days of the Mission, we had many specialists. Some of us specialised in bent propellers. We had specialists in 'ground loops'. We had specialists in trying to take off without removing the tie down weights. That was actually my specialty... and I do **NOT** recommend trying to take off with the tie down weight still attached to the tail. It does not work.

And of course we have specialists today too. Michele... where is Michele? Michele is a specialist in babies and bumps... I remember when she had her first 'baby'... it was a big occasion and she had the baby on a table... in the middle of a dinner at the Grand Palm! Sally Lott was the midwife... and then Gudrun and I adopted that baby doll and she often goes to church with us in Scotland. Matilda - as we call her - is a splendid representation of FM and the children we show her to are always fascinated by all the different flags that cover her small body and demonstrate the combination of nationalities in the Mission.

We have specialists in vultures... But Tim, don't think that that vulture of yours was the first in the history of Flying Mission. The inspiration for FM came partly as a result of being bounced on the back of a truck through the Kalahari Desert and, one day, looking up to see vultures circling effortlessly in a cloudless, blue sky... while we were bumping along uncomfortably on a sand track.

Our current Directors are specialists... I am so glad that John and Yvonne came to take over the Mission. They have been a great blessing. The Flying Mission has developed and grown wonderfully under their leadership. And... they are 'on fire for The Lord'... in fact so much so that - at least twice - their garden shed has, unaccountably, burst into flames all by itself!

Right... let's get to the point. Why are we here?

I believe that we are here because of The Bible.

In 1968, Gudrun and I came to Botswana to serve as medical missionaries at the Scottish Livingstone Hospital in Molepolole. Why? Because we believed that that was what God wanted us to do. To serve Him as medical missionaries, and to bring the Christian Message to people in Botswana.

It is a message of hope. And it is message that changes people.

That is why we are here today.

This lovely aircraft is being dedicated today for medical and mission service. To bring healing and the Christian message of hope to people in Botswana. Even to some folk beyond the borders of Botswana. To anyone who is in need of these things.

Now, let's look for a moment at the registration letters of this aircraft. What I am about to say is particularly for you Flying Mission folk.

The 'A2' of course is for Botswana. A wonderful country.

Then we have 'MJM'. Now I want you to forget what Mark told you the letters stand for. I want to look at this odd collection of letters and think of some Setswana words.

I would like you to look at the two M's and be reminded that these stand for the Setswana words **Mpho** and **Masego**. Mpho and Masego are names that are common in Botswana. Mpho means 'gift' and refers to the fact that the bearer of the name is regarded as a gift from God. That's exactly what this aircraft is. Then Masego means 'blessings'. This aircraft is to be regarded as a gift from God and is to bring people God's blessings.

A2-MJM in the hangar

Now, forget the 'M's... focus on the centre... the 'J'.

Now, forget the 'M''s... focus on the centre... the 'J'. The J here actually stands for John, a name that also means a 'gift from God'. The J is made up of a straight line and at the bottom the line is bent, or bowed. And, whenever you look at that J and the bowed lower end of the 'J', I want you to remember a Bible verse that tells us something important that is going to happen. It is an easy verse for pilots to remember. I remember where the verse is by saying to myself 'P two ten'.

Pilots will think that 'P210' stands for 'pressurised C210'.

But I want 'P210' to remind you of the verse in the Bible in the book of Philippians Chapter 2 Verse 10. This tells us something about bending or bowing. It tells us that 'At the name of Jesus every knee shall bow...' That is a verse - and a prophecy - worth remembering.

Remember too... that this is why you and I are here in Botswana. We are here to proclaim The Way to God, and to worship Him, and to give Him the glory. To proclaim the Christian Message of Jesus' sacrifice on Calvary and the forgiveness of sins for all those who repent of their sins and accept Jesus as their Saviour. We have a wonderful message to proclaim to people... the Christian hope of joy and peace and life. Eternal life!

Let me close with two reminders... about short cuts.

Some of you will know the writings of Eddie Askew. He writes about short cuts in his recent booklet entitled 'Disguises of Love'. It's a book of meditations... and it also includes some of his lovely paintings. In his book he writes about the right to speak... how the right to speak is earned, and how it often takes a long time to attain this right to speak. Then he includes two reminders.

The first reminder is that 'there are no short cuts - except to disappointment'.

And the second reminder is that 'there is no Calvary bypass'.

Flying Mission has been in service here in Botswana for a number of years now. It has brought relief and hope and help to many people.

I believe that we have earned the right to speak out our Christian message of hope. Therefore speak out. But, speak the message at all times with love.

Finally... almost... I have an apology.

I have always been a 'singles' man. If the engine quits in a 'single' there is no fuss... one just has to find somewhere to land. With two engines, if one engine quits then one has a **BIG** problem. Mark and our pilots know what to do and how to handle an 'engine out' situation. They are real experts.

For me that was too complicated. For that reason, too, I always preferred simple, fixed gear undercarriage. When you come in to land you know it's there... fixed down and ready. No nasty surprises on final approach when, in a retractable gear aircraft, one may discover one's wheels are not 'down and locked' or, worse still, won't come down. Yes... for me single engine, fixed gear aircraft were ideal.

But... I have discovered that the Bible teaches differently... In the book of Proverbs it tells us clearly that 'two are better than one'! So it is time for Flying Mission to move into operating twins.

And, finally... and I do mean finally this time... at The Ridge in Kanye I usually have my morning coffee out of a mug that has four words inscribed around the inside of the rim. The first word is WIMPY. That tells you a lot about Gudrun and me! But it is the next three words that I want to pass on to you. They say: *'Enjoy every moment'*.

Last Sunday, John Lawson began his sermon by saying how much he was enjoying himself. He had preached the previous Sunday in Kasane and was due to take services later in the day in Gaborone and soon, too, in Jwaneng. He was enjoying his service for The Lord.

It is my prayer for you that you too will enjoy every moment of your service for The Lord.

MAY GOD BLESS YOU ALL. AND MAY THE LORD BLESS THIS AIRCRAFT, AND ALL WHO FLY IN IT.

Thank you.

-oOo-

Ready & waiting...

'...that they may have life... more abundantly.'
(John 10:10)

POSTSCRIPT

-Δ-

One of the reasons for writing this book is to put on record the way God has looked after Gudrun and me, and others in Flying Mission, by providing for all our needs so incredibly, and abundantly.

The primary reason for writing, however, apart from providing the information indicated at the beginning, is to challenge the reader to step out in faith and put his, or her, life at God's disposal and to commit to serving Him wherever, and in whatever way, He asks. This begins, of course, with the acceptance of Jesus Christ and His sacrifice for sin - our sin - and His Lordship over our individual lives.

If even one reader makes that decision and takes that step, then this book has been worth the time and effort to write it and, I believe, many more exciting stories will be in the making.

If you have not already done so then let me encourage you to, seriously, consider accepting that challenge.

You will be blessed.

Malcolm J. McArthur
Landbeach
31/03/2011

-oOo-

Appendix

Flying Mission Personnel & Important Dates

(1977-2000)

1977 - First donation received (USD 110-00) from Springfield Mennonite Church

1980 - Plot 75 Sebina Close (Dedicated 05/03/83)
- Flying Mission Registered 13/06/1980
Ford, Archie & Fiona (UK) UFCofS
Genheimer, Don & Eileen (US) AEF Admin.
McArthur, Malcolm & Gudrun (UK) UFCofS
Reid, Ngaire (NZ) AEF Nurse
Schultz, Roger & Ruth (US) AEF Pilot

1981 Aeschliman, Jay & Cynthia (US) MM Pilot

1982 Horst, Don & Rachel (US) MM Pilot

1983 Halliday, Margaret (UK) IND STV
Lewney, Richard & Emily (UK) IND STV
Merriweather, Dr Alfred (UK) UFCofS
Yates, Clif & Rose (UK) IND STV

1984 Gallacher, David & Mamie (UK) UFCofS
Reynolds, Anne (UK) IND STV
Stratton, Andy & Margaret (UK) MAF Pilot
Thieszen, Eugene (US) MM Pilot

1985 Fuglestad, Mark (US) Pilot
Pickard, Maurice & Sally (US) MAF Pilot
Walkemeyer, Peter & Paula (UK) IND STV
Weaver, Roger & Jolene (US) MM Pilot

1986 Atkinson, Thomasina (UK) IND STV
Epp, Reg & Mary (US) MAF Pilot
Parkinson, Cherry (UK) IND STV
Sekgwa, Jacob (BW) Board
Griffiths, Dareth (UK) IND STV
Vracaric, Mara (UK) IND STV

1987 Blake, Bob & Sue (US) Pilot
Cannata Mike & Karla (US) Pilot

Fuglestad, Lynley (NZ) IND STV
Kroeker, Bev (CA) AEF Nurse
Chapman, Alice (UK) IND STV
Irvine, Keith & Jo (UK) AEF
Pullenyagum, Malkanthi (UN) IND STV
Sammons, Julia (UK) IND STV
1988 - Hangar keys received 15/08/88
Bagshaw, Irene (ZIM) IND STV
Calhoon, John & Denise (US) Engineer
Goquana, Salome (BW) IND STV
Gureja Nitin, (IN) IND STV
Porteous, Nancy (UK) IND STV
Powell, Robert (UK) IND STV
Schmidt, Fred & Desi (US) MAF Pilot
Seasole, Gaone (BW) IND STV
Tsheko, Patrick (BW) Hangar Assistant
Widdup, Sue (UK) IND STV
- Roger & Jolene Weaver > Maun
1990 Bolthouse, Joel & Sue (US) Engineer
Cobbold, Fiona (UK) IND STV
Mingham, Ngaire (NZ) AEF Nurse
Peterson, John & Cindy (US) AEF Pilot
Seleka, Magda (BW) IND STV
Vermeer, Gerrit & Karla (CA) MAF Pilot
Williams, Geoffrey (UK) Board
Thipe, Neo (BW) Receptionist
1992 Beckwith, Amy (UK) IND STV
Mauwane, Lindah (BW) Secretary
Reid, Adam (UK) IND STV
Savage, Elaine (UK) IND STV
Toise, Neo (BW) Receptionist
1993 Cutler Dan, (US) AEF Engineer
Fahrni, Daniel (CH) SGM Pilot
French, Leslie & Pauline (UK) Accountant
- (Helston, Daniel & Shauna & the Daniel
        Helston Memorial Fund)
McKay, Len & Jeanne (CA) MAF Pilot
Merriweather, Ellah (BW) IND STV
Otukile, Master (BW) Hangar Trainee
Savage, Angela (UK) Board

Spicer, Mark & Debbie (US) Pilot
Thorsen, Fride & Susan (NO) Pilot
Tlhabiwa, Kenneth (BW) Hangar Trainee
Vincent, Claire (UK) IND STV
1994 Ferreira, Manuel & Emma (P) Vehicle
    Mechanic
Keane, Zoe (UK) IND STV
Lawson, Debbie (UK) IND STV
Mingham, Stuart (UK) IND STV
Patterson, Robert & Zel (US) Operations Manager
Patterson, Simon (UK) IND STV
Tallents, Penny (UK) IND STV
1995 Davidson, Bernie (UK) IND STV
Baerg, Ken & Ann-Marie (CA) MAF   Engineer
Breuninger, Markus & Evelyne (DE) MAF Pilot
Farley, Tim (UK) IND STV
Juzi, Daniel (CH) Pilot
Long, Dave & Ginny (US) Board
Owens, Dan (US) IND STV
1996 Grieve, Geraldine (SA) IND STV
Gumper, Bill & Donna (US) Pilot
Kgasa, Kgomotso (BW) Receptionist
Klatt, Ute (DE) DEM Pilot
Megaw, Alan & Gloria (SA) IND STV
Philipsen, Jens (DE) MAF Engineer
Wilson, Bryan (US) Pilot
1997 Dube, Samkelo (BW) IND STV
Fahrni, Roberta (CH) IND STV
Freeman, Dr Steve (AU) Board
Kort, Tina (CA) AEF Orientation Supervisor
Meier, Markus (DE) IND STV
Weiss, Lukas & Brigitta (CH) SGM Pilot
1998 Eimansberger, Veronica (DE) IND STV
Gould, David & Ruth (CA) Accountant
Hunter, Ann (UK) IND STV
Lott, David & Sally (US) Pilot
Marari, Keitshokile (BW) Hangar Assistant
Moshomme, Keneilwe (BW) Hangar
Royce, Jeffrey & Michelle (US) Pilot
Tshinangwe, Thabo (BW) Hangar Trainee